CIVIL STRIFE
IN AMERICA

A Historical Approach
to the Study of
Riots in America

NORMAN S. COHEN

The Dryden Press Inc.
Hinsdale, Illinois

To my mother Lillian
and father Meyer
for whom I never said Kaddish

PREFACE

No period in American history has been so confused or so complex as is our own. Rarely, perhaps only once, has such a deep sense of pessimism pervaded the nation's spirit. The cynic may remark that each generation has echoed this statement, but he has overlooked the accelerating intensity and immediacy of daily living brought to us by a technological revolution, a Cold War and an explosively, expanding population. In ghettoes and *barrios*, a rumbling may swell into a roar immediately; the middle-class, educated, affluent young scream aloud their rejection of parents, traditional values—the old system. The daughter of a Midwestern, small-town, first family destroys herself while constructing bombs for use against her family's society. While sitting in a bar, a chicano reporter is killed by a police bullet fired as a consequence of the riot swirling about outside. Metropolitan police departments plan and train for riot duty, and a lucrative business develops apace to provide police with appropriate weaponry. Washington D. C. is "invaded" by young protestors bringing a small part of the war they protest to the Capitol from which the orders involving their generation in that war were issued. The alternatives to violent action appear to grow inexorably fewer; as nonviolence fails to serve its proponents, violence appears to offer more potential for change.

   This book is about disorder. From the first contact with American Indians by English colonists, civil strife has been a factor in determining the formation and operation of our society. The essays in this volume illustrate this facet of American history. The introduction attempts to provide a unifying overview for *Civil Strife in America*. Comments introduced and interpretations made hopefully will raise questions about such happenings, and about possible alternatives and their meanings for the reader.

Always it is difficult to decide upon those articles to be included when practical considerations force that choice. Conscience and zeal are assuaged by the suggested further readings for each section. These do provide the reader further opportunity to research and make his own interpretation. Many of the "chosen" articles included numerous footnotes which in the interest of space and cost the authors and publishers involved have permitted me to delete. The credit page includes the full citation to the article or book from which the reading was taken. The facts cited, therefore, may easily be certified. Where no indication is given concerning deleted footnotes, none appeared in the original source.

Finally, I would like to make two acknowledgments for the help and encouragement I received. The first is to my colleagues in the Department of History of Occidental College. The second is to Joseph C. Byers of the Dryden Press. His advice, assistance and counsel made this book possible.

Norman S. Cohen

CONTENTS

INTRODUCTION

"If ever the free institutions of America are destroyed, that event may be attributed to the unlimited authority of the majority, which may at some future time urge the minorities to desperation, and oblige them to have recourse to physical force. Anarchy will then be the result, but it will have been brought about by despotism."

Alexis de Tocqueville,
Democracy in America

"Occasionally . . . the violence of the mob appears to be the only method by which a dominant group can be dislodged from a position it holds unjustly through force or unfair legalized privilege."

L. L. Bernard in the
Encyclopaedia of the Social Sciences

"Violence is as American as cherry pie."

H. Rap Brown

" . . . every State is founded on violence and cannot maintain itself save by and through violence. I refuse to make the classic distinction between violence and force. The lawyers have invented the idea that when the state applies constraint, even brutal constraint, it is exercising 'force'; that only individuals or nongovern-

mental groups . . . use violence. This is a totally unjustified distinction. The state is established by violence. . . ."

Jacques Ellul,
Violence: Reflections from a Christian Perspective

Civil disorder has occurred frequently throughout United States history. Riots were common to colonial America. News of the Glorious Revolution (1688-1689) precipitated organized uprisings throughout the colonies. Mob violence was a common problem for the colonial cities. Boston withstood a bread riot in 1713, election brawls were common in Philadelphia, a slave revolt occurred in New York, and impressment struggles were frequent in the port cities. There was also rural unrest. The Regulator Movement in the Carolinas, the Paxton Boys' "revolt" in Pennsylvania, and the tenant uprisings in New Jersey were rural and violent. When the urban crowds demonstrated against the Stamp Act in 1765, and when the Shaysites (a group of western Massachusetts farmers led by Daniel Shays) came together in 1787 to protest the seaboard commercial interests' control of the colony's government, civil strife as a method of protest already existed as a tradition in America.

Since the colonial period mob action has repeatedly occurred in the United States. The single, isolated violent act of a crowd must not be considered along with other acts of mob violence that were purposeful and were a consequence of historical developments. Such events as the abolition crusade, the Civil War, the labor movement, the civil rights movement, and the anti-Viet Nam War movement have produced such emotional and moral commitments to the positions taken by both sides that civil violence resulted and became a part of the larger event's history.

Yet curiously, historians have not studied this aspect of our history in much detail, and they have not offered a great deal to further our understanding of the collective behavior involved. Scholars in other disciplines, such as sociology and social psychology, have made the behavioral interpretations. And so, civil strife is considered an unusual phenomena occurring only rarely. Seldom have the causes of mass violence been seen as an indication of a possible deep conflict underlying the social and/or political system. Indeed for most American historians, civil strife has been so rare and isolated that they have characterized our history as being unique for its lack of conflict.

Furthermore, historians have not, in general, accepted or aptly applied ideas that attempt to explain human behavior.[1] Instead, they have set out to be dispassionate, scientific students of demonstrable facts. Consequently, most of the theories proposed by the behavioral scientists have been ignored by historians.

The influence of Gustave LeBon, resulting from his study of mob behavior, enhanced this neglect. First published in 1895, LeBon's *The Crowd* has ever since significantly influenced our opinions of both rioters and studies of them. It would be fair to say that the opinions of most Americans on this subject are basically those of a nineteenth-century French conservative.

LeBon was theorizing about mob behavior historically drawn from the French Revolution but more specifically the crowds that threatened his own Third Republic. He was intrigued by the differences he saw between a peaceful group of people assembled for whatever reason and a *crowd* which engulfed the individual and made him a part of a fickle, irresponsible collective. "In crowds," he wrote, "it is stupidity and not mother-wit that is accumulated." Or, "in the collective mind the intellectual aptitudes of the individual, and in consequence their individuality are weakened." LeBon dwelt upon the "disappearance of the conscious personality" which took place when the individual identity became lost in the anonymity of a crowd. Such a person became an "automaton who ceased to be guided by his will," and "a grain of sand amid other grains of sand, which the wind stirs up at will."[2]

LeBon's characterization of crowds emphasized "impulsiveness, irritability, incapacity to reason, the absence of judgment and of the critical spirit, [and] the exaggeration of the sentiments . . . which are almost always observed in beings belonging to inferior forms of evolution, in women, savages, and children for instance."[3] He believed that a skillful orator, by playing upon these traits, could easily control a crowd, for it was a "servile flock that is incapable of ever doing without a master."

So influential was LeBon's description of crowds and their behavior that much in his theory has been assumed by other scholars. In 1921, Sigmund Freud took "LeBon's deservedly famous work" as the starting point for his *Group Psychology and the Analysis of the Ego.*

Freud accepted LeBon's observation that man in a crowd regresses to a primitive state marked by the loss of "the particular acquirements of individuals." When in a crowd, man also can reveal new characteristics: "a sentiment of invincible power which allows him to yield to instincts which, had he been alone, he would perforce have kept under restraint;" a contagious feeling "of a hypnotic order" which makes the individual sacrifice his personal interest to the collective interest; and an increased potential for suggestibility, characterized by repression of the "conscious personality," which is exacerbated to an extent that the individual will obey "the operator who has deprived him of it." But Freud was not satisfied to leave this description here, for he was intrigued by a question that he believed LeBon had left unanswered which concerned the source of such a hypnotic influence that could reduce a "cultivated individual" to a "barbarian" in a crowd. Freud derived his answer from his studies of hypnosis and the unconscious. He emphasized the significance of the leader for the crowd. The libidinal constitution of a group is directed towards their leader "in the place of their ego ideal" (conscience) and . . . consequently each person identifies with the other in their ego. Their own critical faculties or their conscience was surrendered to the leader who in turn remained independent and lacking in similar attachments to the crowd.[4] To some extent, students of collective behavior have all been influenced by LeBon. Definitions have been reworked and categories reorganized, but the theoretical framework has remained all but intact. This inheritance is basic to the American public's attitude about mobs and their acts.

Robert Park, Ralph H. Turner, Roger W. Brown, Herbert Blumer, and Neil J. Smelser are a few of the social scientists who have sought to analyze collective behavior. Riots cannot be predicted or experimentally controlled, for they are not uniform in either their causes or consequences. Therefore, objective observations and reports are not absolutely possible. These men have tried to identify constants that are an aspect of the behavior of any crowd. In so doing, it became necessary to differentiate among crowds and to establish limits for studies.

Roger W. Brown,[5] for example, divided groups according to size—small enough to fit in a room or an auditorium, or too large to congregate—and then distinguished them according to frequency of meeting, degree of permanence, polarization of individuals, and the ability of fostering a common identity. These criteria form physical, temporal, and psychological categories which can then be divided into a variety of crowds, mobs, and audiences. Mobs are considered aggressive (lynchings and riots), escapist (panic), acquisitive (looting), and expressive (a revival meeting). The audience is classified according to its goal: casual, intentional, recreational, or informational. In his work, Brown includes other theories, such as mass contagion (which he considers along with the fad and the craze), mass polarization (such as happened to a geographically dispersed crowd, a radio audience, in its reaction to Orson Welles' *The War of the Worlds* in 1938), the social movement, and the mass unorganized collectivity. Such research is based on a careful definition of the field of study according to criteria which explain differences between collective and individual behavior. This approach is, in its methodology, quite like those used by many behavioral scientists. Such studies and their results have clarified the definitions of commonly used terms, and have pointed out vital distinctions among types of crowds and their potential behavior. The theories and the data which have come from this research have elicited more questions and more research. However, until recently, historians as a group have not applied their knowledge and skills to the investigations suggested by social science.

Historical accounts of crowd behavior have generally been descriptive and only rarely interpretive. Interpretations like Joel Tyler Headley's *Account of Riots in New York*, Carl Bridenbaugh's in his *Cities in the Wilderness* and *Cities in Revolt*, Ray Allen Billington's in *The Protestant Crusade*, and Arthur Meier Schlesinger's "Political Mobs and the American Revolution" are exceptional. For the most part historians have not developed the conceptual framework necessary for studying collective behavior. The impetus for new historical analyses and methods grew from two sources. The first was a critical reaction that began in sociology, with C. Wright Mills at its forefront. The second was the reaction to the historical analyses made by a group of European historians who had employed a Marxian approach to their research.

C. Wright Mills attacked the methods and a good portion of the results to which sociologists subscribed as being ahistorical and myopic, especially in their disregard of Marxian technique and analysis:

> The social scientists study the details of small scale mileus; Marx studied such details too, but always within the structure of a total society. The social scientists, knowing little history, study at most short-run trends; Marx, using historical materials with superb mastery, takes as his unit of

study entire epochs. The values of the social scientists generally lead them to accept their society pretty much as it is; the values of Marx lead him to condemn his society—root, stock and branch. The social scientists see society's problems as matters only of "disorganization"; Marx sees problems as inherent contradictions in the existing structure.[6]

At the root of Mills' criticism lay the concept of a value free research. As is implied by the name, the goal for researchers was to eliminate all moral or human judgments from both their investigations and their reports, which should cite and analyze only observable, definable facts. This approach gained dominance in the social sciences in the early years of the twentieth century. It was a consequence of something approaching a national idolatry of that time for science and the scientific method which reinforced a desire common among leading social scientists to prove their methods and findings to be as "scientific" as those of the natural and physical sciences.

Mills, along with many others, believed that this ideal was a phantom which took social science on a wild goose chase, far from its proper pursuit of understanding humanity and the causes of human behavior. The methodology also restricted conclusions. As in the above quotation from Mills, research was directed toward solving society's social ills and not toward finding the basic causes of those ills. The latter emphasis could have involved a condemnation of the social structure along with an advocation of drastic social change.

The proponents for new methods also questioned the narrow functional analysis of Talcott Parsons and others. For their answers, these individuals looked not only to Marx's class analysis, but also to the older writings of Max Weber and Emile Durkheim. These were also re-evaluated and found to be rich in potential for new and more satisfactory answers.

But it was Marx's ideas that were of the most value for crowd studies. This is not surprising, for Marx had seen class struggle as the primary element in historical development. Any study of the historical process would have to deal with mass movements, riots, and the development of class consciousness. Such an undertaking was impossible for most Americans who were not trained in rigorous Hegelian dialectics and economic theory. Without a clear understanding of the terms and definitions involved, serious misapplications of the required technique were made. Broad public misconceptions also resulted from incorrect assignments of terminology, such as equating "economic determinism" with Marxism.[7]

A group of European historians, all Marxists, including Albert Soboul, Edward P. Thompson, George Rude, and E. J. Hobsbawm, applied social-historical methods to their studies of crowds. In so doing, they clarified many of the causes and consequences of civil strife in history.[8]

A careful search of archival materials, when combined with Marxian methodology, proved fruitful for Albert Soboul's understanding of the Parisian *sans-culottes* (urban workers) of the French Revolution. Paralleling this work, E. P. Thompson in England investigated previously neglected sources, such as arrest records, songs, popular literature and advertisements, government papers, and accounts of the activities of secret societies, when he was preparing to write *The Making of the English Working Class*, which reinterpreted broad aspects of that English revolutionary period (1780-1832). Whereas Soboul had found that in Paris the *sans-culottes* did not develop a feeling of class consciousness, Thompson discovered that the opposite was true in England. He also revealed a new dimension of Methodist revivalism of the time by demonstrating how this kept alive the spirit of an earlier radicalism. his writing resulted in a new interpretation of the Luddites, who, thereafter, could not be considered simply as wanton destroyers of England's industrial machinery. The Luddite movement was found to be an organized one which developed from their understanding and comprehension of the impact of technological change. Thompson's accounts of the daily life of early, nineteenth-century English working people are remarkable. Rather than portraying them as passive actors, they came to be seen as aware, active agents of their destinies. Significantly, Thompson demonstrated that popular disturbances of that time were clearly a catalyst for social change.

From an isolated Australia came George Rude's examination of preindustrial crowds in England and France. Many of his sources had also been neglected. Rude proposed that the riotous elements from the lower and middle classes became the strongest effectors for change in their societies. He also denied the popular conception of mobs as capricious, murderous, and destructive. In short, he challenged LeBon's theory of crowds and rejected it.

Intrigued scholars in the United States, reading these accounts and others like them, came to the realization that mob behavior did not vary greatly. Differences that did exist related to the motivations involved with a mob's formation. These differences were understandable only within the historical context of the time, place, and social order pertinent to each incident of mob formation. Whereas American consensus historians had not seen a social and/or political meaning in crowd violence in the United States, a new interpretation of the American Way of Violence which challenged those opinions began to emerge. Venturing onto a new path, a new breed of historian began to re-evaluate the dominant interpretations of their nation's past, using class conflict as a scalpel which cut deeply and made a more telling historical autopsy possible.

In 1831, Alexis de Tocqueville observed that minorities whose aspirations for change appeared hopelessly frustrated by "the unlimited authority of the majority" would resort to physical violence. This is one example of de Tocqueville's "tyranny of the majority," which he believed was potentially a serious problem for our political system. As he first observed, in a democratic state whose population is not homogeneous, any conflicts of interest between a majority and a minority could bring about a serious rupture in that society. This would come from the majority's use of its unfettered power of the ballot, either directly in elections or by its elected representatives, to deny a minority any change or permit only token change. De Tocqueville felt that the United States Constitution gave a degree of power to the majority which had no historical equal.

Frustrations of the sort envisioned by de Tocqueville have time and again brought about the violence he predicted. However, a social revolution has not occurred because, in general, the members of any minority which has been involved believed deeply in the fundamental worth of the ideals and institutions of their society. Still, societal institutions were to them always represented by a state (or establishment) that seemed always to protect the interests of the majority, while ignoring the circumstances which caused the minority to protest. Their alienation and their violence was, for them, an outgrowth of distortion and ocrruption. Therefore, their goals have been to reform social and political functions and to insure the equality and democratic participation in which they believed.

The investigations and reports which inevitably followed a riot were, it seemed, always dominated and dictated by the same interests which precipitated the riots. The historian Barrington Moore, Jr. has noted that, "in any society the dominant groups are the ones with the most to hide about the way society works."[9] So the same interest groups appeared to also determine the historical interpretation of their society and their acts. Recorded as history these judgments are the standard against which minority actions have thereafter been judged.

The following essays concern *Civil Strife in America*. They, however, offer but a cursory examination of a terribly complex subject. The criteria for selecting these articles were that they present a clear narrative of a particular riot, that the interpretation given the events should point clearly to more research, and that the scholarship of all pertinent disciplines receive adequate consideration.

The first section presents several theories of crowd behavior. Most of these appear in the article by Ralph Turner which summarizes the major theories. The article by George Rude offers an alternative interpretation to either the singular historical or behavioral analysis, for it combines elements from both.

The opening section is followed by seven more containing accounts of riots that have occurred from the colonial period through the 1960's. These sections appear in a chronological order. A final section offers suggestions for assessing the significance of civil strife in our history, and raises the question which must finally be considered: is mob violence necessary to bring about social change in our society?

This historical chronology appears to support a number of at least preliminary conclusions. Perhaps the most important of these suggests that mob violence is not an anomaly, since collective behavior is not necessarily deviant behavior. Riotous action is consistently in our past, and it should not be studied apart from that past and its antecedents. Participants in social and/or political disorders have expressed a deep and often widespread discontent with the society they beheld as one unresponsive to their legitimate aspirations. A crowd can serve to mold individual emotions into action and can become a general expression of many frustrations. The leadership role in a riotous group may be important, frequently it has been vital, but in many of the riots described on the following pages a leader, at least an obvious one, was not an essential ingredient.

The term *violence* is associated with mobs and their acts; the term is almost never associated with the actions of those who represent the state. Official violence, a new concept in America, has not been historically considered. Finally, the faces in these crowds were not anti-American, nor have they belonged to criminals. Rather, the faces have been those of Americans who generally had previously been good citizens, but who came to believe that violent action was necessary to bring reform.

Cries for and about law and order are commonly heard again, as they have been periodically before. Popular fear of mobs is real, and LeBon's opinions on crowd behavior still have influence. Unfortunately, fear is easily exploited to encourage the acceptance of simplistic solutions for complex problems. The response of the state when acting in the name of society and order generally has been increased police action. A violent collision usually has resulted. Violence, whatever its source, does tend to promote violence. Then violence itself often becomes a more appealing voice in crisis than does the voice of calm or the voice of a minority seeking to redress its grievances. Unless the ideas which come from many perspectives are not only understood, but also dispassionately considered and applied, civil strife in America can be that unexpected ingredient of our society with the potential for drastically altering not only the society, but also the political system.

So let us consider violence, regardless of its source and the extent to which it has been inflicted, and evaluate the effect this behavior has had on our society. Ultimately, we must ask: Should a society tolerate violence or can it afford its elimination? A society can remove from itself those who commit violent acts rather than risk destruction, but there is a price for either of the extreme alternatives. The price for an examination of causes may prove less than that of treating the consequences alone.

Footnotes

1   In 1939 Robert S. Lynd published his essay, *Knowledge For What?* (Princeton, N.J.; the Princeton University Press, 1939) in which he noted that the historical profession had not developed any theory of human nature or how people behave. Despite the more recent interest in interdisciplinary studies, the contemporary historian is in much the same position as then.

2   Gustave LeBon, *The Crowd: A Study of the Popular Mind* (N.Y.: The Viking Press, 1960).

3   That LeBon should see these traits as found in "women, savages, and children," should not surprise the modern reader, for Freud too accepted this premise—omitting women from his catalog—as indicative of the primitive nature of crowds.

4   Sigmund Freud, *Group Psychology and the Analysis of the Ego* (N.Y.: Bantam Books Inc., 1960).

5   Roger W. Brown, "Mass Phenomena" in *Handbook of Social Psychology*, Vol. II (Cambridge, Mass: Addison-Wesley, 1954).

6   C. Wright Mills, *The Marxists*, (N.Y.: Dell Publishing Co., Inc., 1962), pp. 10-11.

7   See Eugene D. Genovese, "Marxian Interpretations of the Slave South" in Barton J. Bernstein, ed., *Towards a New Past: Dissenting Essays in American History* (N.Y.: Random House, Inc., 1967, 1968).

8 Albert Soboul, *The Parisian Sans-Culottes and the French Revolution, 1793-4* (Oxford: Oxford University Press, 1964); E. P. Thompson, *The Making of the English Working Class* (N.Y.: Vintage Books, 1963); George Rude, *The Crowd in History* (N.Y.: John Wiley & Sons, Inc. 1964); E. J. Hobsbawm, *Primitive Rebels* (N.Y.: W. W. Norton & Company, Inc. 1959); and E. J. Hobsbawm and George Rude, *Captain Swing*, (N.Y.: Pantheon Books, 1968).

9 Barrington Moore, Jr., *Social Origins of Dictatorship and Democracy* (Boston: Beacon Press, 1966), p. 522.

I

VIEWS OF CROWD BEHAVIOR

In 1908, a German sociologist, Georg Simmel, published an essay *Der Streit (Conflict)* which discussed the positive role played by conflict in human relationships. Conflict, not of an interpersonal sort, but that demonstrated by violent crowds is, in our time, a subject which has forced us to ponder questions that strike at the vitals of our society. Can significant change occur without violent social upheaval? Is belief in peaceful progress a myth? Riots of earlier times did not produce basic political or societal change. There have been no *coup d'etats* and, actually, only a few local disruptions. Only if the broadest definition of "riot" is assumed, so as to include both the Revolutionary War and the Civil War, have such events brought dramatic change or even threatened to bring it about. Change has been a consequence of a ritualized response by society to the potential of the riot itself, not as a consequence of an increased sympathy for the conditions which moved a people to violence in the first place.

The official reaction to such events has generally been the creation of committees which were charged with the tasks of finding the causes of such outbreaks and of determining what could be done to prevent their reoccurrence. Prominent citizens making up these boards have historically arrived at their decisions by calling in and questioning government officials, business leaders, police officers, academics—even representative demonstrators; it is as if this procedure is itself part of the solution.

For the public, fear is a basic ingredient of its response to riots. Fear says to call out the militia and all will be well. Fed by the news media, this simplistic reaction is picked up by politicians. In the meantime, the report itself has been authorized, published, and forgotten. The committee has disbanded after its report; civil order, which is deemed essential by the majority, has been restored.

The recent (1969) Skolnick Report, *The Politics of Protest,*[1] prepared for the National Commission on the Causes and Prevention of Violence, saw its task in this light:

> Throughout this report we have concentrated on showing the difficulty of determining what causes and what prevents violence, such as it is, in several protest movements. A common theme has emerged from the analysis of these movements. We have argued that they represent forms of political protest oriented toward significant change in American social and political institutions . . . We believe that conventional approaches to the analysis and control of riots have inadequately understood their social and political significance, and need to be revised.

The two essays that open this volume describe various methods used for such an understanding of civil strife.

The first article, by Ralph H. Turner, a respected sociologist, reviews the theories and the literature of this area of study and attempts to find limits for such research. He presents clearly and precisely several theories for comprehending the complexities of crowd actions. His multi-dimensional viewpoint might be contrasted to the work of Neil J. Smelser.[2]

For Smelser—greatly influenced by the structural-functional analysis of Talcott Parsons—the creation of a theoretical model gives a tool for an analysis and understanding of riots. Such a model, he feels, helps reduce the number of indeterminate factors characteristic of the explanations given for violent collective behavior. A model also permits a step-by-step formula "for organizing [these] determinants into [an] explanatory model." Whereas Smelser sees riots as interruptions in the normal operations of society, Turner sees them as a function of the political process itself. These men represent two of the different approaches used by behavioral scientists in analyzing riots.

The second article in this section is by George Rude, a European historian who has lived much of his life in Australia. An outstanding Marxist scholar, Rude set for himself the task of understanding the role played by crowds in French and English history. His writing has helped to negate the bloodthirsty and destructive image of mob behavior that is under the influence of criminal leadership. His work has struck a blow against LeBon's theories of crowd behavior.

His analytical method is different from that of Turner, Smelser, *et al.* In part, this difference is found in the questions asked. For the social scientist the problem is to find out *why* a riot occurred, and, in the case of Smelser, to offer a method predicting future outbreaks. For the historian, the determining word is *how*. This is best seen in descriptive accounts of "what actually happened," so that the event's historical significance can be understood. For each approach the research sources vary, and for each the other can offer invaluable insight and understanding.

Suggested Further Readings

The works of Gustave LeBon, Sigmund Freud, Roger W. Brown and E. P. Thompson mentioned in the introduction are all basic to the study of collective behavior. Ralph H. Turner has co-edited an important text with Lewis M. Killian entitled *Collective Behavior* (1957), which deals with many aspects of the crowd; both of these authors are greatly indebted to Herbert Blumer whose ideas are best developed in his essay "Collective Behavior" in *Review of Sociology*, Joseph B. Gittler, (ed.), (1957). Neil J. Smelser, *Theory of Collective Behavior* (1962) is difficult reading but indispensable to an understanding of this subject. His long bibliography is of great value. Richard E. Rubenstein, *Rebels in Eden* (1970) questions the myth of peaceful progress in our history. Unfortunately except for the works already cited there is little historical writing on the theory of mob behavior.

Footnotes

1 Jerome H. Skolnick, Director, *The Politics of Protest* (Washington, D. C.: Government Printing Office, 1969), p. 251.

2 See Neil J. Smelser, *Theory of Collective Behavior* (New York: The Free Press, 1962).

1   Ralph H. Turner

COLLECTIVE BEHAVIOR

The assumption that there is a special field of study which can be called "collective behavior" rests primarily upon apparent contrasts with normal social and institutional behavior. It is the unusual character of mob behavior, of social movements in which otherwise meek individuals dare to threaten the established powers, of rumor process in which normally critical people seem to accept the improbable without a second thought, of dancing and revelrous behavior in which modest and sedate people make public spectacles of themselves, and of panic in which usually considerate people trample others to death, which leads investigators to single out a

Ralph H. Turner, "Collective Behavior," in Robert E. L. Farris, (Ed.), *Handbook of Modern Sociology*, © 1964 by Rand McNally & Company, Chicago, pp. 382-97.

special field of study. Formal definitions are efforts to find theoretically sound and empirically objective grounds for the intuitive separation. But the formalization of the distinction is contingent upon some conception of normal behavior, whether explicit or implicit. Conceptions of normal behavior have undergone steady change as the understanding of normal social processes has progressed, and each such change has required a reassessment of the boundaries of collective behavior.

Three such changes have had profound effects on the conception of the field. Initially the subject matter of crowds and related phenomena was approached from the point of view that the individual had come under the sway of the group, yielding his independent judgment in the face of some overpowering collective force. Although this view still plays a large part in popular thinking, the sociological developments, from Bagehot (1869 [1948]) and Sumner (1906 [1940]) to the recent reference group theorists and the psychological research of Sherif (1935) and Asch (1951), have stressed the degree to which normal behavior is under group control and influence. If the entire framework of objects, alternatives, and criteria within which supposedly individual discretion is exercised is itself a group product, constantly reinforced and modified by group process, then the intensification of group control over the individual in collective behavior may be an illusion. The phenomena of collective behavior must then be marked by the *manner* in which social control operates rather than by its presence or degree of effectiveness, if the criterion of control is not to be abandoned entirely.

A second common-sense distinction emphasized the unpredictability of collective behavior. Observers were struck by the discontinuity between the normal behavior of an individual and the tendencies revealed in the crowd. They were also struck by the supposed propensity for a crowd to shift its object suddenly and unpredictably. But developments in psychology and especially the influence of psychoanalysis have convinced most students that much of the behavior of individuals in unusual situations would have been predictable from a sufficient knowledge of the hidden layers of his personality. The resentments that find expression in mobs or revolutionary movements and the selfishness expressed in panic can often be discovered in the individual by sophisticated procedures of psychological detection and used as a basis for prediction. Similarly, a better understanding of schisms in normal community life render many shifts in the course of crowd, public, and movement behavior understandable. The simplest and most prevalent basis for predictions in social sciences is the assumption that whatever people have been observed doing at time *one* they will continue to do at time *two*. As relational paradigms take the place of such simple continuity models in predicting behavior in conventional situations, the problem of predicting collective behavior becomes less distinctive.

A third and more sociologically sophisticated basis for distinguishing the field of collective behavior was aptly stated in Park and Burgess' commentary on the crowd; "The distinction between control in the crowd and in other forms of society is that the crowd has no tradition. It has no point of reference in its own past to which its members can refer for guidance. It has therefore neither symbols, ceremonies, rites, nor ritual: it imposes no obligations and creates no loyalties" (Park & Burgess, 1921, p. 790). But the stress on spontaneity and the discontinuity from conventional norms and social structure (Blumer, 1939 [1946]; Lang & Lang, 1961; Turner & Killian, 1957) seems less clear when the complexity of normal social structure and social norms is recognized. There is seldom only a single rule applicable to a particular situation, and the application of different rules indicates different courses of action. Careful examination of a wide range of collective behavior reveals few instances that are not specifically justified by their participants on the basis of some extant social norm and which cannot be shown to have some continuity with tradition. If there is a reasonable distinction to be made on this score, it must rest on the complex character of the relationship of collective behavior to established norms and social structure and not on a total discontinuity.

There is another type of difficulty in defining collective behavior which derives from the fact that such behavior is often thought to be coexistent with institutional or organized group behavior. While the extreme forms of panic and mob behavior can serve as relatively pure instances of collective behavior, it is necessary to recognize a collective behavior component in such otherwise institutional phenomena as fashion, financial cycles, organizational morale, and intraorganizational power plays. That the course of group life in any particular situation may have to be explained as a product of the simultaneous operation of an institutional causal system and a collective behavior causal system has been explicitly acknowledged (Blumer, 1939 [1946]; Lang & Lang, 1961; LaPiere, 1938; Turner & Killian, 1957). But defining collective behavior as a component of group behavior rather than simply as what happens in designated types of groups requires a refined understanding of its distinctive processes.

The conclusion toward which one is forced by this discussion is that a satisfactory definition depends on successive refinements of inadequate definitions based on the understanding acquired by working with these definitions. At present the most productive developments may stem from consideration of the peculiar character of the relationships between the behavior and organization of collective behavior and the conventional social norms and social organization. It is altogether possible that the search will ultimately undermine all of the traditional dynamic distinctions between collective behavior and organizational behavior and suggest that no special set of principles is required to deal with this subject matter. Past developments suggest that investigators should stress continuity rather than discontinuity with conventional behavior.

The following discussion of collective behavior begins by exploring certain alternative theoretical approaches to the field. Because of its prototypical character, the crowd will be used as the focus for the discussion, and the theories applied to other forms of collective behavior. Next will come an examination of the essential conditions for the emergence of collective behavior and consideration of the simple processes by which people arrive at collective definitions as a basis for collective action. Finally, the factors and processes associated with the transformation of collective behavior into its various developed forms will be reviewed. . . .

THEORY OF COLLECTIVE BEHAVIOR

Treatments of the dynamics of collective behavior reflect three different kinds of theory which have been presented with varying degrees of explicitness. *Contagion* theories explain collective behavior on the basis of some process whereby moods, attitudes, and behavior are communicated rapidly and accepted uncritically. *Convergence* theories explain collective behavior on the basis of the same predispositions and preoccupations. *Emergent norm* theories see collective behavior as regulated by a social norm which arises in a special situation.

Contagion Theory

Some form of contagion, whereby unanimous, intense feeling and behavior at variance with usual predisposition are induced among the members of a collectivity, has been the focal point for most sociological study of collective behavior. From the early work of Bagehot (1869 [1948]), LeBon (1896), and Tarde (1901), through the American tradition of Ross (1921), Park and Burgess (1921), Young (1945), Blumer (1946), and the Langs (1961), this approach has played a major part. The foremost problem which this type of theory sets for the investigator is to explain how people in collectivities come to behave (a) uniformly, (b) intensely, and (c) at variance with their usual patterns. In differing degrees theorists of this bent accept LeBon's "law of the mental unity of crowds." "Under certain given circumstances, and only under those circumstances, an agglomeration of men presents new characteristics very different from those of the individuals composing it. The sentiments and ideas of all the persons in the gathering take one and the same direction, and their conscious personality vanishes" (LeBon, 1896, pp. 23-24). The solutions to this problem focus upon psychological mechanisms such as imitation, suggestion, and emotional contagion, through which dissemination takes place, and anonymity and restricted attention, which neutralize ordinary behavior anchorages.

In summarizing a common view of the process leading to this condition of unanimity and intensity, Blumer (1939 [1946]) contrasted the *circular reaction* of the crowd with the *interpretative interaction* of normal groups. The former "refers to a type of interstimulation wherein the response of one individual reproduces the stimulation that has come from another individual and in being reflected back to this individual reinforces the stimulation" (Blumer, 1946). Responses in the latter form of interaction follow upon interpretation, rather than directly upon the stimulus behavior, and are therefore likely to be different from the stimulus behavior. Since social structure ordinarily makes its impact through the interpretation phase, crowd behavior is thought to exhibit characteristics of herd behavior in animals (Blumer, 1939 [1946]; Trotter, 1919). It is similarly argued that the stripping away of "structured expectations of the participants" means that "psychological categories to supplement the categories of social structure" are required to explain collective behavior (Lang & Lang, 1961, p. 12).

Suggestion is the psychological mechanism upon which reliance has most often been placed. When writers such as Trotter (1919) asserted that suggestion is fundamental to all social behavior or Tarde (1901) that imitation is the basic process, suggestion in the crowd must be distinguished on the basis of the unusual limitation in the sources of suggestion. Tarde, accordingly, made the physical contiguity of crowd members a crucial criterion for the existence of the crowd. Trotter concluded that the degree to which the suggestion appears to emanate from the herd and embody the herd view determines its acceptance. Writers who distinguish the crowd according to the preponderance of suggestion and suggestibility are then led to search for the conditions which determine degrees of suggestibility. McDougall (1927) attributed suggestibility especially to the crowd's sense of power and to emotional excitement. Prestige, either of an individual or of the group, is the source characteristic most consistently viewed as conducive to acceptance of suggestion. Psychological research, beginning with Binet (1900), has accumulated a great deal of evidence on the conditions of suggestibility under laboratory conditions, whose extrapolation to crowd situations need not be of concern here.

Investigators have often asserted an inherent contagiousness of emotionally expressive behavior as the key mechanism in crowd behavior. McDougall enunciated a principle of primitive sympathy that "each instinct . . . is capable of being excited in one individual by the expressions of the same emotion in another" (McDougall, 1927, p. 25). The fact that a situation is one that evokes emotional expression and that the emotion is a simple rather than complex one determines that contagion will take place. Control of a crowd by playing the national anthem, during which people must inhibit all emotional expression, is an effort to interrupt contagiousness of this sort.

The place of leaders in giving direction to crowds has generally been stressed, usually following the tradition of LeBon who asserted that the crowd seeks leaders and that "the leader has most often started as one of the led" (LeBon, 1896, p. 118). The opposite viewpoint, that there must be a leader before a crowd comes into being, was asserted by Gabriel Tarde (1901). Freud (1921) made a similar assumption the basis for a serious attempt to locate a more satisfactory mechanism than suggestion to account for the subservience of members to the group. Freud drew upon the similarity between crowd behavior and neurotic behavior and proposed that the explanation for suggestibility in groups be found in the harnessing of libidinal (or love) energy. An organized group is held together by two kinds of ties: to the leader and among the members. The suppression of the normal ambivalence among members of a group indicates that some new kind of libidinal tie must be at work since no other force would be strong enough to nullify negative reactions. The mechanism which accounts for the readiness of members to accept suggestions uncritically from others in the group is identification. Identification is the earliest form of emotional tie, but one which gives way to object-choice as the individual matures. When object-choice is blocked, however, there is a regression to identification. In groups the members form intense attachments to a common leader. Object-choice is blocked because the leader cannot reciprocate with an exclusive attachment to any of the group members. Consequently the members' attachments are transformed into identifications with the leader and with their fellows. Identification with their fellows is a protective device against special privilege: If I cannot possess the leader, neither must you, and complete uniformity and equality must be the rule among us. It is this two-way identification which makes for the rapid dissemination and uncritical acceptance of suggestion in the crowd.

Social contagion, imitation, suggestion, emotional contagiousness, and identification are the processes variously assumed to come into operation as vehicles for social contagion. In addition there are mechanisms which are believed to neutralize the normal inhibitions and social pressures against types of behavior which occur in the crowd. Normal social control is effective largely because the individual is known and identified and held responsible for his actions. In a large crowd people lose sight of individuals and mix with strangers before whom they can act without shame. Restriction of attention is another device which enables the present crowd to take the place of the normal range of reference groups in legitimating a course of action. If ability to carry out a course of action successfully is often a consideration in judging it legitimate, the apparent power of the crowd adds to its displacement of the usual behavioral anchorages.

While writers from the contagion point of view have in common their conception of crowd behavior as "not volitional but impulsive" (McDougall, 1920 [1927]), they differ in the manner in which they distinguish it from organized group behavior. Freud nowhere made any sharp distinction, while Tarde (1901) and Trotter (1919) differentiated in degree rather than kind. LeBon (1896), on the other hand, made the sharpest distinction on the basis of his law of mental unity. The preponderance of interpretative interaction (Blumer, 1939) and the control of interaction by shared expectations (Lang & Lang, 1961) have also been noted as characteristics of organized groups which distinguish them from crowds. While not denying that there are differences, Park and Burgess cautioned that none of the writers had "succeeded in distinguishing clearly between the organized or 'psychological' crowd, as LeBon calls it, and other similar types of social groups" (Park & Burgess, 1921, p. 876).

There are certain common difficulties in the use of contagion theory as an approach to collective behavior. First, characterizations seem to rely excessively on the extreme and rare instances of behavior which the sociologist has no opportunity to observe for himself. The revivals, riots, demonstrations, and other events that sociologists visit appear to lack the contagiousness that purportedly whips disinterested bystanders into an emotional fury. Since the reports which support the contagion theories best are historical accounts by untrained and horrified observers, it is even conceivable that theorists have merely reconstructed the nightmare experienced by an observer in the face of something threatening and incomprehensible to him. But even if the reports are correct but apply only to rare events, it would be unwise to adopt the exceptional aberration as the model for collective behavior as a whole.

Second, the idea that crowds require a level of psychological explanation which organized groups do not require perpetuates a somewhat dubious conception of the human being as an animal with a removable veneer of socialization. Writers who employ the same level of explanation for crowd and organized groups escape this inconsistency, though they may do so as Freud (1922) did by extending the classical crowd model to include organized groups.

Third, the mechanisms cited to explain contagion appear to resist empirical verification. Least substantiated is the notion that the crowd develops out of love of a leader. There appear to be abundant instances in which shifting leadership is the rule and in which the leader only emerges after considerable crowd development has taken place. There may well be some contagiousness about a state of excitement, but it is doubtful that specific emotions are transmitted apart from some awareness of a situation to which they are appropriate responses. Suggestion is probably the best verified mechanism, but psychological research has led to narrower and narrower circumscription of the conditions under which suggestion takes place.

Fourth, contagion theory affords little basis for predicting the kinds of shifts which occur in crowd behavior. Contagiousness is perhaps the explanation for the existence of the shifting currents which have often been ascribed to crowds. But it affords no clues to the selective response that leads to a shift on one occasion and resistance on another.

Finally, contagion theory has nothing to offer in a study of the organization of collective behavior. Unless the simplistic model of the crowd as an undifferentiated mass of persons accepting suggestions uniformly is correct, a different sort of theory is essential to provide clues to differentiation of function within the crowd.

Convergence Theory

While the most popular interpretations of collective behavior (i.e., contagion) have stressed the temporary transformation of individuals under group influence, there has always been an undercurrent of suspicion that participants were merely revealing their "true selves" and that the crowd served merely as the excuse. When this suspicion is exalted into the key assumption about which the analysis of crowds is focused, the writer is guided by a theory which accounts for crowd behavior on the basis of the *convergence* of a number of persons who share the same predispositions. The predispositions are activated by the event or object toward which their common attention is directed. The course of action of the crowd would have been predictable had the observers known sufficiently the composition of the group and the latent predispositions of its members.

For investigators employing this kind of theory, the problem of identifying a mechanism and specifying conditions under which contagion will create a homogeneous crowd out of a heterogeneous aggregate evaporates, as the product of a faulty assumption. The problems instead become those of identifying relevant latent tendencies in masses of people, the circumstances that will bring people with similar latencies together, and the kinds of events which will trigger these tendencies. There are three major ways in which the assumption of convergence has been used, not all of which merit the designation "theory." These are the identification of a special class or category of persons as crowd-prone, equation of the crowd with psychopathy, and the application of attitude and learning theory.

Popular accounts of crowd behavior lean heavily on the "outsider" theme. The medieval dancing manias were attributed to groups of dancers who entered the villages from outside, the Russian pogroms were attributed to a "barefoot brigade" traveling from place to place, and outside "agitators" are currently blamed for industrial and racial strife. Newspaper reports of race riots in the United States have often stressed the role of uniformed military personnel who come from outside of the local community and who take advantage of the stereotype of the military person on a pass. Such popular accounts vary in the degree to which they acknowledge a supplementary role for contagion.

Serious studies have put less emphasis on outsiders, but have been concerned with categories of people within the community who are not fully committed to the dominant mores. Distinguishing between the active mob participants and others, Cantril (1941) cited the findings of private investigation to show that, in the Leeville, Texas, lynching of 1930, the active members were chiefly from the lowest economic bracket, and several had previous police records. The poorest whites were the class most likely to compete for employment with Negroes and were most likely to find their own status threatened by the presence of Negroes more successful than themselves. The lack of commitment to lawful procedure among criminal elements and the aggravated state of relations between poor whites and Negroes created a reservoir of people who were ready for a lynching upon a minimum of provocation.

The view that man has an evil nature which can show itself upon occasion is an old one which has been given an intellectually respectable imprint by introduction of the psychoanalytic concept of the unconscious. Jung, while invoking a contagion principle by speaking of "a sort of collective possession . . . which rapidly develops into a psychic epidemic," attributed a key role in such manifestations to latent psychotics. They are the dangerous "sources of infection" because, "their chimerical ideas, upborne by fanatical resentment, appeal to the collective irrationality and find fruitful soil there, for they express all those motives and resentments which lurk in more normal people under the cloak of reason and insight" (Jung, 1959, p. 14).

Extensive elaborations of the latent pathology explanation for crowd behavior were made by Martin (1920) and Meerloo (1950). Martin said that "a crowd is a device for indulging ourselves in a kind of temporary insanity by all going crazy together" (Martin, 1920, p. 37). Released in the crowd are the primitive impulses of hate and egotism which in normal circumstances are repressed. For a crowd to develop, it is merely necessary that a sufficient number of persons with the same unconscious wishes assemble and that one person strike the blow that all the others unconsciously want to deliver.

An effort to retain elements of the pathology approach while eliminating some of the extremities of Martin's (1920) and Meerloo's (1950) analyses is found in the frustration-aggression approach. Dollard, Doob, Miller, Mowrer, and Sears (1939) applied the general proposition that frustration universally creates instigations to aggression in proportion to the extent of frustration and that, where aggression against a perceived source of frustration is blocked, aggression will be redirected toward available and safe objects. In a review of lynchings of Negroes in the United States, Dollard et al. showed a connection between the amount of frustration that poor southern whites have experienced, as indicated by economic indices, and the incidence of lynchings directed against Negroes. The high incidence of race riots in the United States during the period of readjustment after World War I and the frequency of wild-cat labor strife and race riots during the second and third years of World War II have likewise been attributed to accumulating frustrations. In such explanations the object of crowd behavior need have nothing directly to do with the source of frustration.

The most careful development of a convergence type of theory is to be found among psychologists working in the learning theory tradition. The classic statement of this view was made by Allport (1924) and has been translated into the language of modern learning theory by Miller and Dollard (1941). Attacking LeBon's (1896) references to crowds in the French Revolution, Allport asserted,

> It was the *individual citizen* who did this—the man who "in a state of isolation" had for many years felt the same hatred and cherished the same spark of vengeance or lust for freedom that was now bursting into flame in the crowd. Nothing new or different was added by the crowd situation except an intensification of the feeling already present, and the possibility of concerted action. The individual in the crowd behaves just as he would behave alone, *only more so* (Allport, 1924, p. 295).

Allport suggested that the term social facilitation is more appropriate than contagion. "By the similarity of human nature the individuals of the crowd are all set to react to their common object in the same manner, quite apart from any social influence. Stimulations from one another release and augment these responses; but they do not originate them" (Allport, 1924, p. 299).

Convergence theorists perform a valuable task in deflating the exaggerated claims of some contagion formulations. A compromise which stresses the importance of pre-existing attitudes while acknowledging that contagion may absorb persons without appropriate predispositions, in extreme circumstances, is logically tenable. The crucial empirical question of the power of contagion remains unanswered, however.

Apart from the unresolved empirical question there are some limitations to convergence theory. First, shifts in crowd behavior are difficult to explain under this approach. If the behavior in the crowd reflects the common predispositions of its members, then the development of the crowd should bring a clearer and more consistent, rather than a shifting, pattern to the fore. The one line of explanation available to convergence theory is that more intense impulses which are also more thoroughly repressed take longer to gain expression than surface impulses. Consequently, a crowd begins by expressing a fairly superficial but thinly repressed tendency, which then gives way to the deeper impulse whose repression is overcome by crowd facilitation. The test of this explanation would require examination of a large number of detailed accounts of actual crowds in which shifts occurred.

Second, like contagion theory, convergence theory offers no framework from which to approach organization in the crowd, unless it be the perpetuation of pre-existing relations within the crowd or the boosting of persons whose repressions are least intense to the positions of leaders.

A third limitation is more serious. It was a discovery of some importance that people have latent tendencies which they do not ordinarily express or recognize in themselves. That behavior in the crowd is an expression of these latencies is an observation that allows a more parsimonious explanation for phenomena that had mystified and terrified observers. But as the understanding of these latencies has progressed, it has also become clear that people have not one but often several latent tendencies which are relevant to a given situation. So long as there was thought to be only a single applicable latency, prediction of crowd behavior on the basis of convergence in connection with an appropriate stimulus situation seemed easy. But with the recognition of multiple latencies the original problem re-emerges in new form: Which of the latencies will make its appearance? The door is reopened for contagion or some other process to select from among several potential courses of action.

Finally, part of the simplification achieved by convergence theory arises from ruling out of analysis a portion of the phenomenon which is crucial in other theories. The Miller-Dollard (1941) formulation, in keeping with other statements from this point of view, concerns itself solely with the intensity of response, taking for granted the kind or direction of response in the crowd. The direction is taken for granted because it is assumed to be an automatic response to the nature of the situation. It is necessary, then, to assume that the situation is self-evident and that it is defined individually. But the "collective" definition of the situation may be the crucial part of crowd development, during which a situation which is ambiguous to individual perceptions is defined as dangerous, as reprehensible, as defenseless, or whatever other characterization serves to indicate the appropriate behavior. If the crowd determines how the situation is defined, the fact that people respond to the situation according to their predispositions may be true but of slight predictive utility.

Emergent Norm Theory

Although convergence theories discount the sometimes exaggerated reports of contagion, they do not ordinarily dispute the unanimity, uniformity, and spontaneity attributed to the crowd by contagionists. A third type of theory makes its departure by challenging the empirical image of the crowd which both of these theories seek to explain. Turner and Killian (1957) suggested that the tendency for an observer to be overwhelmed by any dramatic happening and to see in wholes rather than in details leads to faulty observation and reporting of crowd behavior. The conspicuous actions of a few individuals are attributed to the entire group, and sentiments appropriate to the behavior and the situation are imputed to all of the members.

Observers trained to correct for these tendencies often report that many individuals in a crowd are merely amused or interested bystanders, some are even talking about other matters, and some may be quietly unfriendly to the dominant orientation of the crowd (Lee & Humphrey, 1943). The whole aggregation is characterized by *differential expression,* the behavior of a part of the crowd being taken by observers and crowd members as the sentiment of the crowd, and variant views and sentiments being sufficiently unrecognized to avoid destroying the illusion of unanimity. These observations raise an empirical question, but they also suggest a continuity between simpler and more commonplace phenomena and the dramatic episodes usually stressed. Observations of the former can be used as a basis for generalizations about the latter.

Emergent norm theory defines the key problem not as explaining why an unnatural unanimity develops, but as explaining the imposition of a pattern of differential expression which is perceived as unanimity by crowd members and observers. Taking the cue from the work of Sherif (1935) and Asch (1951), one can explain differential expression as the consequence of a social norm. The shared conviction of right, which constitutes a norm, sanctions behavior consistent with the norm, inhibits behavior contrary to it, justifies proselyting, and requires restraining action against those who dissent. Because the behavior in the crowd is different either in degree or kind from that in noncrowd situations, the norm must be specific to the situation to some degree—hence *emergent* norm. Specific further problems that take pre-eminence when these assumptions are made include accounting for the neutralization or inapplicability of existing norms, specifying the process by which a collectivity comes to acknowledge a norm as the rule of that body, and accounting for the character of the norm.

There are several important differences between emergent norm theory and contagion theory in their characterizations of the crowd. The first concerns the view that complete uniformity is a collective illusion. The image of Nazi crowds attacking Jewish merchants often distorted the true situation in which a few stormtroopers acted while a crowd of persons afraid to voice dissent stood silently by. A "crowd of looters" taking advantage of an overturned ice cream truck in southern California turned out upon careful observation to include many groups of two or three persons who disapproved of the looting, but who by their overt passivity gave some collective support to the activities of the minority.

The second difference is between the spontaneous induction of emotion under contagion and the imposition of conformity under the impact of a norm. Under contagion people find themselves spontaneously infected with the emotions of others so that they want to behave as others do; under a norm people first experience the social pressure against nonconformity and do not necessarily share the emotion themselves, as Asch's (1951) experiments have shown. The crowd suppresses incongruous moods, and a prevalent fear of the crowd expressed both by observers and members of even recreational crowds facilitates the imposition of the norm. Far from being "infected" by the crowd mood, the newcomer observes it, suppresses any inappropriate mood, and then seeks actively to determine the nature of the situation which gives rise to it.

A third difference between normative and contagion theory is that the former is equally applicable to quiet and excited states, while the latter generally views contagion as a direct function of arousal. Moods of dread or of reverence may be as genuinely crowd phenomena as moods of violence and revelry. The observer who ran excitedly into the crowd at the site of a plane crash asking, "What happened?" was promptly silenced by disapproving gestures; students, present at a bonfire which exploded with injury to several persons, even though too far away to have observed the events directly, found it difficult to develop the proper mood for the subsequent homecoming dance.

Fourth, a conspicuous part of the symbolic exchange involved in the development of a crowd is the act of seeking and supplying justifications for the course of action of the crowd, or the recasting of conventional norms in a humorous or outgroup context so as to nullify their impact. Lynchings and riots never occur without extensive preparation, which consists of the development of collective assurance that the intended victims are outside of the ordinary moral order. Students cutting classes for a victory celebration were heard by observers to seek assurance that enough students would join to prevent professors from attempting to hold classes. Much of the content of the discussion and rumor which occurs in the crowd serves to define with group support the "facts" which are specifically necessary to determine the applicability of a particular norm. An empirical test of the two theories could be made by a content analysis of the exchanges that take place in observed crowds. The prime emphasis under contagion theory would be on communications which are expressive of the dominant emotion of the crowd and suggestions for action in accordance with the mood. While the latter would also be anticipated under norm theory, the former would be replaced by communications which have a normative character and which serve to indicate the applicability of a norm.

Fifth, limits to the development of crowd emotion and behavior are more readily explained as a function of a norm than as a product of contagion. The principle of contagion envisages a spiral of mutual reinforcement and neutralization of inhibitions typically leading the crowd to more extreme actions than were envisaged at its beginning. The evidence that southern lynchings were often followed by generalized devastation of Negro neighborhoods or that crowds soon get out of the hands of their original leaders appears to lend support to the spiral nature of contagion. Contradictory examples are available, however, and pose problems for contagion theory. In conventionalized crowds, the person whose expression of religious fervor (in a revival) or of abandonment of conventional mores (in an expressive jazz session) goes too far for the crowd serves to dampen the crowd mood rather than to facilitate its further development. Under contagion theory it might be argued that the crowd is not yet ready for the suggestion in question, but the fact that such crowds regularly reach limits beyond which they do not go calls this explanation into question. The further observation, drawn from careful historical research, that even so classical a crowd action as the storming of the Bastille during the French Revolution failed to follow up its action by attacks on the highly available director of the prison (Rude,1959), suggests that popular imagery of crowds has given insufficient attention to limits on crowd development. If an emergent norm defines behavior which is not usually acceptable as the rule in the crowd, it will usually also define the upper limits of acceptable behavior. Normative theory further gives rise to the hypothesis that many forms of crowd behavior are rendered possible as much by the conviction that behavior will not exceed certain upper limits as by the interstimulation of like-minded participants.

A final difference concerns the stress on anonymity which plays a part in many treatments of the crowd from a contagion viewpoint. Since social identity, by which the individual thinks of himself in certain stable social contexts and is recognizable to others, is a prime link in the chain of social control, its relevance is crucially different. If the crowd is a phenomenon of released impulse, then anonymity—the neutralization of identity—is important in eliminating the controls which ordinarily keep impulses in check. If the crowd represents behavior under an emergent norm, it is important that the individual in the crowd have an identity so that the control of the crowd can be effective over him. The latter assumption gives rise to the hypothesis that the control of the crowd is greatest among persons who are known to one another, rather than among anonymous persons.

Whereas convergence theory stresses the continuity between normal *individual* behavior and crowd behavior, emergent norm theory stresses the continuity between normal *group* behavior and crowd behavior. Just as behavior in normal groups gives rise to, and is governed by, norms, so the crowd generates and is governed by normative control. There is likewise a continuity between crowd norms and the norms which are usually in effect, the crowd supplying an atypical resolution of a long-standing normative conflict, defining a situation in which "emergency" norms can be invoked, or providing collective sanction for the conviction that the usual normative order has ceased to operate.

THE EMERGENCE OF COLLECTIVE BEHAVIOR

The question, "When does collective behavior take place?" must be divided into three more specific parts. First, by the nature of the definition of the field, collective behavior occurs only (but not always) when the established organization ceases to afford direction and supply channels for action. Hence one is led into the theory of social organization and disorganization to uncover the major circumstances which produce such failure affecting considerable numbers of people. Smelser spoke of *structural strain,* "an impairment of the relations among and consequently inadequate functioning of the components of action" (Smelser, 1963, p. 47). The impairment occurs when the problem at hand cannot be handled without reconsidering the more general foundations upon which a specific application of a means, motive, norm, or value is based. Thus the strain which produces collective behavior is distinguished from routine problems by its more far-reaching implications for the culture and organization of the society.

The second question is, "Why action rather than inaction?" In the absence of norms to specify action or organizational means to facilitate action, people may simply fail to act at all. The third problem is to discover the basis for the coordination of individual responses into collective behavior. Individual responses may be so disparate and uncoordinated that orderly procedures are disrupted but no collective response develops.

Although each consideration leads one to a different set of sources for collective behavior, the elements are not in practice fully independent. The social organization is only adequate or inadequate in relation to action tendencies. Similarly, the existence of relationships among people which facilitate coordination can enhance otherwise insufficient action tendencies, which in turn renders an otherwise adequate social organization insufficent.

Developmental Models

Conditions which give rise to collective behavior may be sought either according to a factorial or a developmental model. Factorial studies which relate the incidence of lynchings to decline in the price of cotton, attacks on constituted authority to runaway inflation, panic to low of confidence in leadership, or financial crazes to the opening of seemingly unlimited new opportunities for development supply the starting point for a more refined analysis of causation. But collective behavior is the product of a serial development, such that the conditions which facilitate the transition from stage I to stage II are not identical to the conditions which facilitate transition from stage II to stage III. It is the merit of the oft-used *life-cycle* or *natural history* approach "to permit us to discover the additional conditions that have to be present if a movement (or other collective behavior) is to proceed from any given stage to the next. . . ." (Turner & Killian, 1957, pp. 319-320). In a specific instance the failure of a social movement to develop after an impressive beginning could be attributed to such circumstances as the absence of an established communication network linking the populations whose interests were at stake and the failure to develop a program which did not threaten other values of the relevant population, both of which conditions were not essential to the initial stage of demonstration and enthusiasm (Jackson, Peterson, Bull, Monsen, & Richmond, 1960). While explicitly denying that order of occurrence is crucial, Smelser (1963) translates concepts from the development approach into the distinctive *value added* approach. He suggested a set of stages having general applicability to a wide range of collective behavior, each stage taking a specific form which is somewhat different for each type of collective behavior. The stages are structural *conduciveness* of the social order to collective behavior, social *strain, crystallization of beliefs* appropriate to the particular form of collective behavior, *precipitating factors, mobilization* for action, and efforts at *social control* of the collective behavior by outside persons and agencies. The specific implication of the developmental model is that the conditions leading to the development of collective behavior cannot be ascertained wholly apart from an examination of the actual process of development of the behavior.

Convergence Approaches

Under the parsimonious convergence approach, collective behavior culminates in the simultaneous development in many people of a sufficiently intense action tendency. Such development is achieved through learning or frustration of impulse, which is then activated by an appropriate incident. Social organization enters into the explanation as (1) the source of tension and (2) the basis for uniform tendencies in a collection of people. Frustrations leading to accumulating aggression and arising out of disadvantageous economic conditions or political subordination (Dollard et al., 1939; Hovland & Sears, 1949) and anxiety accumulating out of a succession of experiences which shake confidence in the future (Cantril, 1940) are among the conditions most frequently cited.

The incident which precipitates the crowd is often of minor apparent importance, or unrelated to the source of accumulated tension. An extended period of learning is required to connect incident with tension. Thus, although the southern poor white's troubles stemmed from economic, technological, and political conditions largely beyond his control and understanding, he had learned over the years to identify the unsubservient Negro as his primary threat (Cantril, 1941). The incident of Negro transgression of the color line was sometimes all that was then necessary to set in motion the community clamor for a lynching. The traditional religious teachings and the consequences of permitting only Jews to engage in money-lending during a period of growing demand for risk capital made it easy to see the pogrom in magico-religious terms as expiatory and in instrumental terms as the redistribution of ill-gotten wealth.

Contagion Approach

Social unrest is often viewed as a preparatory stage for translating individual action tendencies into collective action and preparing people to accept new forms of behavior. For individual unrest to be incorporated into circular reaction and become social unrest (Blumer, 1946), individuals must be sensitized to one another. Aggregations, audiences, and casual crowds, awareness of undergoing derangement of living routines together, and prior interaction supply the initial sensitization. Possible evidence for the effect of prior sensitization, though subject to alternative interpretation, is supplied by French's (1944) experimental study in which groups, consisting of basketball teams, developed fear in response to a threat of fire more quickly than other groups of five students who had not previously known one another. Social unrest leads to milling, which in turn sets the stage for collective excitement and then social contagion. These stages involve increasing suggestibility and declining critical facility, and increasingly exclusive preoccupation with persons engaged in the common milling process. The focus of the milling process about an exciting event provides the basis for translation into crowd behavior.

The Langs, speaking of mass contagion, add that "the emergence of a leader who represents the 'typical' qualities of his following is the essential feature in the transformation of behavior in the elementary collectivity" (Lang & Lang, 1961, p. 228). Earlier, in the discussion of Freud, the contradictory evidence regarding leadership was noted; it should now be added that "typical" must be employed in a very limited and special sense if the statement is to be accepted. While the leader must reflect the same preoccupations and some of the same weaknesses as his followers, he must radiate a sense of competence, assuredness, and self-righteousness which the followers lack. But with the latter characteristics, acceptance of his leadership takes on less of the character of suggestibility and contagion and more of the quality of response to a definer of norms.

Emergent Norm Approach

A normative approach places equal weight on prior sensitization and shared derangement, less dependence on suggestibility and excitement or the psychological mechanism of identification, and greater stress on locating the conditions and sequences under which a new or special rule comes to be recognized and accepted as the basis for a coordinated response. From the normative viewpoint, situations of collective behavior are of varying complexity. In the simplest situation an event occurs for which the social organization offers insufficient directives or means for action. The normative implications are slightly complicated when the necessity to replace a temporarily inoperative social order must be set aside and when it must be actively opposed as a condition for carrying out the indicated action. It is useful to examine these situations in order of increasing complexity.

The occurrence of events which are inadequately defined in the group culture or for which there is no prior organization is endemic in all societies. Analysis of how collective behavior arises, if at all, in such situations as an automobile accident or failure of a teacher to arrive promptly at the beginning of a class period should reveal the elementary requirements for collective action.

Illustrative accounts of such episodes indicate that very little action is entirely individual, but that the coordination of behavior tends to remain limited to subgroups rather than to encompass the entire aggregation. Students typically leave the unstaffed class in groups after making decisions among themselves, and spectators at an automobile accident or fire form small groups, not necessarily limited to persons who have known each other previously. At the same time, in cases in which some action is required of people, a striking awareness of the larger group is common, and focus of attention on the actions of a few conspicuous individuals is general. In all cases some reduction of the usual barriers to interaction among strangers seems to occur. Collective action of the whole is largely a matter of registering approval or disapproval of actions and suggestions from individuals or small groups.

Participants in such episodes are primarily concerned with three types of cues. First, there is much concern with rules—what people are supposed and not supposed to do in such situations, except when the rule is universally understood.

Second, there are attempts to define the situation, explain the teacher's absence, account for the accident, and the like, which often take the form of assigning fault or absolving from blame. When the rule is clear-cut, these considerations become the dominant ones, and a satisfactory definition appears to be as essential to action as the rule. Third, there is attention to, and search for, leadership, with appraisal of leader credentials, and with heavy dependence upon leaders to legitimate rules and assume the onus of starting action (Redl, 1945). The importance of finding a rule and formulating a conception of the situation with group sanction as a precondition to collective action is suggested by the instance of a university class in which members were still milling in the classroom and the hall without leaving, one-half hour after the professor walked out without explanation in the middle of his lecture. In more complex situations, the requirement of comprehensibility probably takes the form of demand for an ideology which will supply a basis for action.

There is greater complexity when the necessity to act in a situation of collective significance without adequate organizational direction and means is combined with a disruption of existing organization. Here is the typical disaster situation in which police, civilian defense officials, militia, fire departments, and other such groups should normally be directing action, but in which the organization of these groups has been impaired by the disaster. The emergence of such behavior cannot be explored apart from the relationships with the existing order. A similar situation exists when the social order is disrupted by rebellion, leaving elemental economic and social functions uncared for.

Beginning with the wartime studies of the effects of bombing on civilian morale and organization, there has been a concerted program of study of the effects of natural and man-made disasters (Disaster Research Group, 1961). A certain amount of effort has been devoted simply to dispelling popular misconceptions of mass panic, widespread looting, bitter conflict, and far-reaching mental illness in the wake of these episodes (Form & Loomis, 1956; Fritz & Williams, 1957). The greatest attention has been to strictly psychological effects, to effects on the normal social organization, and to the administrative and planning aspects of disaster rather than to the emergence and nonemergence of collective behavior.

When disasters strike with a warning, there is a period characterized by reluctance on the part of officials to issue advance information for fear of creating panic and a tendency on the part of the populace to discount warnings. Evidence points toward a dominating tendency, both individual and collective, to cling to the established order and resist efforts to invoke innovative behavior until the threat is directly and dramatically apparent. Even in evacuation people stop to dress respectably and carry articles which provide symbolic linkage with the conventional order but lack survival utility.

When the disaster strikes, particularly if it is without warning, there is a brief stage of immobility in which people underreact to the event, failing to comprehend its magnitude, and either fail to act at all or act in grotesquely inappropriate fashion (Moore, 1956). A stage of vigorous activity then follows with emphasis on activity for its own sake. A spirit of generosity and compassion breaks down many conventional barriers, though help is often given to those who need it least and in an inefficient manner. Form and Nosow (1958) found an initial preoccupation with helping and searching for specific persons, such as family and close friends. After these had been located or assisted, attention shifted toward all others in need, irrespective of personal ties. Only after these two phases did people generally turn attention to their own injuries and losses. The initial concern about family and intimates, even to the extent of overlooking others in greater need and close at hand, has been well documented, and is the reason for much of the failure of local organizations to work effectively during this period (Killian, 1952). Barton noted, however, that it has never been adequately established that the majority of people actually participate in the rescue activities (Baker, 1962), and self-reports gathered by interviews may well be biased in a favorable direction.

Perhaps the most interesting observation about this stage of activity is the special character of the solidarity which develops. Professional rescue workers and other "outsiders" complain of noncooperation and often meet bitter hostility at the same time that residents of the disaster area are showing exceptional compassion toward one another. An outside group, however, such as the Salvation Army, whose workers participate in the sentiments of the victims, is readily accepted (Form & Nosow, 1958). The solidarity seems to be of the mechanical type (Durkheim, 1893 [1947]), based upon similarity of experience and sentiment rather than upon an interdependent division of labor. A sharp ingroup-outgroup dichotomy carries resentment against those who behave and feel as outsiders. When the complex social order may proceed best by instituting first the simpler, more "primitive" mechanical solidarity as a transitional step toward a new or reinstated organic solidarity.

Completion of the immediate tasks of rescue and decline of the heightened mechanical solidarity mark the transition to the reorientation stage during which time there is a general tendency to restore customary controls, and old hostilities reawaken within the community. The beginning of this stage sometimes incorporates such vigorous expressions of criticism and complaint that it has been called the brick-bat phase (Moore, 1956). With surprising rapidity the pre-disaster social order is reinstated with little immediate evidence of the more profound long-run changes which Sjoberg (Baker, 1902) believed may occur later.

The principal details of disaster response have been gleaned from the study of temporary crises in relatively smoothly functioning social orders where largely naturalistic definitions of events prevailed. Hence one can only guess at the answers to some of the most crucial questions for collective behavior research. Except for the well-known disorganization of behavior on occasions when the location and nature of danger cannot be identified, there seems to be only a brief period for comprehending and defining the situation before some kind of action gets underway. Where magical and teleological conceptions prevail, there may be a longer period of definition required as a prelude to even limited collective action. Observers have reported surprise at how little looting and deliberate selfishness occurs under these circumstances. But their reports deal with basically solidary communities in which the disaster is not likely to be experienced as an opportunity to unseat an oppressive system or seek revenge. Although propriety forestalled open expression of such sentiments, there were abundant rumblings in poorer sections of Los Angeles at the time of the 1962 fire in the wealthy Bel Air and Brentwood neighborhoods, to the effect that "it couldn't have happened to a better group."

Still a further level of complexity is introduced when collective behavior takes place in the presence of a functioning social situation which does not supply avenues for the expression of certain strong action tendencies. Collective behavior then involves setting aside the established organization, usually temporarily. Reports of the frontier revivals in the United States during the early nineteenth century suggest the importance of these events in removing men and women from the daily routine and creating the occasion for abandonment of the usual restraints on behavior. Huizinga's (1924 [1954]) account of the late middle ages describes recurrent excesses of collective behavior. Because of the general sameness of life, people overreacted to small variations from the routine and made up for a general boredom by entering wholeheartedly into widely unrestrained collective behavior of many sorts. Vigilante actions often have this character, being viewed by the participants as temporary supplanting of constituted organization in response to an event (crime wave, or exceptionally heinous crime) which cannot be handled quickly or drastically enough by the accepted organization, or because incumbents are unwilling or unable to make the organization function effectively. Here, in addition to requirements noted already, symbolic legitimation from the established order seems to be essential. Expressions of tolerance from representatives of the established order, participation by people who provide a link to the established order, and adherence to ritual borrowed from the established order are nearly universal elements in such collective behavior.

The difference is only one of degree between collective behavior which develops because of strong impulses for which the social order provides no outlet and collective behavior which develops because the social order must be actively opposed. The bulk of riots, wildcat strikes, violent demonstrations, and the like fall in this group; though many incorporate much less real opposition to the social order than is supposed.

Common to all forms of collective behavior are (a) the discovery of a special but legitimate rule and (b) the development of a conception of the situation to which the rule is the appropriate guide. The nearer the situation is to the complex end of the continuum, the more complex is the fashion in which three general conditions must be met. First, there must be justification from the existing order, even in antiorganization behavior. The impact of an established order upon the normative conceptions of its members is such that value conflict or value change, within the established culture, the opportunity to borrow legitimating rituals from the traditional order, and defection or support from some representatives of the order are generally necessary to give the collective behavior legitimacy. Second, there must be justification for repudiating the established order. The more extreme collective behavior seldom develops except as the culmination of long-standing divisions in society involving groups that are set apart from the main order by double lines of division, such as duplicating class and regional lines. Communication breakdown is crucial because lack of access to the legitimate order is a prime justification for use of exceptional means; but even then extreme collective behavior seldom occurs without incidents interpreted as repudiation of appeals and good faith by the established order. Third, there must be a conviction of ingroup rightness and effectiveness. This conviction is supplied through the opportunity to establish mechanical solidarity and through the prior development of an ideology which supplies the necessary definition of the situation and of the significance of the collectivity's action.

2   George Rudé

THE CROWD AND ITS PROBLEMS

Perhaps no historical pehnomenon has been so thoroughly neglected by historians as the crowd. Few would deny that the crowd has, in a rich variety of guises, played a significant part in history. Yet it has, over many years, been considered a subject fit to be studied by the psychologist or the sociologist rather than by the historian. This book is a historian's attempt to do something to redress the balance.

Of course, I have no intention of attempting to deal with the crowd as a whole, and I shall begin by explaining my subject and defining its limits. In the first place, I am assuming the crowd to be what sociologists term a "face-to-face" or "direct contact" group[1] and not any type of collective phenomenon, such as a nation, a clan, caste, political party, village community, social class, the general "public," or any other "collectivity too large to aggregate." This would seem evident enough, had not some writers in the field (and there are eminent names among them) chosen to extend the crowd's boundaries to encompass far wider horizons. Gustave Le Bon, for example, the founding father of modern crowd psychology, being preoccupied with mental states rather than physical phenomena, includes in his crowd not only castes, clans, and classes but electoral "crowds," criminal juries, and parliamentary assemblies.[2] And Dr. Canetti, a newcomer in the field, discusses "the

George Rudé, "Introduction," in *The Crowd in History: A Study of Popular Disturbances in France and England, 1730-1848* (New York: John Wiley & Sons, Inc., Publishers, 1964), pp. 3-16. Reprinted by permission of the publisher.

crowd in history" (such is the subheading to one of his chapters) in terms of the various national symbols that he considers most appropriate to Englishmen, Frenchmen, Dutchmen, Germans, Jews, and Italians.[3]

This, however, can only be a first step in the process of delimitation. Any sort of crowd may, exceptionally, be termed suitable material for history; yet the "historical" crowd is more likely to be found among some of the sociologists' neat categories than among others. I say "more likely" quite deliberately, as we shall see that one type of crowd is liable, by the intrusion of the unexpected or of forces outside itself, to be converted into another. Nevertheless, in general, we may exclude from our present considerations crowds that are casually drawn together, like sight-seers; crowds assembled on purely ceremonial occasions or crowds taking part in religious or academic processions; or "audience" crowds (as they have been termed) who gather in theaters or lecture halls, at baseball matches or bullfights, or who used to witness hangings at Tyburn Fair or in the Place de Greve in Paris. Equally, we should generally exclude those more active, or "expressive" crowds that come together for Mardi Gras, participate in dancing orgies or student "rags," or attend revivalist meetings to hear Billy Graham or Father Divine, as they listened two hundred years ago to George Whitefield and the Wesleys. Certain "escape" or "panic" crowds (again to use the sociologist's jargon) are more likely to fall within our province: such manifestations have sometimes accompanied food riots and runs on banks, and these may be the very stuff of social history. Other outbursts of mass hysteria—from the convulsions around St. Medard's tomb in eighteenth-century Paris or the self-immolating orgies of Russia's Old Believers to the more recent frenzies stirred by Orson Welles' "Martian" broadcast—are fascinating material for the student of crowd psychology, but they may be of only casual interest to the historian. In fact, our main attention will be given to political demonstrations and to what sociologists have termed the "aggressive mob" or the "hostile outburst"[4]— to such activities as strikes, riots, rebellions, insurrections, and revolutions.

Even now, without further limitation, the subject would be far too vast to cover in a single volume. It is not the "crowd in history" in general that I propose to deal with, but the crowd within a limited period and within a limited area. For this purpose, I have chosen the period of the 1730's to 1840's in French and English history: apart from their importance as having seen the great political revolution in France and the industrial revolution in England, they were years of transition leading to the new "industrial" society.

Some may object to so arbitrary a division of what I am calling the "pre-industrial" and the "industrial" ages. Admittedly, my starting point is a somewhat arbitrary one, and the 1730's are chosen as much for convenience as to mark any sudden change in the pattern of social and political development. There is, however, a stronger case, in considering these two countries, for drawing a line somewhere around the 1840's. By then the effects of both the political and industrial revolutions were (earlier in the city and later in the village) transforming old institutions, uprooting the old society, changing old habits and modes of thinking, and imposing new techniques. To name only a few innovations, factory towns, railways, stable trade unions, a labor movement, socialist ideas, and the new Poor Law and police force in England were evidence that a new age was not only in the making but in being.

Such breaks with the past could not fail to leave their mark on the form and content of the crowd's activities; and we may as sharply (or as broadly) distinguish the typical popular disturbance of the new industrial society from that of the "pre-industrial" age as we may distinguish the latter from that of earlier times. In industrial society, the disturbances most prone to be historically significant take the shape of strikes and other labor disputes, or of public mass meetings and demonstrations conducted by political organizations; their objects tend (though by no means always) to be well defined, forward looking, and rational enough, even if only acceptable, in the first instance, to one side in the dispute; and participants tend, except in distinct peasant communities, to be wage earners or industrial workers. Similarly, the "pre-industrial" age has its own type of disturbance whose objects, behavior, forms of actions, and participants are, more or less, peculiar to the times. In our transitional period the typical form of social protest is the food riot, not the strike of the future or the millenarial movement or the peasant *jacquerie* of the past. Those engaging in popular disturbances are sometimes peasants (as in the past), but more often a mixed population of what in England were termed "lower orders" and in France *menu peuple* (or, for a short period in the 1790's, sans-culottes); they appear frequently in itinerant bands, "captained" or "generaled" by men whose personality, style of dress or speech, and momentary assumption of authority mark them out as leaders; they are fired as much by memories of customary rights or a nostalgia for past utopias as by present grievances or hopes of material improvement; and they dispense a rough-and-ready kind of "natural justice" by breaking their enemies of the moment in effigy, firing hayricks, and "pulling down" their houses, farms, fences, mills, or pubs, but rarely by taking lives. The riot, then, is the characteristic and ever-recurring form of popular protest which, on occasion, turns into rebellion or revolution.

It would be ridiculous, of course, to press this general distinction too far. Strikes were frequent enough in the eighteenth and early nineteenth centuries in France and England, particularly after the 1770's; and, on occasion, they assumed forms almost identical with those of more recent times. Londoners demonstrated and signed petitions in St. George's or Copenhagen Fields, and Parisians in the Champ de Mars or Place de Grève, as they might today in Trafalgar Square or Downing Street, around the "Bastille Column" or in the Place de la Concorde. Race riots today are not unlike religious riots of an earlier period. Outbursts of mass hysteria provoked by rumors of Flying Saucers or Martian invaders, recall similar manifestations in the past. Revivalist orgies and the antics of "Holy Rollers" (though little known in present-day Western Europe) are by no means strangers to modern industrial society. Again, in 1914, German bakers' shops in the East End of London were pillaged and wrecked as they might have been in Paris in the Revolution; and mythical Russians with "snow on their boots" were then as much a figment of popular imagination as the dreaded "brigands" of the Great Fear of

1789. And, if we need any further reminder that past or "archaic" forms may spill over into the present, we have but to turn to Dr. Hobsbawm's studies on millenarial, "populist-legitimist," and "Robin Hood" types of movement in southern Europe today.[5] The overlap between periods is, then, considerable and extends into fields that are as much the concern of the historian as of the sociologist; yet, in my view, they are not sufficient to invalidate the general distinction that I am seeking to establish.

The "crowd" of the "industrial" age has the advantage of having been relatively well served by historians (and, more recently, by sociologists): labor history and popular movements of this period have attracted a fair crop of reputable historians from the Webbs and Cole in England to Duveau, See, and Dolleans in France. The "pre-industrial" crowd has, in this respect, been less fortunate. There are honorable exceptions: the Hammonds in England and Jaures and Lefebvre in France come to mind. But, generally, the treatment of such movements has been bedeviled by one or other of two stereotyped approaches. The one—the more liberal, humane, and "democratic"—has taken one of two forms. The first is to read history backwards and ascribe such activities, without further investigation, to the "working class": J. M. Thompson in England, Tarle in the Soviet Union and Levasseur in France have all, in one form or another, done this. More frequently, the writer shows his sympathy for the objects of a movement by labeling its participants "the people." In France, the great protagonist of this school of writing was Michelet, whose generous impulses led him, quite simply and in defiance of all sociological niceties, to see *le peuple* as the sole agent of revolutionary action. Who captured the Bastille? he asks: not Marat's *pauvres ouvriers* or Dickens' *Saint-Antoine*; but, even less specifically, "*le peuple, le peuple tout entier*."[6] The tradition has survived. Similar approbatory labels are appended by liberal historians to Greek, Italian, and Spanish nationalist rebels of the nineteenth century and, if their cause is considered just (but then alone), to the "patriots" and "freedom fighters" of today.

The other stereotype—more fashionable among conservative writers—is to pin the label "mob" or "rabble" without discrimination on all participants in popular disturbance. The usage goes back to the seventeenth century at least, but we shall not attempt to trace its origins. It was certainly already fashionable in this "pre-industrial" age in France and England, when rioters and other disturbers of the peace were generally dismissed by contemporaries as "banditti," "desperadoes," "mob," "convicts," or "canaille";* and even a revolutionary democrat like Robespierre, though passionately devoted to "the people," was inclined to see food rioters (as on a famous occasion in February 1793) as agents of the English or the

* For an interesting exception, see Lord Granville's speech in the House of Lords on February 10, 1737, when commenting on the popular disturbances of 1736: "The People seldom or never assemble in any riotous or tumultuous manner, unless they are oppressed, or at least imagine they are oppressed" (*Gentleman's Magazine*, 1737, p. 374). But Granville, like Michelet in 1847, was in opposition to the government.

aristocracy. Burke, to whom the "lower orders" were a "swinish multitude," could not fail to look on the revolutionary crowds of 1789 as being composed of the most undesirable social elements: thus the Parisians invading the royal chateau at Versailles in the October "days" become "a band of cruel ruffians and assassins, reeking with . . . blood"; and the King and Queen, on their return journey to the capital, are escorted by "all the unutterable abominations of the furies of hell, in the abased shape of the vilest of women."[7] Yet Burke's invective, colorful as it is, is far surpassed by the French historian Taine, who, though a liberal in 1848, had, before he wrote his account of the Revolution, been soured by his experience of the Paris Commune. To him the revolutionaries of 1789 and the captors of the Bastille were the lowest social scum: "dregs of society," "bandits," "savages," and "raggamuffins"; the insurgents of October were "street prowlers," "thieves," "beggars," and "prostitutes"; and those of August 1792, who drove Louis XVI from the Tuileries palace, were bloodthirsty adventurers, "foreigners," "bullies," and "agents of debauchery."[8] So rich a flood of expletives has never, it is true, been matched by later historians; but the tradition launched by Burke and Taine has found its more recent echoes in such generalized labels attached to "No Popery" rioters, English Jacobins, political demonstrators, rural incendiaries, machine wreckers, and strikers as "criminal elements," "the slum population," or, more usually, just "the mob."* And the "mob" in question, having no ideas or honorable impulses of its own, is liable to be presented as the "passive" instrument of outside agents— "demagogues" or "foreigners"—and as being prompted by motives of loot, lucre, free drinks, bloodlust, or merely the need to satisfy some lurking criminal instinct.

Of course, there is all the difference in the world between these two approaches—that of Michelet, which sees the crowd as "the people," and that of Burke and Taine, which presents the crowd as "rabble"—and I do not hide my own preference for the first rather than the second; yet, in relation to my present argument, they have an important element in common. It is that they both are stereotypes and both present the crowd as a disembodied abstraction and not as an aggregate of men and women of flesh and blood. In short, they both reduce the participants in crowds and popular movements to what Carlyle called a "dead logic-formula" and thus, for the purpose of our present study, beg all the relevant questions.

Sociologists, having learned from Marx and Weber, have, on the whole, a better record. This is hardly surprising; the crowd has often been their particular field of study and, in recent years, American sociology in particular has done invaluable work on mixed communities, racial minorities, and racial riots. To them the crowd has not been, as it so often has to the historian, a merely generalized abstraction: they have rather tended to break it down and classify it according to its goals, behavior, or underlying beliefs."[9] Again, their concern for the collective attitudes of crowds is a salutary reminder to those liberal historians to whom the crowd has

* Even serious students of popular movements are not immune from this: see, for example, J. P. de Castro, *The Gordon Riots* (London, 1926); and M. Beloff, *Public Order and Popular Disturbances 1660-1714 (London, 1938).*

appeared as merely an aggregate of individuals that the whole is often not simply the sum total of its parts. Yet the crowd psychologists among them have often been guilty of creating their own stereotypes. Le Bon allowed that crowds differed according to "race" (most often, he appears to mean nationality) and that a crowd could be heroic as well as cowardly and might even possess virtues denied to many of the individuals who composed it. But he was inclined to treat the crowd in *a priori* terms: as irrational, fickle, and destructive; as intellectually inferior to its components; as primitive or tending to revert to an animal condition.[10] His prejudices led him to equate the "mob" with the lower classes in society; and, though critical of Taine in some respects, he took from him his fanciful picture of the French revolutionary crowd, which (as Le Bon claimed) tended to be formed of criminal elements, degenerates, and persons with destructive instincts, who blindly responded to the siren voices of "leaders" or "demagogues."[11] So, in spite of the author's profession to distinguish between one type and another, he arrives at a generalized conception of the crowd that, disregarding all social and historical development, would be equally appropriate to all times and to all places.

It would, of course, be absurd to suggest that the study of crowd behavior has stood still since Le Bon wrote over sixty years ago; and, though he is still revered for his pioneering efforts, many of his aristocratic prejudices and racial notions have been discarded by his successors. Even his insistence on the crowd's "irrational" behavior (though it has been further developed by Freud and Pareto), has been questioned; Dan Katz has been inclined to identify crowds according to class and has urged that account be taken of such stubborn historical realities as hardship and persecution in determining the collective actions of feudal serfs and working men; and Alexander Mintz has gone so far as to find reason in the actions of "panic" crowds.[12] More recently, Professor Smelser has turned his back even more firmly on the old shibboleths and urged that the defining characteristics of collective behavior should be seen as social rather than psychological, and he has stressed the importance in such matters of what he terms "generalized beliefs."[13] These are welcome signs and are, at least, the beginning of wisdom; for to be content to classify the crowd—and certainly the *historical* crowd—by mere patterns of behavior is rather like classifying political leaders according to their tricks of oratory, their sartorial habits, or their amatory exploits. And yet one of the old stereotypes still remains: the social psychologist, like the historian, continues to show reluctance to abandon the old concept of the crowd as "mob,"* with all its disparaging connotations. He has a better excuse than the historian, as much of his "live" material, concerned with lynchings, crazes, and panics, may condition him to see humanity in its collective manifestations as fickle, irrational, and destructive. For his knowledge of the past he has to rely on the historian; and if the latter sees fit to relay the hoary old preconceptions of those nurtured in the tradition of a Burke or a Taine, he can only expect to have them served back to him in double measure.

---

* See L. L. Bernard's definition of "mob" as "a highly excited form of crowd" in the *Encyclopaedia of Social Sciences*, X, 552.

How, then, do we escape from these stereotypes; and how, in particular, do we propose to study the crowd in the "pre-industrial" age? In the first place, by asking a number of questions, beginning with: what actually happened, both as to the event itself, and as to its origins and its aftermath? That is, we should attempt from the start to place the event in which the crowd participates in its proper historical context; for, without this, how can we hope to get beyond the stereotypes and probe into the crowd's outlook, objects, and behavior? Next: how large was the crowd concerned, how did it act, who (if any) were its promoters, who composed it, and who led it? Such questions are important, as they will help us to determine not only the general nature of the crowd and its behavior but also its components—by picking out what Asa Briggs has called "the faces in the crowd" in terms of the individuals and groups that compose it, their social origins, ages (sometimes), and occupations. Next: who were the target or the victims of the crowd's activities? This is also important, as it may help to throw further light on the event itself and tell us something of the social and political aims of those that took part in it.* But, more specifically, we need also to enquire: what were the aims, motives, and ideas underlying these activities? This is where Professor Smelser's "generalized beliefs" come in: without such enquiry we shall have to fall back on the purely "psychological" and "behaviorist" explanations of the crowd. A further relevant question is: how effective were the forces of repression, or of law and order? It is evident that in strikes, riots, or revolutionary situations the success or failure of the crowd's activities may largely depend on the resolution or reluctance of magistrates or on the degree of loyalty or disaffection of constables, police, or military. Finally: what were the consequences of the event, and what has been its historical significance? And so, having dissected the crowd and its components, its leaders and its victims, we return to the question from which we started—the nature and importance of an event in history.

It is, of course, one thing to ask such questions and quite another to find reasonably adequate answers to them. The degree to which our curiosity may be satisfied will depend both on the event itself and on the availability of suitable records. Obviously, we cannot afford to neglect the traditional sources, the historian's stock in trade: memoirs, correspondence, pamphlets, provincial and national newspapers, parliamentary reports and proceedings, the minutes and reports of local government and political organizations, and the previous findings of other historians, chroniclers, and antiquarians. Yet, even if we have the patience to consult them all, they may not take us very far; for they will often tend to present the question exclusively from the point of view of the government, the official political opposition, the aristocracy, or the more prosperous middle class—in short, from the angle of more elevated groups and classes than those to which the participants will generally belong. They will, in fact, rarely tell us much about the identity of either the rioters or their victims and remarkably little (as a rule) about the more

---

* For its relevance to the study of the London Gordon Riots of 1780 and the English agrarian disturbances of 1830, see Chapters 3 and 10.

detailed pattern of events, or about the motives or behavior of those most actively involved. These participants, unfortunately, rarely leave records of their own in the form of memoirs, pamphlets, or letters; and to identify them—and their victims—and probe into their motives and behavior, we shall have to rely on other materials. They may include police, prison, hospital, and judicial records; Home Office papers and Entry Books and the Treasury Solicitor's reports; tax rolls; poll books and petitions; notarial records; inventories; parish registers of births, deaths, and marriages; public assistance records; tables of prices and wages; censuses; local directories and club membership lists; and lists of freeholders, jurymen, church wardens, and justices of the peace. The record is by no means exhaustive: in fact, in considering this kind of history it would be foolish to attempt one. It is intended rather to give an idea of the sort of document where answers may be sought.

Yet, in their use, we must be prepared for disappointments. For one thing, such records are often housed in local depots, where they have not been classified or preserved with the same diligent care as those in central archives. Many have, in the course of time, tended to disappear or to fall victim to fire or flood, civil disturbance, enemy action, local ignorance, the misplaced zeal of collectors, or even (in the case of some judicial and transportation records) to the desire of some to cover up the seamy past. In England, few parliamentary petitions have been preserved; some were destroyed in the House of Commons fire of 1834. Similarly, in Paris, taxation and municipal records up to 1870 were largely destroyed by fire during the street-fighting at the time of the Commune;* others, in French provincial collections, have been obliterated in the course of two World Wars. Australian transportation records (invaluable for the study of English and Irish social movements of the early nineteenth century) have not escaped the attentions of collectors or other interested parties. English judicial records are piecemeal and incomplete for quite another reason; respectable enough in itself but with frustrating consequences for the researcher. Whereas the French police system of the eighteenth century was already highly developed, the English system was not; and whereas the French have accumulated substantial records of the cross examination of prisoners before trial, the English system, being concerned to protect the defendant from self-incrimination, did not allow him to be cross examined even in open court. As a result, English records of Assizes, quarter sessions, and consistory courts are not comparable in value for the researcher in this field with those that may be found in French national and departmental archives.

Even where such records are reasonably complete, however, they cannot possibly help us to identify all "the faces in the crowd." This can only be done on those rare occasions when the names and descriptions of all the persons concerned appear on some contemporary list or register. We know, for example, from lists in the French National Archives, the names, addresses, and occupations of all the

* An interesting survivor is the rolls of the Poor Tax (*taxe des pauvres*) of 1743, discussed by F. Furet in "Structures sociales parisiennes au XVIII siècle", *Annales (Economies-Sociétes-Civilisations)*, 1961, pp. 939-58.

800-odd citizens who were able to establish their claim to have been actively engaged in the final assault on the Bastille. Again, if we are willing to follow Le Bon in stretching the meaning of "crowd" beyond our earlier limitation, we can tell from the poll books of 1768 and 1769 the names and parishes of every one of those who voted for the radical John Wilkes in the Middlesex elections of those years, and from the Land Tax or Poor Rate books we may tell what properties they owned or rented. But these are quite exceptional cases. To identify the crowd, we usually have to supplement what we can learn from the one-sided accounts of eyewitnesses with such samples of those killed, wounded, or arrested in disturbances as we may find in police, judicial, and hospital records. Such samples have to be treated with caution as they are often too small to permit us to draw general conclusions; and there is often little to tell us whether those shot down or arrested were curious bystanders or active participants. Moreover, even if the sample is adequate, we may be left in doubt, as in studying English sessions papers, whether the term "laborer" denotes a journeyman, a domestic servant, or a small tradesman, or the term "yeoman" a small farmer, a shepherd, or an agricultural laborer. To say the least, the task of identifying "faces" is beset with obstacles and problems.

Even greater problems may face us when trying to establish the causes, motives, and mental and social attitudes underlying the crowd's activities. But these will no doubt become evident from what appears in later chapters, and I shall not elaborate them here. Enough has perhaps already been said to convince the reader that, in such a field of enquiry, the historian needs to tread warily, to look out for constant pitfalls, to avoid snap judgments, and to be more tentative in his conclusions than the historian of later labor movements and, even more, the modern field worker whose materials are not elusive parchment but living human beings. Yet the historian must use what evidence he can lay his hands on; and documents such as these, with all their imperfections, enable him, at least, to fill in a part of his picture and to answer some, if not all, of the questions with which he started.

In this book, it is with the help of similar materials, drawn from my own researches and from those of others,* that I have attempted to portray the "pre-industrial" crowd in action and to analyze its components and characteristics. To do this, I have, in the first place, divided its activities into a dozen selected categories and then in turn treat French and English rural and provincial riots of the eighteenth century, French and English city riots, industrial disturbances, the crowd in the French Revolution of 1848, and Chartism in England. No particular virtue is claimed for these precise divisions, which are bound to be somewhat arbitrary and to reflect "values" and conceptions that may be acceptable to some and not to others. Besides, they are evidently those of a historian rather than a sociologist. Where some might prefer to classify crowds solely according to their modes of behavior or motives and beliefs, I have chosen to take account not only of these factors but of others, such as the country and period in which disturbances

---

* My considerable debt to other writers in this field will be evident from the references and bibliography.

took place and the composition of their participants: for example, were they peasants or city dwellers? This will at least help to place the crowd in its geographical and historical as well as in its purely behaviorist or sociological setting; besides, it is not a rigid classification, and the reader will easily see for himself where there is an overlap between one selected category and another. This will appear more clearly in Part 2, where I have attempted a critical analysis of the crowd in its various manifestations, discussed the part played by the forces of law and order and the crowd's allies in other social classes, and drawn some general conclusions from the whole field of my inquiry. Such conclusions certainly do not claim to have any universal validity: at most, they are relevant to the crowd at a single stage of its history. Yet I hope that they may also encourage others to study the crowd in other periods and in other places. So, by such combined efforts, the crowd may eventually appear not as an abstract formula but as a living and many-sided historical phenomenon.

Footnotes

1 See articles by L.L.Bernard on "Crowd" and "Mob" in *Encyclopaedia of Social Sciences* (15 vols. New York, 1931-5), IV, 612-13; X, 552-4.

2 Gustave Le Bon, *The Crowd: A Study of the Popular Mind* (English translation, 6th impression, London, 1909), pp. 181 ff.

3 Elias Canetti, *Crowds and Power* (London, 1962), pp. 169-200.

4 See R.W. Brown, "Mass Phenomena," in *Handbook of Social Psychology* (2 vols. Cambridge, Mass., 1954), II, 847-58; and N.J. Smelser, *Theory of Collective Behavior* (London, 1962), pp. 222-69.

5 E.J. Hobsbawm, *Primitive Rebels: Studies in Archaic Forms of Social Movement in the 19th and 20th Centuries* (Manchester, 1959).

6 J. Michelet, *La Revolution francaise* (9 vols. Paris, 1868-1900), I, 248.

7 E. Burke, *Reflections on the Revolution in France* (London, 1951), pp. 66-9.

8 H. Taine, *Les origines de la France contemporaine. La Revolution* (3 vols. Paris, 1878), I, 18, 53-4, 130, 272.

9 See R.W. Brown, *op. cit.*, pp. 840-67 (especially the table of "varieties of crowds" on p. 841); and N.J. Smelser, *op. cit.*, pp. 4-22. Dr. Canetti (perhaps hardly a sociologist) has his own peculiar method of classification (*op. cit.*, pp. 48-63.)

10 Le Bon, *op. cit.*, pp. 25-88.

11 Le Bon, *La Revolution francaise et la psychologie des revolutions*(Paris, 1912), pp. 55-61, 89-93.

12 See Brown, *op. cit.*, pp. 342-5.

[13] Smelser, *op. cit.*, p. 16.

[14] For the foregoing, see my article, "The Study of Popular Distrubances in the 'Pre-Industrial' Age," *Historical Studies* (Melbourne), May 1963, pp. 457-69.

II

THE COLONIAL EXPERIENCE

Increasingly, as historians consider the past in terms of conflict, a question has arisen about their orientation toward the present and relevance of the past: Has the appeal of relevance prostituted objectivity? Years ago, Robert S. Lynd, the author of *Middletown*, warned that "history . . . voyaging forth with no pole star except the objective recovery of the past becomes a vast wandering enterprise.[1] His son, Staughton Lynd, has argued further that it would be irresponsible to study the past for its own sake; research must speak to the living. A historian can find himself in a unique position enabling him a look backward and forward simultaneously. He can study events not as isolated occurrences, but as parts of a process in which the present must be placed in the context of the past in order for it to be understood.

The disturbances of the past decade have shaken our confidence in the institutions and structures of this society so that we have been witnessing a severe questioning of our past and our relationship to it. In an essay written shortly before his death, Richard Hofstadter denied that a tradition of violence existed in the United States, because it lacks an "ideological and geographical center" and because the country has historical amnesia regarding violence. Yet, equally certain, we have a long, voluminous history concerning civil unrest. The growing awareness of this aspect of our history, as viewed in the light of recent experience, has resulted in a new and growing pessimism about the future.

The colonial period was a time of change and demonstrations, disorder and violence. But as a result of historical detachment, we know relatively little about this story today. Lacking any unifying theory of human behavior, historians have not been successful in placing mob activities into a conceptual, theoretical, whole. For the most part, civil unrest in early America has been related in some way to the Revolution. Seldom, if ever, have such events been considered relative to the social-political structure in which they occurred. The participants in disorders have been considered alike insofar as their socio-economic statuses and their relationships to the existing institutions and political units were concerned. The social-functional aspects of their lives and actions have been little noticed and less studied.

In 1955, a book, *Middle-Class Democracy and the Revolution* by Robert E. Brown,[2] was published. Equating widespread property holdings with social and political democracy, Brown held that the American Revolution was essentially a struggle to maintain rights already won by such "holders" during the Massachusetts colonial period. Essentially a conservative interpretation holding that the revolutionaries desired no fundamental social change, Brown's work has been attacked by various critics, many of whom have challenged his methodological approach involving economic indicators of class, the statistics upon whcih he rested his case and his use of terms not strictly in accord with commonly-held definitions. The present awareness of the role of conflict in human affairs makes some scholars wary of any theory ignoring, as Brown did, the significance of crowd behavior. Further, his conception and use of the terms *class* and *democracy* have been criticized. As late as 1965, a similar definitional or conceptual problem, specifically, the notion of a static class, caused another major study of the period to be downgraded. This was Jackson Turner Main's *The Social Structure of Revolutionary America.*[3] So what are examples of class in colonial America, and how can they be considered important?

In the winter of 1763-1764, Pennsylvania frontiersmen called the Paxton Boys, after one of their leaders, marched armed on the Quaker-controlled legislature in Philadelphia demanding stronger defensive measures be taken by the colony to protect them from an increasing number of Indian attacks along the frontier Their peaceful pleas had received only inaciton in reply, so they turned to armed petition. Several years later a German farmer, Frederick Stump, killed ten unarmed Indians and was subsequently arrested for murder. Another mob formed and by threat of armed violence freed him. Stump's actions were considered heroic in western Pennsylvania. There, the villain was the eastern-dominated assembly that ignored the farmers' requests for military protection. These acts were political and reached the point where rebellion was likely only when no other method brought a serious hearing.

Agrarian conflicts in colonial New York between tenant farmers and land owners were marked by a sense of class consciousness. The common impressment disorders, such as the one which took place in Boston in 1747, revealed deep social antagonism; they also demonstrated the effectiveness of mob action as a means of response to royal policies. Some colonial crowds were better organized than others, and these had a lasting impact on the history of the period. The Regulator movement in South Carolina, for example, grew out of the formation of a vigilante group to bring law and order to a backcountry plagued by cattle rustlers, thieves and roaming bands of outlaws. They, in turn, influenced the creation of Regulators in North Carolina, who were upset by a corrupt court system, underrepresentation in the colonial assembly, and higher taxes. So, from a vigilante group, the Regulator Movement grew into a western rebellion against the established government. In 1771, about one thousand militia men ended the Regulator Rebellion at the Battle of Alamance Creek.

Bernard Bailyn, in his *Pamphlets of the American Revolution,*[4] briefly attempted to explain events such as the Regulator uprising. He wrote that:

> . . . in the colonies, popular disturbances, occurring almost continuously in the eighteenth century, had been aimed at specific, limited targets and had expressed immediate grievances, which the regular processes of government seemed incapable of satisfying.

Whereas Bailyn saw significant political motivation behind revolutionary mobs, he interpreted earlier disturbances as ideologically inert and seldom expressing "deep-lying social distress." A different account might emerge if we could experience the daily life of that time as did those frustrated farmers and artisans who lived it; perhaps we can understand their actions and interpret them more correctly by attempting to re-construct as precisely as possible that daily life. It should be noted that Bailyn was not seeking such answers, but rather was trying to find precedents for the Stamp Act Riots of 1765 and for the Revolution. One of Professor Bailyn's students, Mrs. Pauline Maier, followed with a comprehensive study of American disturbances preceding the Revolution. Her article, which opens this section, is a broad survey of such uprisings; her findings support the interpretation given by Bailyn. She argues that mob action was then common to American life, and in this respect it was not much different from life in England. Colonial riots were seldom excessively violent. In general, she feels that the crowd was looked upon as an "extralegal arm of the community's interest," and was not "anti-authortarian in any general sense." As the mob often expressed the wishes of a large segment of the population, it became a quasi-legal means of political expression, and its membership, far from being seamen, servants, Negroes, and criminals, was taken from individuals who formed a cross section of the society.

The second essay looks at an urban disturbance and shows the significance of anti-authoritarian and anti-elite feeling commonly expressed during an election. Here, it is indicated that there was a sense of class consciousness in Pennsylvania, a colony which had an essentially undemocratic colonial government. This article emphasizes the spontaneity of such outbreaks and the discontent expressed by the disaffected elements of the colonial society.

Though these two interpretations differ, both raise serious questions about society and power in eighteenth-century America, and illustrate the important role that mob action played in bringing social change.

Suggested Further Readings

On the whole, the colonial crowd has been neglected by scholars, though Brooke Hindle, "The March of the Paxton Boys," *The William and Mary Quarterly*, III (1946), 461-86 and Patrick Henderson "Smallpox and Patriotism: The Norfolk Riots, 1768-1769," *The Virginia Magazine of History and Biography*, LXXIII (1965), 413-24 are interesting examples of what can be done. A book length study by Richard Maxwell Brown deals with *The South Carolina Regulators* (1963). Wilcomb E. Washburn, *The Governor and the Rebel* (1957) is an exciting account of a seventeenth-century rebellion and of the role which the mob played. Important insights into urban riots are found throughout Carl Bridenbaugh's *Cities in the Wilderness* (1938) and *Cities in Revolt* (1955). Most of the readings in the following section should also be consulted for additional insight into eighteenth-century disturbances.

Footnotes

1 The essay Robert S. Lynd, *Knowledge for What?* (New York: Grove Press, Inc., 1964) deserves to be better known; his comments on history are found on pp. 129-38. See also, Staughton Lynd, "The Historian as Participant." in Robert Skotheim, (ed.), *The Historian and the Climate of Opinion* (Reading, Mass.: Addison-Wesley Publishing Company, 1969), pp. 105-19.

2 Robert E. Brown, *Middle-Class Democracy and the Revolution in Massachusetts, 1691-1780* (Ithaca, N. Y.: Cornell University Press, 1955).

3 Jackson Turner Main, *The Social Structure of Revolutionary America* (Princeton, N. J.: Princeton University Press, 1965).

4 Bernard Bailyn, *Pamphlets of the American Revolution, 1750-1776*, Vol. 1 (Cambridge, Mass.: The Belknap Press of Harvard University Press, 1965), p. 582.

3   Pauline Maier

POPULAR UPRISINGS AND CIVIL AUTHORITY IN EIGHTEENTH-CENTURY AMERICA

It is only natural that the riots and civil turbulence of the past decade and a half have awakened a new interest in the history of American mobs. It should be

Reprinted from *William and Mary Quarterly*, XXVII (January, 1970), pp. 3-35, and by permission of the publisher.

emphasized, however, that scholarly attention to the subject has roots independent of contemporary events and founded in long-developing historiographical trends. George Rude's studies of pre-industrial crowds in France and England, E. J. Hobsbawm's discussion of "archaic" social movements, and recent works linking eighteenth-century American thought with English revolutionary tradition have all, in different ways, inspired a new concern among historians with colonial uprisings. This discovery of the early American mob promises to have a significant effect upon historical interpretation. Particularly affected are the Revolutionary struggle and the early decades of the new nation, when events often turned upon well-known popular insurrections.

Eighteenth-century uprisings were in some important ways different than those of today—different in themselves, but even more in the political context within which they occurred. As a result they carried different connotations for the American Revolutionaries than they do today. Not all eighteenth-century mobs, simply defied the law: some used extralegal means to implement official demands or to enforce laws not otherwise enforceable, others in effect extended the law in urgent situations beyond its technical limits. Since leading eighteenth-century Americans had known many occasions on which mobs took on the defense of the public welfare, which was, after all, the stated purpose of government, they were less likely to deny popular upheavals all legitimacy than are modern leaders. While not advocating popular uprisings, they could still grant such incidents an established and necessary role in free societies, one that made them an integral and even respected element of the political order. These attitudes, and the tradition of colonial insurrections on which they drew, not only shaped political events of the Revolutionary era, but also lay behind many laws and civil procedures that were framed during the 1780's and 1790's, some of which still have a place in the American legal system.

1

Not all colonial uprisings were identical in character or significance. Some involved no more than disorderly vandalism or traditional brawls such as those that annually marked Pope's Day on November 5, particularly in New England. Occasional insurrections defied established laws and authorities in the name of isolated private interests alone—a set of Hartford County, Connecticut, landowners arose in 1722, for example, after a court decision imperiled their particular land titles. Still others—which are of interest here—took on a broader purpose, and defended the interests of their community in general where established authorities failed to act. This common characteristic linked otherwise diverse rural uprisings in New Jersey and the Carolinas. The insurrectionists' punishment of outlaws, their interposition to secure land titles or prevent abuses at the hands of legal officials followed a frustration with established institutions and a belief that justice and even security had to be imposed by the people directly. The earlier Virginia tobacco insurrection also illustrates this common pattern well: Virginians began tearing up young tobacco plants in 1682 only after Governor Thomas Culpeper forced the quick adjournment of their assembly, which had been called to curtail tobacco planting during an economic crisis. The insurrections in Massachusetts a little over a century later represent a variation on this theme. The insurgents in Worcester, Berkshire, Hampshire, Middlesex, and Bristol counties—often linked together as members of "Shays's Rebellion"—forced the closing of civil courts, which threatened to send a major portion of the local population to debtors' prison, only until a new legislature could remedy their pressing needs.

This role of the mob as extralegal arm of the community's interest emerged, too, in repeated uprisings that occurred within the more densely settled coastal areas. The history of Boston, where by the mid-eighteenth century "public order . . . prevailed to a greater degree than anywhere else in England or America," is full of such incidents. During the food shortage of 1710, after the governor rejected a petition from the Boston selectmen calling for a temporary embargo on the exportation of foodstuffs one heavily laden ship found its rudder cut away, and fifty men sought to haul another outward bound vessel back to shore. Under similar circumstances Boston mobs again intervened to keep foodstuffs in the colony in 1713 and 1729. When there was some doubt a few years later whether or not the selectmen had the authority to seize a barn lying in the path of a proposed street, a group of townsmen, their faces blackened, levelled the structure and the road went through. Houses of ill fame were attacked by Boston mobs in 1734, 1737, and 1771; and in the late 1760's the *New York Gazette* claimed that mobs in Providence and Newport had taken on responsibility for "disciplining" unfaithful husbands. Meanwhile in New London, Connecticut, another mob prevented a radical religious sect, the Rogerenes, from disturbing normal Sunday services, "a practice they . . . [had] followed more or less for many years past; and which all the laws made in that government, and executed in the most judicious manner could not put a stop to."

Threats of epidemic inspired particularly dramatic instances of this community oriented role of the mob. One revealing episode occurred in Massachusetts in 1773-1774. A smallpox hospital had been built on Essex Island near Marblehead "much against the will of the multitude" according to John Adams. "The patients were careless, some of them wantonly so; and others were suspected of designing to spread the smallpox in the town, which was full of people who had not passed through the distemper." In January 1774 patients from the hospital who tried to enter the town from authorized landing places were forcefully prevented from doing so; a hospital boat was burned; and four men suspected of stealing infected clothes from the hospital were tarred and feathered, then carted from Marblehead to Salem in a long cortege. The Marblehead town meeting finally won the proprietors' agreement to shut down the hospital; but after some twenty-two new cases of smallpox broke out in the town within a few days "apprehension became general," and some "Ruffians" in disguise hastened the hospital's demise by burning the nearly evacuated building. A military watch of forty men were needed for several nights to keep the peace in Marblehead.

A similar episode occurred in Norfolk, Virginia, when a group of wealthy residents decided to have their families inoculated for smallpox. Fears arose that the lesser disease brought on by the inoculations would spread and necessitate a general inoculation, which would cost "more money than is circulating in Norfolk" and ruin trade and commerce such that "the whole colony would feel the effects." Local magistrates said they could not interfere because "the law was silent in the matter." Public and private meetings then sought to negotiate the issue. Despite a hard-won agreement, however, the pro-inoculation faction persisted in its original plan. Then finally a mob drove the newly inoculated women and children on a five-mile forced march in darkness and rain to the common Pest House, a three-year old institution designed to isolate seamen and others, particularly Negroes, infected with smallpox.

These local incidents indicate a willingness among many Americans to act outside the bounds of law, but they cannot be described as anti-authoritarian in any general sense. Sometimes in fact—as in the Boston bawdy house riot of 1734, or the Norfolk smallpox incident—local magistrates openly countenanced or participated in the mob's activities. Far from opposing established institutions, many supporters of Shays's Rebellion honored their leaders "by no less decisive marks of popular favor than elections to local offices of trust and authority." It was above all the existence of such elections that forced local magistrates to reflect community feelings and so prevented their becoming the targets of insurrections. Certainly in New England, where the town meeting ruled, and to some extent in New York, where aldermen and councilmen were annually elected, this was true; yet even in Philadelphia, with its lethargic closed corporation, or Charleston, which lacked municipal institutions, authority was normally exerted by residents who had an immediate sense of local sentiment. Provincial governments were also for the most part kept alert to local feelings by their elected assemblies. Sometimes, of course, uprisings turned against domestic American institutions—as in Pennsylvania in 1764, when the "Paxton Boys" complained that the colony's Quaker assembly had failed to provide adequately for their defense against the Indians. But uprisings over local issues proved *extra-institutional* in character more often than they were anti-institutional; they served the community where no law existed, or intervened beyond what magistrates thought they could do officially to cope with a local problem.

The case was different when imperial authority was involved. There legal authority emanated from a capital an ocean away, where the colonists had no integral voice in the formation of policy, where governmental decisions were based largely upon the reports of "king's men" and sought above all to promote the king's interests. When London's legal authority and local interest conflicted, efforts to implement the edicts of royal officials were often answered by uprisings, and it was not unusual in these cases for local magistrates to participate or openly sympathize with the insurgents. The colonial response to the White Pines Acts of 1722 and 1729 is one example. Enforcement of the acts was difficult in general because "the various elements of colonial society . . . seemed inclined to violate the pine laws—legislatures, lumbermen, and merchants were against them, and even the royal governors were divided." At Exeter, New Hampshire, in 1734 about thirty men prevented royal officials from putting the king's broad arrow on some seized boards; efforts to enforce the acts in Connecticut during the 1750's ended after a deputy of the surveyor-general was thrown in a pond and nearly drowned; five years later logs seized in Massachusetts and New Hampshire were either "rescued" or destroyed. Two other imperial issues that provoked local American uprisings long before 1765 and continued to do so during the Revolutionary period were impressment and customs enforcement.

As early as 1743 the colonists' violent opposition to impressment was said to indicate a "Contempt of Government." Some captains had been mobbed, the Admiralty complained, "others emprisoned, and afterwards held to exorbitant Bail, and are now under Prosecutions carried on by Combination, and by joint Subscription towards the expense." Colonial governors, despite their offers, furnished captains with little real aid either to procure seamen or "even to protect them from the Rage and Insults of the People." Two days of severe rioting answered Commodore Charles Knowles's efforts to sweep Boston harbor for able-bodied men in November 1747. Again in 1764 when Rear Admiral Lord Alexander Colville sent out orders to "procure" men in principal harbors between Casco Bay and Cape Henlopen, mobs met the ships at every turn. When the *St. John* sent out a boat to seize a recently impressed deserter from a Newport wharf, a mob protected him, captured the boat's officer, and hurled stones at the crew; later fifty Newporters joined the colony's gunner at Fort George in opening fire on the king's ship itself. Under threat to her master the *Chaleur* was forced to release four fishermen seized off Long Island, and when that ship's captain went ashore at New York a mob seized his boat and burned it in the Fields. In the spring of 1765 after the *Maidstone* capped a six-month siege of Newport harbor by seizing "all the Men" out of a brigantine from Africa, a mob of about five hundred men similarly seized a ship's officer and burned one of her boats on the Common. Impressment also met mass resistance at Norfolk in 1767 and was a major cause of the famous *Liberty* riot at Boston in 1768.

Like the impressment uprisings, which in most instances sought to protect or rescue men from the "press," customs incidents were aimed at impeding the customs service in enforcing British laws. Tactics varied, and although incidents occurred long before 1764—in 1719, for example, Caleb Heathcote reported a "riotous and tumultuous" rescue of seized claret by Newporters—their frequency, like those of the impressment "riots," apparently increased after the Sugar Act was passed and customs enforcement efforts were tightened. The 1764 rescue of the *Rhoda* in Rhode Island preceded a theft in Dighton, Massachusetts, of the cargo from a newly seized vessel, the *Polly* by a mob of some forty men with blackened faces. In 1766 again a mob stoned a customs official's home in Falmouth (Portland), Maine, while "Persons unknown and disguised" stole sugar and rum that had been impounded that morning. The intimidation of customs officials and of the particularly despised customs informers also enjoyed a long history. In 1701 the South Carolina attorney general publicly attacked an informer "and struck him several times, crying out, this is the Informer, this is he that will ruin the country."

Similar assaults occurred decades later, in New Haven in 1766 and 1769, and New London in 1769, and were then often distinguished by their brutality. In 1771 a Providence tidesman, Jesse Saville, was seized, stripped, bound hand and foot, tarred and feathered, had dirt thrown in his face, then was beaten and "almost strangled." Even more thorough assaults upon two other Rhode Island tidesmen followed in July 1770 and upon Collector Charles Dudley in April 1771. Finally, customs vessels came under attack: the *St. John* was shelled at Newport in 1764 where the customs ship *Liberty* was sunk in 1769—both episodes that served as prelude to the destruction of the *Gaspee* outside Providence in 1771.

Such incidents were not confined to New England. Philadelphia witnessed some of the most savage attacks, and even the surveyor of Sassafras and Bohemia in Maryland—an office long a sinecure, since no ships entered or cleared in Sassafras or Bohemia—met with violence when he tried to execute his office in March 1775. After seizing two wagons of goods being carried overland from Maryland toward Duck Creek, Delaware, the officer was overpowered by a "licentious mob" that kept shouting "Liberty and Duck Creek forever" as it went through the hours-long rituals of tarring and feathering him and threatening his life. And at Norfolk, Virginia, in the spring 1766 an accused customs informer was tarred and feathered, pelted with stones and rotten eggs, and finally thrown in the sea where he nearly drowned. Even Georgia saw customs violence before independence, and one of the rare deaths resulting from a colonial riot occurred there in 1775.

White Pines, impressment, and customs uprisings have attracted historians' attention because they opposed British authority and so seemed to presage the Revolution. In fact, however, they had much in common with many exclusively local uprisings. In each of the incidents violence was directed not so much against the "rich and powerful" as against men who—as it was said after the Norfolk smallpox incident—"in every part of their conduct . . . acted very inconsistently as good neighbors or citizens." The effort remained one of safeguarding not the interests of isolated groups alone, but the community's safety and welfare. The White Pines Acts need not have provoked this opposition had they applied only to trees of potential use to the Navy, and had they been framed and executed with concern for colonial rights. But instead the acts reserved to the Crown all white pine trees including those "utterly unfit for masts, yards, or bowsprits," and prevented colonists from using them for building materials or lumber exportation even in regions where white pine constituted the principal forest growth. As a result the acts "operated so much against the convenience and even necessities of the inhabitants," Surveyor John Wentworth explained, that, "it became almost a general interest of the country" to frustrate the acts' execution. Impressment offered a more immediate effect, since the "press" could quickly cripple whole towns. Merchants and masters were affected as immediately as seamen: the targeted port, as Massachusetts' Governor William Shirley explained in 1747, was drained of mariners by both impressment itself and the flight of navigation to safer provinces, driving the wages for any remaining seamen upward. When the press was of long duration, moreover, or when it took place during a normally busy season, it could mean serious shortages of food or firewood for winter, and a general attrition of the commercial life that sustained all strata of society in trading towns. Commerce seemed even more directly attacked by British trade regulations, particularly by the proliferation of customs procedures in the mid-1760's that seemed to be in no American's interest, and by the Sugar Act with its virtual prohibition of the trade with the foreign West Indies that sustained the economies of colonies like Rhode Island. As a result even when only a limited contingent of sailors participated in a customs incident officials could suspect—as did the deputy collector at Philadelphia in 1770—that the mass of citizens "in their Hearts" approved of it.

Because the various uprisings discussed here grew out of concerns essential to wide sections of the community, the "rioters" were not necessarily confined to the seamen, servants, Negroes, and boys generally described as the staple components of the colonial mob. The uprising of Exeter, New Hampshire, townsmen against the king's surveyor of the woods in 1754 was organized by a member of the prominent Gillman family who was a mill owner and a militia officer. Members of the upper classes participated in Norfolk's smallpox uprising, and Cornelius Calvert, who was later attacked in a related incident, protested that leading members of the community, doctors and magistrates, had posted securities for the good behavior of the "Villains" convicted of mobbing him. Captain Jeremiah Morgan complained about the virtually universal participation of Norfolkers in an impressment incident of 1767, and "all the principal Gentlemen in Town" were supposedly present when a customs informer was tarred and feathered there in 1766. Merchant Benedict Arnold admitted leading a New Haven mob against an informer in 1766; New London merchants Joseph Packwood and Nathaniel Shaw commanded the mob that first accosted Captain William Reid the night the *Liberty* was destroyed at Newport in 1769, just as John Brown, a leading Providence merchant, led that against the *Gaspee*. Charles Dudley reported in April 1771 that the men who beat him in Newport "did not come from the . . . lowest class of Men," but were "stiled Merchants and the Masters of their Vessels"; and again in 1775 Robert Stratford Byrne said many of his Maryland and Pennsylvania attackers were "from Appearance . . . Men of Property." It is interesting, too, that during Shays's Rebellion—so often considered a class uprising—"men who were of good property and owed not a shilling" were said to be "involved in the train of desperado's to suppress the courts."

Opposition to impressment and customs enforcement in itself was not, moreover, the only cause of the so-called impressment or customs "riots." The complete narratives of these incidents indicate again not only that the crowd acted to support local interests, but that it sometimes enforced the will of local magistrates by extralegal means. Although British officials blamed the *St. John* incident upon that ship's customs and impressment activities, colonists insisted that the confrontation began when some sailors stole a few pigs and chickens from a local miller and the ship's crew refused to surrender the thieves to Newport officials. Two members of the Rhode Island council then ordered the gunner of Fort George to detain the schooner until the accused seamen were delivered to the sheriff, and "many People went over the Fort to assist the Gunner in the Discharge of his Duty." Only after this uprising did the ship's officers surrender the accused men. Similarly, the 1747 Knowles impressment riot in Boston and the 1765 *Maidstone* impressment riot in Newport broke out after governors' request for the release of impressed seamen had gone unanswered, and only after the outbreaks of violence were the governors' requests honored. The crowd that first assembled on the night the *Liberty* was destroyed in Newport also began by demanding the allegedly drunken sailors who that afternoon had abused and shot at a colonial captain, Joseph Packwood, so they could be bound over to local magistrates for prosecution.

In circumstances such as these, the "mob" often appeared only after the legal channels of redress had proven inadequate. The main thrust of the colonists' resistance to the White Pines Acts had always been made in their courts and legislatures. Violence broke out only in local situations where no alternative was available. Even the burning of the *Gaspee* in June 1772 was a last resort. Three months before the incident a group of prominent Providence citizens complained about the ship's wanton severity with all vessels along the coast and the colony's governor pressed their case with the fleet's admiral. The admiral, however, supported the *Gaspee*'s commander, Lieutenant William Dudingston; and thereafter, the *Providence Gazette* reported, Dudingston became "more haughty, insolent and intolerable, ... personally ill treating every master and merchant of the vessels he boarded, stealing sheep, hogs, poultry, etc. from farmers round the bay, and cutting down their fruit and other trees for firewood." Redress from London was possible but time-consuming, and in the meantime Rhode Island was approaching what its governor called "the deepest calamity" as supplies of food and fuel were curtailed and prices, especially in Newport, rose steeply. It was significant that merchant John Brown finally led the Providence "mob" that seized the moment in June when the *Gaspee* ran aground near Warwick, for it was he who had spearheaded the effort in March 1772 to win redress through the normal channels of government.

2

There was little that was distinctively American about the colonial insurrections. The uprisings over grain exportations during times of dearth, the attacks on brothels, press gangs, royal forest officials, and customsmen, all had their counterparts in seventeenth- and eighteenth-century England. Even the Americans' hatred of the customs establishment mirrored the Englishman's traditional loathing of excise men. Like the customsmen in the colonies, they seemed to descend into localities armed with extraordinary prerogative powers. Often, too, English excisemen were "thugs and brutes who beat up their victims without compunction or stole or wrecked their property" and against whose extravagances little redress was possible through the law. Charges of an identical character were made in the colonies against customsmen and naval officials as well, particularly after 1763 when officers of the Royal Navy were commissioned as deputy members of the customs service, and a history of such accusations lay behind many of the best-known waterfront insurrections. The Americans' complaints took on particular significance only because in the colonies those officials embodied the authority of a "foreign" power. Their arrogance and arbitrariness helped effect "an estrangement of the Affections of the People from the Authority under which they act," and eventually added an emotional element of anger against the Crown to a revolutionary conflict otherwise carried on in the language of law and right.

The focused character of colonial uprisings also resembled those in England and even France where, Rude has pointed out, crowds were remarkably single-minded and discriminating. Targets were characteristically related to grievances: the Knowles rioters sought only the release of the impressed men; they set free a captured officer when assured he had nothing to do with the press, and refrained from burning a boat near Province House for fear the fire would spread. The Norfolk rioters, driven by fear of smallpox, forcefully isolated the inoculated persons where they would be least dangerous. Even the customs rioters vented their brutality on customs officers and informers alone, and the Shaysite "mobs" dispersed after closing the courts which promised most immediately to effect their ruin. So domesticated and controlled was the Boston mob that it refused to riot on Saturday and Sunday nights, which were considered holy by New Englanders.

When colonists compared their mobs with those in the Mother Country they were struck only with the greater degree of restraint among Americans. "These People bear no Resemblance to an English Mob," John Jay wrote of the Shaysites in December 1786, "they are more temperate, cool and regular in their Conduct— they have hitherto abstained from Plunder, nor have they that I know of committed any outrages but such as the accomplishment of their Purpose made necessary." Similar comparisons were often repeated during the Revolutionary conflict, and were at least partially grounded in fact. When Londoners set out to "pull down" houses of ill fame in 1688, for example, the affair spread, prisons were opened, and disorder ended only when troops were called out. But when eighteenth-century Bostonians set out on the same task, there is no record that their destruction extended beyond the bordellos themselves. Even the violence of the customs riots—which contrast in that regard from other American incidents—can sometimes be explained by the presence of volatile foreign seamen. The attack on the son of customsman John Hatton, who was nearly killed in a Philadelphia riot, occurred, for example, when the city was crowded by over a thousand seamen. His attackers were apparently Irish crew members of a vessel he and his father had tried to seize off Cape May, and they were "set on," the Philadelphia collector speculated, by an Irish merchant in Philadelphia to whom the vessel was consigned. One of the most lethal riots in the history of colonial America, in which rioters killed five people, occurred in a small town near Norfolk, Virginia, and was significantly perpetrated entirely by British seamen who resisted the local inhabitants' efforts to reinstitute peace. During and immediately after the Revolutionary War some incidents occurred in which deaths are recorded; but contemporaries felt these were historical aberrations, caused by the "brutalizing" effect of the war itself. "Our citizens, from a habit of putting . . . [the British] to death, have reconciled their minds to the killing of each other," South Carolina Judge Aedanus Burke explained.

To a large extent the pervasive restraint and virtual absence of bloodshed in American incidents can best be understood in terms of social and military circumstance. There was no large amorphous city in America comparable to London, where England's worst incidents occurred. More important, the casualties even in eighteenth-century British riots were rarely the work of rioters. No deaths were inflicted by the Wilkes, Anti-Irish, or "No Popery" mobs, and only single fatalities resulted from other upheavals such as the Porteous riots of 1736. "It was authority rather than the crowd that was conspicuous for its violence to life and limb": all 285 casualties of the Gordon riots, for example, were rioters. Since a regular army was less at the ready for use against colonial mobs, casualty figures for American uprisings were naturally much reduced.

To some extent the general tendency toward a discriminating purposefulness was shared by mobs throughout western Europe, but within the British Empire the focused character of popular uprisings and also their persistence can be explained in part by the character of law enforcement procedures. There were no professional police forces in the eighteenth century. Instead the power of government depended traditionally upon institutions like the "hue and cry," by which the community in general rose to apprehend felons. In its original medieval form the "hue and cry" was a form of summary justice that resembled modern lynch law. More commonly by the eighteenth-century magistrates turned to the *posse commitatus* literally the "power of the country," and in practice all able-bodied men a sheriff might call upon to assist him. Where greater and more organized support was needed, magistrates could call out the militia. Both the *posse* and the militia drew upon local men, including many of the same persons who made up the mob. This was particularly clear where these traditional mechanisms failed to function effectively. At Boston in September 1766 when customsmen contemplated breaking into the house of merchant Daniel Malcom to search for contraband goods, Sheriff Stephen Greenleaf threatened to call for support from members of the very crowd suspected of an intent to riot; and when someone suggested during the Stamp Act riots that the militia be raised Greenleaf was told it had already risen. This situation meant that mobs could naturally assume the manner of a lawful institution, acting by habit with relative restraint and responsibility. On the other hand, the militia institutionalized the practice of forcible popular coercion and so made the formation of extralegal mobs more natural that J. R. Western has called the militia "a relic of the bad old days," and hailed its passing as "a step towards . . . bringing civilization and humanity into our [English] political life."

These law enforcement mechanisms left magistrates virtually helpless whenever a large segment of the population was immediately involved in the disorder, or when the community had a strong sympathy for the rioters. The Boston militia's failure to act in the Stamp Act riots, which was repeated in nearly all the North

American colonies, recapitulated a similar refusal during the Knowles riot of 1747. If the mob's sympathizers were confined to a single locality, the governor could try to call out the militias of surrounding areas, as Massachusetts Governor William Shirley began to do in 1747, and as, to some extent, Governor Francis Bernard attempted after the rescue of the *Polly* in 1765. In the case of sudden uprisings, however, these peace-keeping mechanisms were at best partially effective since they required time to assemble strength, which often made the effort wholly pointless.

When the disorder continued and the militia either failed to appear or proved insufficient, there was, of course, the army, which was used periodically in the eighteenth century against rioters in England and Scotland. Even in America peacetime garrisons tended to be placed where they might serve to maintain law and order. But since all Englishmen shared a fear of standing armies the deployment of troops had always to be a sensitive and carefully limited recourse. Military and civil spheres of authority were rigidly separated, as was clear to Lord Jeffery Amherst, who refused to use soldiers against antimilitary rioters during the Seven Years' War because that function was "entirely foreign to their command and belongs of right to none but the civil power." In fact troops could be used against British subjects, as in the suppression of civil disorder, only upon the request of local magistrates. This institutional inhibition carried, if anything, more weight in the colonies. There royal governors had quickly lost their right to declare martial law without the consent of the provincial councils that were, again, usually filled with local men.

For all practical purposes, then, when a large political unit such as an entire town or colony condoned an act of mass force, problems were raised "almost insoluble without rending the whole fabric of English law." Nor was the situation confined to the colonies. After describing Englands's institutions for keeping the peace under the later Stuarts, Max Beloff suggested that no technique for maintaining order was found until nineteenth-century reformers took on the task of reshaping urban government. Certainly by the 1770's no acceptable solution had been found—neither by any colonists, nor "anyone in London, Paris, or Rome, either," as Carl Bridenbaugh has put it. To even farsighted contemporaries like John Adams the weakness of authority was a fact of the social order that necessarily conditioned the way rulers could act. "It is vain to expect or hope to carry on government against the universal bent and genius of the people," he wrote, "we may whimper and whine as much as we will, but nature made it impossible when she made man."

The mechanisms of enforcing public order were rendered even more fragile since the difference between legal and illegal applications of mass force was distinct in theory, but sometimes indistinguishable in practice. The English common law prohibited riot, defined as an uprising of three or more persons who performed what Blackstone called an "unlawful act of violence" for a private purpose. If the act was never carried out or attempted the offense became unlawful assembly; if some effort was made toward its execution, rout; and if the purpose of the uprising was public rather than private—tearing down whore houses, for example, or destroying all enclosures rather than just those personally affecting the insurgents—the offense became treason since it constituted a usurpation of the king's function, a "levying war against the King." The precise legal offence lay not so much in the purpose of the uprising as in its use of force and violence "wherein the Law does not allow the Use of such Force." Such unlawful assumptions of force were carefully distinguished by commentators upon the common law from other occasions on which the law authorized a use of force. It was, for example, legal for force to be used by a sheriff, constable, "or perhaps even . . . a private Person" who assembled "a competent Number of People, in Order with Force to suppress Rebels, or Enemies, or Rioters"; for a justice of the peace to raise the *posse* when opposed in detaining lands, or for Crown officers to raise "a Power as may effectually enable them to over-power any . . . Resistance" in the execution of the King's writs.

In certain situations these distinctions offered at best a very uncertain guide as to who did or did not exert force lawfully. Should a *posse* employ more force than was necessary to overcome overt resistance, for example, its members acted illegally and were indictable for riot. And where established officials supported both sides in a confrontation, or where the legality of an act that officials were attempting to enforce was itself disputed, the decision as to who were or were not rioters seemed to depend upon the observer's point of view. Impressment is a good example. The colonists claimed that impressment was unlawful in North America under an act of 1708, while British authorities and some—but not all—spokesmen for the government held that the law had lapsed in 1713. The question was settled only in 1775, when Parliament finally repealed the "Sixth of Anne." Moreover, supposing impressment could indeed be carried on, were press warrants from provincial authorities still necessary? Royal instructions of 1697 had given royal governors the "sole power of impressing seamen in any of our plantations in America or in sight of them." Admittedly that clause was dropped in 1708, and a subsequent parliamentary act of 1746, which required the full consent of the governor and council before impressment could be carried on within their province, applied only to the West Indies. Nontheless it seems that in 1764 the Lords of the Admiralty thought the requirement held throughout North America. With the legality of impressment efforts so uncertain, especially when opposed by local authorities, it was possible to see the press gangs as "rioters" for trying *en masse* to perpetrate an unlawful act of violence. In that case the local townsmen who opposed them might be considered lawful defenders of the public welfare, acting much as they would in a *posse*. In 1770 John Adams cited opposition to press gangs who acted without warrants as an example of the lawful use of force; and when the sloop of war *Hornet* swept into Norfolk, Virginia, in September 1767 with a "bloody riotous plan . . . to impress seamen, without consulting the Mayor, or any other magistrate," the offense was charged to the pressmen. Roused by the watchman, who called out "*a riot by man of war's men,*" the inhabitants rose to back the magistrates, and not only secured the release of the impressed men but also imprisoned ten members of the press gang. The ship's captain, on the other hand, condemned the townsmen as "Rioters." Ambiguity was present, too, in Newport's *St. John* clash, which involved both impressment and criminal action on the part of royal seamen and culminated with Newporters firing on the king's ship. The Privy Council in England promptly classified the incident as a riot, but the Rhode Island governor's report boldly maintained that "the people meant nothing but to assist [the magistrates] in apprehending the Offenders" on the vessel, and even suggested that "their Conduct be honored with his Majesty's royal Approbation."

The enforcement of the White Pines Acts was similarly open to legal dispute. The acts seemed to violate both the Massachusetts and Connecticut charters; the meaning of provisions exempting trees growing within townships (act of 1722) and those which were "the property of private persons" (act of 1729) was contested, and royal officials tended to work on the basis of interpretations of the laws that Bernhard Knollenberg has called farfetched and, in one case, "utterly untenable." The Exeter, New Hampshire, "riot" of 1734, for example, answered an attempt of the surveyor to seize boards on the argument that the authorization to seize logs from allegedly illegally felled white pine trees in the act of 1722 included an authorization to seize processed lumber. As a result, Knollenberg concluded, although the surveyors' reports "give the impression that the New Englanders were an utterly lawless lot, . . . in many if not most cases they were standing for what they believed, with reason, were their legal and equitable rights in trees growing on their own lands."

Occasions open to such conflicting interpretations were rare. Most often even those who sympathized with the mobs' motives condemned its use of force as illegal and unjustifiable. That ambiguous cases did arise, however, indicates that legitimacy and illegitimacy, *posses* and rioters, represented but poles of the same spectrum. And where a mob took upon itself the defense of the community, it benefited from a certain popular legitimacy even when the strict legality of its action was in doubt, particularly among a people taught that the legitimacy of law itself depended upon its defense of the public welfare.

Whatever quasi-legal status mobs were accorded by local communities was reinforced, moreover, by formal political thought. "Riots and rebellions" were often calmly accepted as a constant and even necessary element of free government. This acceptance depended, however, upon certain essential assumptions about popular uprisings. With words that could be drawn almost verbatim from John Locke or any other English author of similar convictions, colonial writers posited a continuing moderation and purposefulness on the part of the mob. "Tho' innocent Persons may sometimes suffer in popular Tumults," observed a 1768 writer in the *New York Journal*, "yet the general Resentment of the People is principally directed according to Justice, and the greatest Delinquent feels it most." Moreover, upheavals constituted only occasional interruptions in well-governed societies. "Good Laws and good Rulers will Always be obey'd and respected"; "the Experience of all Ages proves, that Mankind are much more likely to submit to bad Laws and wicked Rulers, than to resist good ones." "Mobs and Tumults," it was often said, "never happen but thro' Oppression and a scandalous Abuse of Power."

In the hands of Locke such remarks constituted relatively inert statements of fact. Colonial writers, however, often turned these pronouncements on their heads such that observed instances of popular disorder became *prima facie* indictments of authority. In 1747, for example, New Jersey land rioters argued that "from their Numbers, Violences, and unlawful Actions" it was to be "inferred that . . . they are wronged and oppressed, or else they would never *rebell agt. the Laws*." Always, a New York writer said in 1770, when "the People of any Government" become "turbulent and uneasy," it was above all "a certain Sign of Maladministration." Even when disorders were not directly levelled against government they provided "strong proofs that something is much amiss in the state" as William Samuel Johnson put it; that—in Samuel Adams's words—the "wheels of good government" were "somewhat clogged." Americans who used this argument against Britain in the 1760's continued to depend upon it two decades later when they reacted to Shays's Rebellion by seeking out the public "Disease" in their own independent governments that was indicated by the "Spirit of Licentiousness" in Massachusetts.

Popular turbulence seemed to follow so naturally from inadequacies of government that uprisings were often described with similes from the physical world. In 1770 John Adams said that there were "Churchquakes and state-quakes in the moral and political world, as well as earthquakes, storms and tempests in the physical." Two years earlier a writer in the *New York Journal* likened popular tumults to "Thunder Gusts" which "commonly do more Good than Harm." Thomas Jefferson continued the imagery in the 1780's, particularly with his famous statement that he liked "a little rebellion now and then" for it was "like a storm in the atmosphere." It was, moreover, because of the "imperfection of all things in this world," including government, that Adams found it "vain to seek a government in all points free from a possibility of civil wars, tumults and seditions." That was "a blessing denied to this life and preserved to complete the felicity of the next."

If popular uprisings occurred "in all governments at all times," they were nonetheless most able to break out in free governments. Tyrants imposed order and submission upon their subjects by force, thus dividing society, as Jefferson said, into wolves and sheep. Only under free governments were the people "nervous," spirited, jealous of their rights, ready to react against unjust provocations; and this being the case, popular disorders could be interpreted as "Symptoms of a strong and healthy Constitution" even while they indicated some lesser shortcoming in administration. It would be futile, Josiah Quincy, Jr., said in 1770, to expect "that pacific, timid, obsequious, and servile temper, so predominant in more despotic governments" from those who lived under free British institutions. From "our happy constitution." he claimed, there resulted as "very natural Effects" an "impatience of injuries, and a strong resentment of insults."

This popular impatience constituted an essential force in the maintenance of free institutions. "What country can preserve it's [*sic*] liberties if their rulers are not warned from time to time that their people preserve the spirit of resistance?" Jefferson asked in 1787. Occasional insurrections were thus "an evil . . . productive of good": even those founded on popular error tended to hold rulers "to the true principles of their institution" and generally provided "a medecine necessary for the sound health of government." This meant that an aroused people had a role not only in extreme situations, where revolution was requisite, but in the normal course of free government. For that reason members of the House of Lords could seriously argue—as A. J. P. Taylor has pointed out—that "rioting is an essential part of our constitution"; and for that reason, too, even Massachusetts's conservative Lieutenant Governor Thomas Hutchinson could remark in 1768 that "mobs a sort of them at least are constitutional."

3

It was, finally, the interaction of this constitutional role of the mob with the written law that makes the story of eighteenth-century popular uprisings complexity itself. If mobs were appreciated because they provided a check on power, it was always understood that, insofar as upheavals threatened "running to such excesses, as will overturn the whole system of government," "strong discouragements" had to be provided against them. For eighteenth-century Americans, like the English writers they admired, liberty demanded the rule of law. In extreme situations where the rulers had clearly chosen arbitrary power over the limits of law, men like John Adams could prefer the risk of anarchy to continued submission because "anarchy can never last long, and tyranny may be perpetual," but only when "there was any hope that the fair order of liberty and a free constitution would arise out of it." This desire to maintain the orderly rule of law led legislatures in England and the colonies to pass antiriot statues and to make strong efforts—in the words of a 1753 Massachusetts law—to discountenance "a mobbish temper and spirit in . . . the inhabitants" that would oppose "all government and order."

The problem of limiting mass violence was dealt with most intensely over a sustained period by the American Revolutionary leadership, which has perhaps suffered most from historians' earlier inattention to the history of colonial uprisings. So long as it could be maintained—as it was only fifteen years ago—that political mobs were "rare or unknown in America" before the 1760's, the Revolutionaries were implicitly credited with their creation. American patriots, Charles McLean Andrews wrote, were often "lawless men who were nothing more than agitators and demagogues" and who attracted a following from the riffraff of colonial society. It now seems clear that the mob drew on all elements of the population. More important, the Revolutionary leaders had no need to create mob support. Instead they were forced to work with a "permanent entity," a traditional crowd that exerted itself before, after, and even during the Revolutionary struggle over issues unrelated to the conflict with Britain, and that, as Hobsbawm has noted, characteristically aided the Revolutionary cause in the opening phases of conflict but was hard to discipline thereafter.

In focusing popular exuberance the American leaders could work with long-established tendencies in the mob toward purposefulness and responsibility. In doing so they could, moreover, draw heavily upon the guidelines for direct action that had been defined by English radical writers since the seventeenth century. Extralegal action was justified only when all established avenues to redress had failed. It could not answer casual errors or private failings on the part of the magistrates, but had to await fundamental public abuses so egregious that the "whole people" turned against their rulers. Even then, it was held, opposition had to be measured so that no more force was exerted than was necessary for the public good. Following these principles colonial leaders sought by careful organization to avoid the excesses that first greeted the Stamp Act. Hutchinson's query after a crowd in Connecticut had forced the resignation of stampman Jared Ingersoll—whether "such a public regular assembly can be called a mob"—could with equal appropriateness have been repeated during the tea resistance, or in 1774 when Massachusetts *mandamus* councillors were forced to resign.

From the first appearance of an organized resistance movement in 1765, moreover, efforts were made to support the legal magistrates such that, as John Adams said in 1774, government would have "as much vigor then as ever" except where its authority was specifically under dispute. This concern for the maintenance of order and the general framework of law explains why the American Revolution was largely free from the "universal tumults and all the irregularities and violence of mobbish factions [that] naturally arise when legal authority ceases." It explains, too, why old revolutionaries like Samuel Adams or Christopher Gadsden disapproved of those popular conventions and committees that persisted after regular independent state governments were established in the 1770's. "Decency and Respect [are] due to Constitutional Authority," Samuel Adams said in 1784, "and those Men, who under any Pretence or by any Means whatever, would lessen the Weight of Government lawfully exercised must be Enemies to our happy Revolution and the Common Liberty."

In normal circumstances the "strong discouragements" to dangerous disorder were provided by established legislatures. The measures enacted by them to deal with insurrections were shaped by the eighteenth-century understanding of civil uprisings. Since turbulence indicated above all some shortcoming in government, it was never to be met by increasing the authorities' power of suppression. The "weakness of authority" that was a function of its dependence upon popular support appeared to contemporary Americans as a continuing virtue of British institutions, as one reason why rulers could not simply dictate to their subjects and why Britain had for so long been hailed as one of the freest nations in Europe. It was "far less dangerous to the Freedom of a State" to allow "the laws to be trampled upon, by the licence among the rabble . . . than to dispence with their force by an act of power." Insurrections were to be answered by reform, by attacking the "Disease"—to use John Jay's term of 1786—that lay behind them rather than by suppressing its "Symptoms." And ultimately, as William Samuel Johnson observed in 1768, "the only effectual way to prevent them is to govern with wisdom, justice, and moderation."

In immediate crises, however, legislatures in both England and America resorted to special legislation that supplemented the common law prohibition of riot. The English Riot Act of 1714 was passed when disorder threatened to disrupt the accession of George I; a Connecticut act of 1722 followed a rash of incidents over land title in Hartford County; the Massachusetts act of 1751 answered "several tumultuous assemblies" over the currency issue and another of 1786 was enacted at the time of Shays's Rebellion. The New Jersey legislature passed an act in 1747 during that colony's protracted land riots; Pennsylvania's Riot Act of 1764 was inspired by the Paxton Boys; North Carolina's of 1771 by the Regulators; New York's of 1774 by the "land wars" in Charlotte and Albany Counties. Always the acts specified that the magistrates were to depend upon the *posse* in enforcing their provisions, and in North Carolina on the militia as well. They differed over the number of people who had to remain "unlawfully, riotously, and tumultuously assembled together, to the Disturbance of the Publick Peace" for one hour after the reading of a prescribed riot proclamation before becoming judicable under the act. Some colonies specified lesser punishments than the death penalty provided for in the English act, but the American statutes were not in general more "liberal" than the British. Two of them so violated elementary judicial rights that they were subsequently condemned—North Carolina's by Britain, and New York's act of 1774 by a later, Revolutionary state legislature.

In one important respect, however, the English Riot Act was reformed. Each colonial riot law, except that of Connecticut, was enacted for only one to three years, whereas the British law was perpetual. By this provision colonial legislators avoided the shortcoming which, it was said, was "more likely to introduce *arbitrary Power* than even an *Army* itself," because a perpetual riot act meant that "in all future time" by "reading a Proclamation" the Crown had the power "of hanging up their Subjects wholesale, or of picking out Those, to whom they have the greatest Dislike." If the death penalty was removed, the danger was less. When, therefore, riot acts without limit of time were finally enacted—as Connecticut had done in 1722, Massachusetts in 1786, New Jersey in 1797—the punishments were considerably milder, providing, for example, for imprisonment not exceeding six months in Connecticut, one year in Massachusetts, and three years in New Jersey.

Riot legislation, it is true, was not the only recourse against insurgents, who throughout the eighteenth century could also be prosecuted for treason. The colonial and state riot acts suggest, nonetheless, that American Legislators recognized the participants in civil insurrections as guilty of a crime peculiarly complicated because it had social benefits as well as damages. To some degree, it appears, they shared the idea expressed well by Jefferson in 1787: that "honest republican governors" should be "so mild in their punishments of rebellions, as not to discourage them too much." Even in countering riots the legislators seemed as intent upon preventing any perversion of the forces of law and order by established authorities as with chastising the insurgents. Reform of the English Riot Act thus paralleled the abolition of constitutent treasons—a traditional recourse against enemies of the Crown—in American state treason acts of the Revolutionary period and finally in Article III of the Federal Constitution. From the same preoccupation, too, sprang the limitations placed upon the regular army provided for in the Constitution in part to assure the continuation of republican government guaranteed to the states by Article IV, Section IV. Just as the riot acts were for so long limited in duration, appropriations for the army were never to extend beyond two years (Article I,

Section viii, 12); and the army could be used within a state against domestic violence only after application by the legislature or governor, if the legislature could not be convened (Article IV, Section iv).

A continuing desire to control authority through popular action also underlay the declaration in the Second Amendment that "a well regulated Militia being necessary to the security of a free State," citizens were assured the "right . . . to keep and bear arms." The militia was meant above all "to prevent the establishment of a standing army, the bane of liberty"; and the right to bear arms—taken in part from the English Bill of Rights of 1689—was considered a standing threat to would-be-tryants. It embodied "a public allowance, under due restrictions, of the *natural right of resistance and self preservation*, when the sanctions of society and laws are found *insufficient* to restrain the *violence of oppression*." And on the basis of their eighteenth-century experience, Americans could consider that right to be "perfectly harmless . . . If the government be equitable; if it be reasonable in its exactions; if proper attention be paid to the education of children in knowledge, and religion," Timothy Dwight declared, "few men will be disposed to use arms, unless for their amusement, and for the defence of themselves and their country."

The need felt to continue the eighteenth-century militia as a counterweight to government along with the efforts to outlaw rioting and to provide for the use of a standing army against domestic insurrections under carefully defined circumstances together illustrate the complex attitude toward peacekeeping that prevailed among the nation's founders. The rule of law had to be maintained, yet complete order was neither expected nor even desired when it could be purchased, it seemed, only at the cost of forcefully suppressing the spirit of a free people. The constant possibility of insurrection—as institutionalized in the militia—was to remain an element of the United States Constitution, just as it had played an essential role in Great Britain's.

This readiness to accept some degree of tumultuousness depended to a large degree upon the lawmakers' own experience with insurrections in the eighteenth century, when "disorder" was seldom anarchic and "rioters" often acted to defend law and justice rather than to oppose them. In the years after independence this toleration declined, in part because mass action took on new dimensions. Nineteenth-century mobs often resembled in outward form those of the previous century, but a new violence was added. Moreover, the literal assumption of popular rule in the years after Lexington taught many thoughtful Revolutionary partisans what was for them an unexpected lesson—that the people were "as capable of despotism as any prince," that "public liberty was no guarantee after all of private liberty." With home rule secured, attention focused more exclusively upon minority rights, which mob action had always to some extent imperiled. And the danger that uprisings carried for individual freedom became ever more egregious as mobs shed their former restraint and burned Catholic convents, attacked nativist speakers, lynched Mormons, or destroyed the presses and threatened the lives of abolitionists.

Ultimately, however, changing attitudes toward popular uprisings turned upon fundamental transformations in the political perspective of Americans after 1776. Throughout the eighteenth century political institutions had been viewed as in a constant evolution: the colonies' relationship with Britain and with each other, even the balance of power within the governments of various colonies, remained unsettled. Under such circumstances the imputations of governmental shortcoming that uprisings carried could easily be accepted and absorbed. But after Independence, when the form and conduct of the Americans' governments were under their exclusive control, and when those governments represented, moreover, an experiment in republicanism on which depended their own happiness and "that of generations unborn," Americans became less ready to endure domestic turbulence or accept its disturbing implications. Some continued to argue that "distrust and dissatisfaction" on the part of the multitude were "always the consequence of tyranny or corruption." Others, however, began to see domestic turbulence not as indictments but as insults to government that were likely to discredit American republicanism in the eyes of European observers. "Mobs are a reproach to Free Governments," where all grievances could be legally redressed through the courts or the ballot box, it was argued in 1783. They originated there "not in Oppression, but in Licentiousness," an "ungovernable spirit" among the people. Under republican governments even that distrust of power colonists had found so necessary for liberty, and which uprisings seemed to manifest, could appear outmoded. "There is some consistency in being jealous of power in the hands of those who assume it by birth . . . and over whom we have no control . . . as was the case with the Crown of England over America," another writer suggested. "But to be jealous of those whom we chuse, the instant we have chosen them" was absurd: perhaps in the transition from monarchy to republic Americans had "bastardized" their ideas by placing jealousy where confidence was more appropriate. In short, the assumptions behind the Americans' earlier toleration of the mob were corroded in republican America. Old and new attitudes coexisted in the 1780's and even later. But the appropriateness of popular uprisings in the United States became increasingly in doubt after the Federal Constitution came to be seen as the final product of long-term institutional experimentation, "a momentous contribution to the history of politics" that rendered even that most glorious exertion of popular force, revolution itself, an obsolete resort for Americans.

Yet this change must not be viewed exclusively as a product of America's distinctive Revolutionary achievement. J. H. Plumb has pointed out, that a century earlier, when England passed beyond her revolutionary era and progressed toward political "stability," radical ideology with its talk of resistance and revolution was gradually left behind. A commitment to peace and permanence emerged from decades of fundamental change. In America as in England this stability demanded that operative sovereignty, including the right finally to decide what was and was not in the community's interest, and which laws were and were not constitutional, be entrusted to established governmental institutions. The result was to minimize the role of the people at large, who had been the ultimate arbiters of those questions in English and American Revolutionary thought. Even law enforcement was to become the task primarily of professional agencies. As a result in time all popular upheavals alike became menacing efforts to "pluck up law and justice by the roots," and riot itself gradually became defined as a purposeless act of anarchy, "a blind and misguided outburst of popular fury," of "undirected violence with no articulated goals."

4   Norman S. Cohen

THE PHILADELPHIA ELECTION RIOT OF 1742

"Wee are thoroughly sensible of the Great Disadvantage Sir William Keith's management has been to our Interest," the Pennsylvania Proprietors wrote to James Logan, "but we hope now he is in England the People will Coole in their Zeal to his Party, so that we may get a good Assembly Chose." Their hope was already a reality. Keithian politics no longer had any significance; the old coalition which had gathered around the fiery and independent Governor ceased to exist almost with his departure for England in 1728. Only five of his supporters were returned to the legislature in 1729, and by the following year but three remained. The issues which created the controversies during the 1720's were already *passe*. The old leadership either died off, or gave up its positions of power, and in turn was supplanted during the next decade by a group of talented and younger men—Benjamin Franklin, Isaac Norris II, Israel Pemberton, Jr., William Allen, and James Hamilton.

While party organization may have been more advanced in Pennsylvania than in any other colony, it still depended upon personal relationships with control in the hands of a few wealthy families. The ruling elite of both proprietary and antiproprietary factions were of the same class, and the struggles that existed were between members of the identical socio-economic sector of society. Both were opposed to democracy. They fought for power, place, and preferment and the resulting privileges. The wishes of the people counted for little, and were heard but once a year—on October 1, election day. Both the Proprietors and their political opponents expressed concern for the people, but neigher side sought to share power or profits with them.

From the beginning factionalism developed over specific issues: land policy, executive *versus* legislative power, mercantile advantages, judicial tenure, responsi-

From *The Pennsylvania Magazine of History and Biography* XCII (July, 1968), 306-19. Reprinted by permission of the author and publisher.

bility for defense, paper money, proprietary prerogative, and quitrents. But such disputes as existed never lasted beyond the immediate problems which had created the conflict. This was true in the seventeenth century; it was true of the Keithian disturbances. Only with the outbreak of war in 1739, and after the Philadelphia election of 1742, did the coalitions become formalized and the issues solidified.

At the conclusion of the Keithian period the membership in the Assembly was not totally Quaker, nor even Quaker controlled; contested elections were fewer than usual, and party disputes on the ebb. The colony was calm. No rift existed between east and west, nor between Quaker and Presbyterian. Andrew Hamilton, despite his position in the proprietary faction, was continually elected to represent Bucks County, and he was time and again chosen Speaker. It was only in time of crisis, of war or economic dislocation, that antiproprietary opposition developed in the Assembly. Peace and prosperity brought with them political tranquility.

Yet old wounds remained, and the apparent serenity was only surface deep. With news of war in 1739 the harmonious spirit collapsed. There had, to be sure, been earlier indications of discord. In 1736 Governor Patrick Gordon had died, and the president of the Council presided over the Assembly. Flare-ups ensued over the nature of the interim government and the question of providing funds for an Indian meeting. When Governor George Thomas finally arrived, he assessed the situation and expressed his desire for a peaceful administration and the "stiffling [of] all Party Disputes," but instead he was challenged by a money bill which begot troublesome conflict for him with the Assembly. A compromise was arranged, though a formidable opposition of eight Assemblymen out of twenty-five objected to any seeming surrender to proprietary privilege.

These were obvious signs of awakening factionalism. Yet in 1739 proprietary leader Andrew Hamilton announced his retirement from all public office, and his son-in-law William Allen followed suit. "I had served on the Assembly these Nine Years past," Allen explained to John Penn, "& as most of our Disputes seem to be at an End & the Province's Affairs upon very good Footing I choose to Decline being concerned this Year as . . . Mr. Hamilton & several others of our Friends have done." This proprietary exodus is all the more remarkable as news of the approaching war had already reached the colony. Quakers quickly filled the vacated seats in the Assembly.

So it was that Governor Thomas faced a thoroughly Quaker Assembly, one opposed to taking any steps toward preparing the colony for war. They would do "nothing but Trust in the Lord," as William Allen expressed it. Acting on his own initiative, Thomas began enlisting indentured servants into a hastily organized militia. This step enraged a large segment of the voters whose opposition found expression in the Assembly. All pledges of money for the King's use were held up until compensation could be arranged for the masters who had been deprived of their property, and legislative proceedings came to a halt. The Assembly appealed its case to England, and withheld financial assistance from the harassed Governor, who had to be dissuaded from resigning.

The proprietary members who had given up their seats believed they could return to the Assembly whenever they so desired. They were mistaken. William Allen, who replaced his father-in-law as head of the proprietary party in the 1740 elections, felt certain he could break the Quaker control in Bucks and Philadelphia, but he was overwhelmed by the sudden appearance of a large number of pro-Quaker German voters who had never before cast a ballot. Allen himself had solicited the German vote, which he felt was the key to political supremacy in the province. Bitter in defeat, his plea for immediate defensive works along the Delaware was offset by the Quaker do-nothing policy.

The legislative deadlock continued in the Assembly, while the Quakers sought to have Thomas removed from office and the colony placed under the Crown. The proprietary party attempted to counter the Quakers by initiating a petition making it illegal for Friends to hold office during time of war. Meanwhile, a small group of Quakers under James Logan, working closely with Allen, attempted to wrench control of the Yearly Meeting out of pacifist hands, and to drive a wedge between the Quaker-German alliance. Failure met both efforts; the elections of 1741 were fought tooth and nail, and once again the Quakers won. In Philadelphia, Quaker and proprietary leaders exchanged blows at the ballot box.

Throughout 1742 the major attention in the colony was focused on the fate of the proprietary petition, but as the elections approached news arrived that the petition had met with ill success at a hearing before the Board of Trade. Members of the proprietary party, disappointed in their hopes to gain control, advocated strong measures in the coming contest. The violence of their suggestions fits in with the violence of the times; war fright, lawlessness, rumored election disorders, increasing bread prices, personal and political strife all made for frayed nerves. To aggravate the situation further, the need for defense played heavily upon the fears of the inhabitants and sailors in the port city.

Elections in Philadelphia were held at the Court House at Market and Second Streets. Inns and grog shops abounded in the area, and it was but a few blocks to the wharves where idle sailors congregated. Rumors were rampant, but two stood out: one, that the Quakers were planning to bring unnaturalized Germans from the country to vote in the election; the other, that the proprietary party had hired armed sailors to drive the Quakers from the Court House. Adding to the confusion was the expiration of the 1739 election law which had provided a simplified system for choosing inspectors. Inspectors were extremely important. They were the judges of the legality of the election process, and they alone could open a suspect ballot, depriving the voter of his secrecy, or challenge his right to participate.

Now inspectors would be selected by the old method whereby the electorate would gather at the polling places to hear the sheriffs call off the names of candidates for that office. The voters would then have to push and shove their way through the throng to stand by their choice. This meant the intermingling of the mob in a crowded area. Mob, rum, and rumors added up to a volatile mixture that William Allen attempted to head off by a compromise. He urged each party to choose four inspectors, but the Quakers, sure of victory, were not interested.

On election eve a Quaker meeting was held to make some last minute plans and to establish a slate of candidates. William Allen sent four of his own party with his compromise suggestion, which was again turned down as illegal; the lawful means of electing inspectors lay with the people. To no avail Allen's men pointed out unnaturalized Germans who were present and who planned to vote; the Quaker party would take no action.

On election morning groups of sailors were observed throughout the city, and one person reported that he had overheard them say that they intended to "knock down the broad Brims." The Quakers became nervous, and sent a small delegation to Mayor Clement Plumsted, while another group went to see William Allen, who, as Recorder, was expected to maintain the peace. Plumsted was asleep, but Allen received the committee which demanded he break up all gatherings of "strangers." Resenting the manner in which he was addressed, Allen angrily charged the Quakers with relying on the votes of unqualified Germans. Just then thirty unarmed sailors approached, and Allen went over to talk with them. When asked what business they had in the city, the mariners replied that they were on holiday and "were going out of Town to be merry." After being warned not to interfere with the elections in any way, they were allowed to proceed, but the Quakers were not convinced that Allen had done his duty.

By this time Plumsted has arisen and met with them. He did not see what he could do as no overt act had taken place, and, he emphasized, the sailors had "as much Right at the Election as the Dutchmen." However, the Mayor did draw up a proclamation ordering everyone to keep the peace, and his message was subsequently read aloud by the Sheriff as the polls opened.

While these activities were taking place, some of the sailors had gathered at the Indian King tavern, where the Quaker Thomas Lloyd claimed to have overheard the cry, "every Man his Dram; and then march." Recognizing a Captain Mitchell as the leader of the men, Lloyd, now joined by Israel Pemberton, Jr., walked over and demanded that he act more like a gentleman and not so demean himself as to appear at the head of such a mob. This tactless approach aroused Mitchell and an argument followed. Pemberton then decided to take matters under his control, and calling over the tavern keeper, Peter Robinson, "desired he would not give the Sailors any Liquor, as they appeared too warm." Like Mitchell, Robinson objected to the Quaker's remarks and heatedly replied that he ran a public house and would serve whomever he pleased, proving the point by pouring out a large glass of rum for Captain Mitchell.

Returning to Mitchell's table, Pemberton desired another word with him. "Damn you," responded Mitchell angrily "what do you want with me." Pemberton wanted Mitchell to disperse his men, or else "find sureties for their good behaviour, or be committed." "Damn you," Mitchell sputtered, "commit Me!" Then, according to Pemberton, Mitchell reached under his coat and withdrew a cudgel; the peace-loving Quakers beat a hasty retreat. From the Indian King they returned to Allen's house, and ordered the Recorder to bind Mitchell over. Allen replied that the "Sailors had as much right to walk the Streets as the unnaturalized Dutch." Again an argument ensued, and Pemberton somewhat presumptuously proclaimed that Allen's refusal to act against the sailors made him responsible for their actions.

By now well fortified with rum, and enraged at being charged with disturbing the peace, Mitchell sought out Pemberton, and this time, according to the Quaker, threatened him. The aristocratic Pemberton and the lowly sea captain shouted heated insults back and forth before words gave way to blows. Joseph Turner, an Alderman and Allen's business partner, was in the crowd that gathered, and he soon added to the confusion by becoming involved in an altercation with the elder Pemberton.

These disputants descended upon the Court House at ten o'clock when John Hyatt, the Sheriff of Philadelphia, opened the elections. Shouting through an amplifying horn, he put forward the name of William Allen for inspector. When this produced few votes, Allen claimed that his supporters were unable to pass through the dense crowd. He suggested that the proceedings might be made easier if everyone left the vicinity and reassembled according to party. The Quakers refused this plan, putting it down as a ruse. Again Hyatt unsuccessfully put forward Allen as a candidate. He then put up Isaac Norris who obtained a large number of votes, and was proclaimed a duly elected inspector.

As if on signal, some fifty to seventy sailors, armed with clubs, appeared, marching from the Jersey Markets one block to the east. When they drew near they gave a loud huzza and began swinging at the Quakers in an effort to clear them away from the Court House steps and so prevent them and the Germans from voting. While the electorate retreated before this assault, the Sheriff issued constables' staffs to those citizens willing to defend their rights. In the resulting melee quite a few persons were severly injured, including old Israel Pemberton whose hand was broken. However, this attack by the sailors was driven back.

During the riot, William Allen was around the corner, so surrounded by his friends, he claimed, that he neither saw nor heard the "Disorders committed by the Sailors." Word of it was brought to him by James Morris, a Quaker, who informed him of what was happening "with a haughty menacing Air." Upset by the manner in which he was ordered to do his duty, "as he did not esteem himself entirely under Mr. Morris's Direction," Allen went with Morris to the Court House. By the time he arrived the sailors had withdrawn and all he saw was Charles Willing returning the blows of a servant who had given him a sound kick during the fracas.

The sailors in the meanwhile regrouped for a second assault. This time they gained their objective, and some of the Quakers retreated into the Court House bolting the doors behind them. The attackers, believing that some of their fellows were being held prisoner inside, increased their efforts. Windows were smashed, and the area completely emptied of all but the wounded and the belligerents. At the height of the battle a Quaker spokesman convinced the sailors that none of their shipmates were being held. This, serving to break the assault's momentum, aided a counterattack by armed Germans and Quakers, seemingly without their usual regard for pacifism, which carried the day. The sailors were driven from the field and the elections were then completed in peace.

During this second disturbance Allen had tried to suppress the riot at the high point of the attack. Bricks were flying, people were in full flight, and Allen could obtain no assistance. Nevertheless, he disregarded the pleas of his friends and "singly went among the Sailors, and told them they were a Parcel of Villains." One of these "Villains," a "squat, full-faced, Pock fretten Man, with a light Wig, and red breeches," shouted "Let's give Mr. Allen a Whorrah." The Recorder angrily replied he wanted none of their "huzzas" and ordered them away from the Court House.

Though the riot was over, its repercussions were just beginning. For the proprietary party the election proved to be a disaster; many voters had altered their ballots, crossing out Allen's name and replacing it with that of a Quaker opponent. Allen's defeat was credited to the disorders, and it was noted, "he has suffered much as to popularity." Again the "broad brims" had won at the polls. In the aftermath of the riotous day fifty-four sailors and their leaders were cast into jail. A watch was posted, and the doctors kept busy that night.

Political factionalism was not healed as quickly as were the broken bones resulting from the riot for the Assembly saw political gains to be made from the disorders of the day. The proprietary party had been in difficulties on many fronts: the governor had been unpaid for more than two years; the proprietary petition to remove the Quakers from the Assembly had failed; no funds had been granted for the war effort; and the Assembly was completely under Quaker control with the able John Kinsey as Speaker. On top of all this the riot was now used to discredit Allen, the proprietary leader.

In an attempt to clear his name, Allen, with "unrighteous indignation" sued Israel Pemberton, Jr., for having openly declared that Allen had plotted with the sailors. Kinsey was hired by Pemberton to defend him in the suit for slander. Finally, the entire investigation of the riot was turned over to the Assembly. Allen objected to this as the procedural rules did not allow the accused to face his accusers, nor to cross-examine witnesses. Only after all depositions had been taken would they be allowed to give their own accounts. To Allen, the Quaker party

> left no stone unturned to Distress & Render a Man uneasy by Slander & most base Calumny. Their Printed Minutes is a fresh Instance of this, in which they have Published a Parcel of Ex-parte Affirmations Taken when these People were in Heat which Contain the grossest Falsehoods & a Suppression of the Truth & every Thing that did not Suit the Party.

To mask the Assembly's intent, a petition was arranged making it appear that the investigation had risen from the demand of an outraged public. Eighteenth-century petitions were seldom expressions of the public will, but were useful devices by which the ruling elite could give that impression. As this fact was well understood by all concerned, it was considered more important to know *who* had signed the document, rather than *how many*.

Three days after receiving the petition, the Assembly opened its hearings. With but few exceptions, the forty-nine witnesses were of the Quaker party. None of the sailors nor sea captains involved testified; the question regarding the presence of unqualified Germans was considered irrelevant. Contradictions in statements went unchallenged; testimony which was so similar in its wording as to suggest collusion passed unquestioned. The investigations were carried out to show that Allen, his business partner Joseph Turner, Mayor Clement Plumsted, and two others had been negligent in their duties and had thereby subverted the Pennsylvania Charter. In addition, Allen was proclaimed the instigator of the riot. Each of the five accused persons was allowed to make a statement in his own behalf, but only at the end of the proceedings, and without information regarding the nature of the charges against them. The burden of proof was upon them.

The investigation proceeded through the winter. Allen and his friends had their remonstrances disallowed as casting aspersions on the Assembly's proceedings. Then the legislature recommended that the collected statements be turned over to the Quaker-dominated Supreme Court for legal action. The Governor, on advice of his Council and Attorney General, expressed the opinion that the Mayor's Court of the city had legal jurisdiction. There the Mayor, Recorder, and Aldermen would hear the case. Naturally, the Assembly objected to the accused sitting in their own judgment and the proceedings between Governor and Assembly once more were deadlocked.

But a move toward compromise was underway. John Kinsey suggested to the Governor that in return for Thomas' signature on certain bills he would receive his salary, so much for each act. The charges against Allen and the others were dropped, the slander charges against Pemberton withdrawn, Kinsey was made Chief Justice of the Supreme Court, and steps were taken to prevent future riots. Contrary to Allen's suspicions, the Assembly seemed earnestly desirous of making this compromise work, and of ending their differences with the Governor. Allen continued to believe that this "peaceable disposition" would not be of "long continuance," and in this he was correct.

In interpreting this episode, commentators, both then and now, have accepted the Assembly's account without too much question. For fourteen years after the riot William Allen was not re-elected to the Assembly, and when he did return it was as a representative of the frontier county of Cumberland. It was believed that, in attempting to offset German assistance to the Quaker party during the war, Allen had resorted to violent means. Yet sufficient proof to support this view has never existed, and certainly Allen had nothing to gain by the riot. William Allen was a clever politician who never in his long career had to use such crass methods. Always careful of his reputation, in the 1742 election he lost both at the polls and in the esteem of the public. If the riot could not benefit Allen or his party, it is also true that the Quakers, already certain of victory, had nothing to gain by it either and did not instigate it willfully. An aid to understanding its cause is found in the remonstrance of Joseph Turner when he asserted that the Quakers' haughty confrontation with Captain Mitchell "in a great Measure, occasioned the ensuing Disorders of the Day."

Political struggles in Pennsylvania had been between contending aristocratic forces, fighting for power, wealth, and preferment. When an issue arose which affected them as a group, they worked together for their common interest. But when an individual privilege was at stake, it was an internecine, intra-class contest which ignored the mass of the population. When the populace was solicited for its vote, the only choice offered was between members of the elite. In addition, the electorate was normally small, and seldom expressive of the popular will. But the relationship between the ruling elite and the people was changing. Quite often this was expressed in disturbing outbreaks, such as the demonstrations during the Keithian decade, and the not unusual riots in colonial port cities. However, these were not conscious nor well-articulated protests. Adequate leadership was often lacking, though the complaints were real. Consequently, the governing class did not recognize the growing demand for political power; what it continued to expect from the people was mere acquiescence.

In the election of 1742, Israel Pemberton and the Quakers were aware of the riot rumors and were desirous of preventing the outbreak of violence. They demanded that the sailors leave the city limits, that they not drink, that they disperse their gatherings. According to their own testimony they proceeded to act against the sailors in an arrogant, haughty, and insolent manner. It was in this mood, believing his social position demanded instant submission, that the twenty-four-year-old Pemberton pounced upon Captain Mitchell. Turner, in his remonstrance, indicated how this stirred up ill feelings, and he was supported by other testimony. One witness remembered that in the midst of the riot Pemberton was a special target for the seamen: "By God, we'll kill Pemberton," one shouted, and this was answered by cries of "so we will." The natural antipathy to "Quaker Sons of Bitches . . . Men with broad Hats and no pockets" was also a factor in war time. When the mariners were ordered to return to their ships, they replied, "You are Damned Quakers, you are Enemies to King George, and we will knock you all in the Head."

This episode was the result of forces little understood by the participants or onlookers. In war time it was as important to provide defensive works on the Delaware as it was to arm the frontiersmen. River fortifications were essential, yet the Quaker Assembly had refused to act. The Allen party backed strong military steps and undoubtedly had the support of the voteless sailors. On election day the unruly sailors, exasperated by Quaker arrogance, failed to respond to the voice of authority. They cast their "ballots" by the only means possible—violence born of frustration.

The aftermath of riot was compromise and apparent political calm. Isaac Norris thought the colony had passed through a "revolution of Uncommon Size." The proprietary party seemed broken. In the next election Allen received but three votes, and indeed for the next ten years "no parties powerful Enough to make any Considerable Opposition" existed. Debarred from elective office, Allen and his followers maintained their appointive positions. Their political power was entirely dependent upon proprietary favor, whereas their Quaker opposition found support among the electorate, and thereby came to identify itself more readily with a democratic basis. It was this separation between "in and out" that solidified the two groups into strong coalitions. With the growing influx of non-Quakers on the frontier, and with the outbreak of war in 1754, the proprietary party emerged stronger than ever. It gained important allies in the frontier communities and found itself once more represented in the Assembly.

The leadership and to some extent the issues remained the same. Two parties struggled for power while the masses of the populace were effectively barred from participation in government. Only with the Revolution was a genuinely democratic system established, superseding the coalitions forged in the forties.

III

THE REVOLUTION

Theoreticians of revolution from Machiavelli to Lenin to Jerry Rubin have insisted that there can be no revolution without violence. But there are many kinds of violence: that of the oppressor and that of the oppressed, the terrorists and the policemen, the criminal killing and the political assassination, the destruction of property, and the destruction of human life. These are useful distinctions to keep in mind when studying civil strife, for all too often historians seem to use the words "riot" and "violence" interchangeably. An author searching for synonyms goes from "urban rioting" in one sentence to "urban violence" in the next and, thereby, confounds his reader. This confusion in terms is more damaging to an understanding of collective behavior than is bewilderment over the use of "mob," "crowd," "collectivity," "disorder" and the like, for it seems to equate the acts of the rape murderer, the thrill killer, the criminal mugger, or even international war with the acts of political and social protesters. Of course, these acts can be related: the Vietnamese War has led to an increase in public disturbances and, therefore, to a growing crime rate. But violence and mob disorder must be distinguished from one another. The slogan "law and order" as used politically is often associated with heinous acts. A recent public statement that the American people prefer the policeman's night stick to the terrorist's bomb is reminiscent of a New York police inspector's remark made in the 1880's: "There is more law in the end of a policeman's night stick than in a decision of the Supreme Court." Both are simplistic statements expressing only fear and glorifying only official violence. To a serious analysis of crowd behavior, they contribute nothing.

But what of the American Revolution? The majority of American historians who believe that the nation's past lacked significant conflict must face this apparent contradiction in their assessment. They argue that the violence and riots of the American Revolution were mild when compared with those which occurred in Europe: "Not a single murder resulted from the activities of the Revolutionary mobs in America" wrote Bernard Bailyn, "and when blood was accidentally spilled, it was made to go a very long way."[1] Here, the American mob was unique because of its restraint; its refrain from personal violence. But to the Loyalists, land holders, merchants, and agents of the aristocracy, the years from 1765 to 1776 were ones of serious, unparalleled disorder. So significant was the role played by the crowd in this period that it may be said that without urban mobs the Revolution would not have occurred, much less succeeded. Arthur Meier Schlesinger pointed out that, "mass violence played a dominant role at every significant turning point of the events leading up to the War for Independence."

How then can we get at the meaning of these events; how can we reconstruct this complex period and find a meaning for our own time? How can we study the eighteenth-century mob as part of a process, a historical continuum connecting these past events to those of Watts, Newark, and Detroit? Will this better enable us to deal with the problems of tomorrow? How can we separate mass violence and its negative connotations from the important political and social implications of disorder?

Even a casual knowledge of the American Revolution reveals the mob's power in the fight for Independence. The Stamp Act Riots and Sam Adams' Sons of Liberty, The Boston Tea Party, The Boston Massacre, and the burning of the *Gaspee* are episodes indicative of the colonial protests against English policies. But do these disorders, and the many others like them, indicate the presence of class conflict within the colonies? Is there any evidence of a class consciousness? Why was there so little personal violence? These questions reach beyond the obvious and do bear on our time.

Professor Jesse Lemisch, in an essay "The American Revolution Seen from the Bottom Up," attempts to answer some of these questions. He argues that too many social scientists draw conclusions about entire societies on the basis of examining a society's elite. Research based on such data, Lemisch feels, has not advanced in the last fifty years; rather, he believes, the role of the modern scholar must be to see events from the point of view of the "inarticulate" persons who lived them. Though Lemisch's suggestion is hardly new, it did help to reorient historical thinking about the past (and this even though his work has been severely criticized). He practiced what he preached in his essay, "Jack Tar in the Streets" in which he describes colonial seamen and their role in the Revolutionary mob. Lemisch found that colonial sailors were "surprisingly like the Negro stereotype," (jolly, childlike, and irresponsible), and they were treated in the law as children. But when the sailors took to the streets in defense of their liberties or in opposition to impressment, they acted as political beings. Thus, for Lemisch, Jack Tar and other lower class participants in civil disorders were active, aware agents of social change.[2]

The selection from Edmund S. and Helen M. Morgan, "The Stamp Act Crisis" also in this section, demonstrates that a careful reading of existing sources can penetrate many of the mysteries surrounding civil disturbances. Edmund S. Morgan is a leading historian of American Puritanism. Here he gives a readable, exciting view of the Revolutionary mob in Boston. His conclusions are those characteristic of the 1950's. To Morgan, the Revolutionary crowd was representing the majority's will even though it was directed by upper-class leaders.

The essay by Gordon Wood, another student of Bernard Bailyn, owes a great deal to Sir George Rude, for Professor Wood finds that the description of the European crowd as it appears in Rude's work, resembles closely his description of the American mob. Professor Woods finds the uniqueness of our colonial experience an adequate explanation for the lack of violence during the Revolution. These articles raise many questions concerning early American crowds meaningful to us today, especially regarding the governmental use or non-use of force against demonstrators.

Suggested Further Readings

Jesse Lemisch's essays "The American Revolution Seen from the Bottom Up" in *Towards A New Past: Dissenting Essays in American History* (1967) and "Jack Tar in the Streets: Merchant Seamen in the Politics of Revolutionary America," *The William and Mary Quarterly*, XXV (1968), 371-407 offer a new approach to the study of crowd behavior. However, critics such as Eugene Genovese and Aileen Kraditor suggest that he has tried to idealize the inarticulate and has just distorted the picture from the bottom up rather than from the top down. Pauline Maier "The Charleston Mob and the Evolution of Popular Politics in Revolutionary South Carolina, 1765-1784" in *Perspectives in American History*, IV (1970), 173-98 carries her research one step further. All students of this period should read Arthur Meier Schlesinger, "Political Mobs in the American Revolution, 1765-1776," *Proceedings of the American Philosophical Society*, IC (1955), 244-50. Two recent book length studies are Benjamin Woods Larabee, *The Boston Tea Party* (1964), and Hiller B. Zobel, *The Boston Massacre* (1970).

Footnotes

1 Bernard Bailyn, *Pamphlets of the American Revolution, 1750-1776* p. 581; Arthur Meier Schlesinger, "Political Mobs and the American Revolution, 1765-1776," *Proceedings of the American Philosophical Society,* IC (1955), p. 244.

2 Jesse Lemisch, "Jack Tar in the Streets: Merchant Seamen in the Politics of Revolutionary America," *The William and Mary Quarterly*, XXV (1968), pp. 371-407.

5 Edmund S. and Helen M. Morgan

BOSTON SETS THE PACE

The resolutions which the clerks of colonial and intercolonial assemblies were recording in the summer and fall of 1765 were outspoken denials of Parliament's right to tax the colonies. But only in Rhode Island did the Assembly approve outright resistance. It was one thing to define a right and another to fight for it, particularly if you must fight against a body which you had hitherto accepted as supreme and to which you still acknowledged "all due subordination." Nevertheless, while men like James Otis blew hot and cold, now for colonial rights and now for Parliamentary supremacy, and while others followed Daniel Dulany in affirming colonial rights but wishing only passive resistance, a substantial number of men in every colony recognized that the time had come when more than talk was needed. They had been convinced by Dulany and Otis and by the Virginia Resolves and the declarations of the Stamp Act Congress that Parliament had no right to tax them. They also knew that there was no branch of government higher than Parliament to prevent Parliament's doing what it had no right to do. The burden therefore was left to those whose rights were endangered: they must resist Parliament to preserve their rights, and if that meant an end to Parliamentary supremacy, then that was what it meant.

It would be too much to say that these men wished to throw off the authority of Parliament altogether. Perhaps some of them did, but there is no reason to suppose that they were not content with the constitutional position which their representatives had defined, denying Parliament's right to tax but allowing its right to regulate trade and to pass other general legislation affecting the empire at large. The only point at which they went a step further than the resolutions was in their determination to prevent the supreme legislature from doing what it had no right to do. In this determination they ignored the distinction which Dulany had drawn between propriety and power. But if anyone had told them that in spite of the impropriety of its action, Parliament's power was supreme, they might have answered that supremacy in power cannot be determined by argumentation or declaration. If Parliament lacked the authority to tax America, then its power to do so would have to be tested in American fields and streets. And this was precisely where they proposed to test it.

Although the Virginians had been first to suggest resistance, it was not in Williamsburg but in Boston that argument first gave way to action. The Massachusetts radicals saw that if the colonists were to defeat Parliament's attempt to tax

From Edmund S. Morgan and Helen M. Morgan, *The Stamp Act Crisis: Prologue to Revolution* (Chapel Hill, North Carolina: The University of North Carolina Press, 1953), pp. 119-43. This book was published for The Institute of Early American History and Culture. Reprinted by permission of The University of North Carolina Press.

them, they could not rely on their representative assemblies to do the job. The assemblies might resolve, as that of Rhode Island did, that officers of government should carry on business as usual, as though the Act had never been passed. But what if the officers of government who had to use the stamps lay beyond the immediate control of the assemblies? Most of the documents which would require stamps after November first were papers used in legal proceedings. In some colonies the assemblies might withhold the salaries of the judges as a means of bringing them into line, but in others the judges of the superior courts were not appointed by the assemblies, and in all the colonies the independence of the judiciary was regarded as a principle of the British constitution which could be tampered with only at the peril of civil liberty. The assemblies were also powerless to control the royally appointed customs officers who must issue clearances for all ships leaving American harbors. According to the Stamp Act, clearance papers issued after November 1 would have to bear a stamp. If the customs officers chose to comply with the law, and as royal officials they doubtless would comply, what could the assemblies do about it? The duties of customs officers did not fall within their jurisdiction, and royal governors would certainly have vetoed any orders from the assemblies which attempted to regulate matters beyond their authority.

Clearly the radicals who had determined to turn from words to deeds could expect little more than words from their assemblies. For action they must look elsewhere, and where was not hard to guess. In Boston particularly the answer was clear, for in the past the good people of that city had frequently turned from the niceties of theological controversy to achieve some necessary social reform in their own way. Perhaps a few inhabitants could recollect with some amusement how they had laid out a street through Jonathan Loring's barn near Love Street some thirty years before. The selectmen had surveyed the proposed street and found Loring's barn square in the way. There was some doubt whether they had a right to seize the barn, but a gathering of the townspeople resolved the question without argument. Under cover of night and with blackened faces, a technique they had already learned and would employ again in 1773, they levelled the building, and the road went through. In 1747 Boston had demonstrated that even the British Navy must watch its step in Massachusetts. Commodore Knowles in that year anchored his fleet off Nantasket and sent press gangs ashore to fill gaps in his crews. When the Governor and Council would not, as they could not, prevent him, a mob arose in Boston which ruled the city until Commodore Knowles released the men he had seized.

Bostonians sometimes seemed to love violence for its own sake. Over the years there had developed a rivalry between the South End and the North End of the city. On Pope's Day, November 5, when parades were held to celebrate the defeat of Guy Fawkes' famous gunpowder plot, the rivalry between the two sections generally broke out into a free-for-all with stones and barrel staves the principal weapons. The two sides even developed a semi-military organization with recognized leaders, and of late the fighting had become increasingly bloody. In 1764 a child was run over and killed by a wagon bearing an effigy of the pope, but even this had not stopped the battle. Despite the efforts of the militia, the two sides had battered and bruised each other until the South End finally carried the day.

When Boston had to face the problem of nullifying the Stamp Act, it was obvious that men who fought so energetically over the effigy of a pope might be employed in a more worthy cause. The problem was to make them see the threat to their liberties that the Stamp Act presented and to direct their energies accordingly. Sometime in the early summer of 1765 a group of men got together in Boston to prepare for the day when the Stamp Act was supposed to go into effect, November 1. An organization was formed which first called itself The Loyal Nine and later, when its ranks had expanded, the Sons of Liberty. The Nine were John Avery, Jr., Thomas Crafts, John Smith, Henry Welles, Thomas Chase, Stephen Cleverly, Henry Bass, Benjamin Edes, and George Trott. They were not the most prominent citizens of Boston, nor were they the men who did most of the talking against the Stamp Act. In general they were artisans and shopkeepers, and they shunned publicity. The names of James Otis and Samuel Adams were conspicuously missing from the list. So was that of John Adams. Perhaps this division of labor was deliberate, in order to keep the radical leaders of the Assembly, who were always conspicuously in the public eye, from bringing too much attention to the group. Or perhaps the effectiveness of the radical leaders in the Assembly might have been impaired if they were openly associated with an organization engaged in the treasonable activities which the Loyal Nine envisaged. Whatever the reason, no conclusive alliance can be proved between the leaders of the Assembly and the organizers of the popular demonstrations, but it is probable that the Nine maintained close communications with both Otis and Sam Adams, and on one occasion at least, John Adams spent an evening with them at their headquarters in Chase and Speakman's distillery on Hanover Square.

Only two members of the Loyal Nine enjoyed any local distinction: John Avery, Jr., was a Harvard graduate, class of 1759, and both his father and grandfather were also Harvard men—a sufficient pedigree in Boston; Benjamin Edes was the printer, along with John Gill, of the *Gazette*, Boston's most enterprising newspaper. Avery's membership lent respectability to the group; Edes's gave it a mouthpiece. Of the two, Edes's contribution was doubtless the more valuable, for his paper published a continuous stream of articles to stir up feeling against the Stamp Act.

By August 14 the Nine felt that Boston was ready for action. They were confident that the well-to-do stood behind the moves which they were contemplating, and that the propaganda published in the *Gazette* had aroused the mass of the people. More important, they had enlisted the services of the man who had led the South End mob to victory over the North-Enders the preceding November. Ebenezer McIntosh, a South-End shoemaker, was soon to become notorious as a man who could control his two thousand followers with the precision of a general. The Nine had persuaded him that he might do his country a real service by forgetting local quarrels and directing his strength against that hated Act which was designed to rob Americans of their constitutional rights.

On the morning of August 14 the signal for impending action was given by the hanging of an effigy on a tree near Deacon Elliot's house on Newbury Street. It represented Andrew Oliver, the man who, according to reports from England, had been appointed Distributor of Stamps for Massachusetts; alongside hung a piece of symbolism designed to connect Oliver and the Stamp Act with the most hated man in England. It was a large boot (a pun on the Earl of Bute), with the devil crawling out of it. When Governor Bernard heard of the event he took it seriously. Some members of his council assured him that it was only a boyish prank, not worthy the notice of the government, but in view of the incendiary pieces appearing in the newspapers Bernard thought otherwise. So did Lieutenant-Governor Hutchinson. Hutchinson, as Chief Justice of the Colony, ordered the Sheriff to cut the image down; Bernard took an easier way out: he summoned the Council and turned the problem over to them. Before the Council could gather together in the afternoon, the Sheriff returned with the breathless news that his men could not take down the image without endangering their lives.

Governor Bernard urged upon the Council the seriousness of the situation, but for various reasons they preferred to do nothing about it. Some thought it a trifling matter which would subside by itself if no notice were taken of it. Others admitted its seriousness, but felt that the government was not strong enough to force the issue and had better not risk the attempt. Unwilling, however, to have it go on record that they had done nothing, they passed the problem on to the Sheriff, advising that he be instructed to summon the peace officers. They could scarcely have expected the peace officers to have any effect on the crowd that was gathering about the tree where the image hung, but some gesture must be made in order to save face. Even as they sat in the Council Chamber the gentlemen could hear the rising voices outside, for the effigy had been cut down from the tree, and taking it with them the mob marched ominously to the Town House, gave three huzzas to let the Council know who was running the town of Boston, and then passed on.

Andrew Oliver had recently constructed a building at his dock on Kilby Street, intending to divide it into shops and rent them. Under the circumstances it was plausible enough to suggest that this was the office where he intended to distribute the stamps. From the Town House then, with McIntosh in the lead, the mob moved on to Kilby Street, and in five minutes Oliver's venture in real estate had gone the way of Jonathan Loring's barn. The next stop was Oliver's house, in the nearby street which bore the family name. Standing in the street the leaders presented those inside with a bit of pantomime, in which Oliver's effigy was beheaded, while the rest of the crowd showered stones through the windows. From here Fort Hill was only a step, and taking what was left of the effigy the mob moved on to the summit where they ceremoniously "stamped" on the figure and burned it in a bonfire, made appropriately of wood which they had carried from the building on Kilby Street.

For the more genteel members of the mob, disguised in the trousers and jackets which marked a working man, this seems to have been the last stop on the evening's excursion. But McIntosh had not yet completed his work. With his followers he now returned to Oliver's house. Both Oliver and his family had meanwhile retired to a friendly neighbor's, leaving the house in charge of a few trusted friends, who barricaded the doors. Finding the entrance blocked, the mob proceeded to de-molish the garden fence and then systematically beat in the doors and windows and entered the house, swearing loudly that they would catch Oliver and kill him. The trusted friends quickly departed, and the mob were preparing to search the neigh-boring houses when a gentleman informed them that Oliver had gone to Castle William and thus saved his life.

It was possible to take revenge on his house, and this they did, destroying the furniture, including "a looking glass said to be the largest in North-America," and a large part of the wainscoting. Governor Bernard meanwhile had sent a message to the Colonel of the Militia ordering him to beat an alarm. The Colonel, a realistic man, replied that any drummer sent out would be knocked down and his drum broken before he could strike it—and besides the drummers were probably all up at Oliver's house engaged in what they would consider more worthwhile activities. With this, having made his gesture, Governor Bernard retired to Castle William, safely isolated from mobs by the waters of Boston harbor.

Lieutenant-Governor Hutchinson was more foolhardy. About eleven o'clock, when the tumult seemed to be subsiding, he took the Sheriff with him and went to Oliver's house to persuade the mob to disperse. He had no sooner opened his mouth than one of the ringleaders, perhaps McIntosh, recognized him. "The Governor and the Sheriff!" went the cry, "to your Arms my boys," and a rain of stones de-scended on the two men as they hurried off into the darkness. The mob was thus left to have its way and continued to make sport of the Stamp Distributor's house until about midnight, when McIntosh evidently decided to call it an evening.

Thus ended the opening move in the program to defeat the Stamp Act. Every-one agreed that it was the most violent riot the town had ever seen. The next day a number of gentlemen called on Andrew Oliver and persuaded him that what had occurred was only the beginning and suggested that he immediately resign his office. Oliver, like other stamp distributors who later followed his example, must have been somewhat confused by the fact that he had not received his commission and thus really had nothing to resign. He promised, however, to write home for leave to resign and in the meantime to do nothing toward executing the Act. This satisfied the Loyal Nine, but their followers could not understand this devious language. In the evening they built another fire on Fort Hill—Governor Bernard, watching from Castle William, knew that the mob was out again—but the leaders who had produced the previous evening's entertainment were able to dissuade their followers from turning the site of Oliver's house into a vacant lot. Instead the mob diverted themselves by surrounding the house of the Lieutenant-Governor. Hutchin-son listened to them beating on the doors and shouting for him to come out, until finally a neighbor convinced them that he had fled, and they gradually drifted away.

During the next ten days McIntosh proved his worth by keeping his followers quiet, and the Loyal Nine could rejoice in a job well done. They had obtained the resignation of the Stamp Distributor a good two and a half months before the Act was scheduled to take effect. Moreover they had made plain what would happen to anyone who dared take Oliver's place. When one gentleman let it be known that he would not have been intimidated had he been the stamp master, they gave him a chance to see how Oliver had felt by fixing the date when his house should be pulled down. The gentleman quickly recovered from his courage and retracted his statement. Few people could be found in Boston who would condemn the proceedings of the fourteenth. Even some of the ministers gave their blessing, and the Loyal Nine, feeling their oats, began to think of other grievances that needed redressing. The officers of the customs and of the admiralty court were obvious targets, and during these days there was much talk of the malicious reports they had sent home about the Boston merchants. Then there was Thomas Hutchinson, a man to reckon with.

The conduct of the Lieutenant-Governor, in ordering the images cut down and in attempting to stop the pillage at Oliver's house, marked him as a friend of the Stamp Act and an enemy of colonial rights. It was insinuated that his letters home had encouraged passage of the Act. Still, the Loyal Nine may not have intended to give Hutchinson the treatment they had handed Oliver. On the evening of the twenty-sixth, Hutchinson himself heard the rumor that the mob was to be out that night, and that the officers of the customs and of the admiralty court were to suffer, but that nothing was contemplated against him. On the other hand, Ebenezer Parkman, the minister of Westborough, thirty-five miles from Boston, heard on the twenty-sixth that Governor Bernard, Lieutenant-Governor Hutchinson, and Mr. Story, the Deputy Register of the Admiralty Court would be attacked. The information came in a letter from a friend in Boston, dated the twenty-fourth.

Neither Hutchinson's nor Parkman's information proved entirely correct. On the evening of the twenty-sixth the mob rallied around a bonfire on King Street and then proceeded in two separate bodies. One went to William Story's, and in spite of the fact that Story had published an advertisement in that day's papers denying that he had written home ill reports of the Boston merchants, they destroyed a great part of his public and private papers and damaged his house, office, and furniture. The other group went after the Comptroller of Customs, Benjamin Hallowell. His house was acknowledged to be one of the finest in town—before they got there. Afterwards the windows, sashes, shutters, and doors were gone, the furniture broken, the wainscoting ripped off, the books and papers carried away, and the wine cellar all but empty.

It is possible that the men who originated the program for this evening had intended that it should go no further, but the letter which Parkman received shows that someone at least had planned what now occurred. McIntosh, who was still master of ceremonies, after the work at Story's and Hallowell's was completed, united his two companies and led them to the Lieutenant-Governor's. Whether he did this on his own initiative or at the request of the Loyal Nine or at the request of some other group will probably never be known. In later years William Gordon, who came to Boston in 1768 and knew most of the persons who were active in the revolutionary movement there, stated that " . . . the mob was led on to the house, by a secret influence, with a view to the destruction of certain papers, known to be there, and which, it is thought, would have proved, that the grant to the New Plymouth Company on Kennebec River, was different from what was contended for by some claimants." The connection between the New Plymouth Company and the riot remains a secret. It may be that McIntosh saw no harm in killing two birds with one mob. He may have attacked the customs and admiralty officers for the Loyal Nine and Hutchinson for someone else.

Certainly in leading the attack on Hutchinson he had an enthusiastic following. Hutchinson was a cool and haughty man, about whom it was easy to believe any evil. McIntosh and company went about the work of wrecking his house with a zeal that far surpassed their previous height of August 14. They destroyed windows, doors, furniture, wainscoting, and paintings, and stole 900 pounds in cash, as well as clothing and silverware. They cut down all the trees in the garden, beat down the partitions in the house and had even begun to remove the slate from the roof when daylight stopped them.

The fury of the attack on Hutchinson alarmed the best people in town. It looked as though the mob had got out of control and was bent upon transforming a commendable hostility to the Stamp Act into a levelling revolution. Rich men began to send their most valuable possessions to the homes of poorer neighbors where they might be safer. The town of Boston held a meeting and disavowed the attack on Hutchinson, though many of the participants in the pillaging must have been present at the meeting. Hutchinson himself concluded that "The encouragers of the first mob never intended matters should go this length, and the people in general express the utmost detestation of this unparalleled outrage." Three companies of militia and a company of cadets were called out to patrol the town and thereafter for many weeks the streets of Boston echoed with the steps of marching men. Even the children were caught up in the excitement. As one harassed parent complained, "the hussa's of the mobbs, the rattleing of drums, the clamour of the soldiers—who comes there—we are all well—and the continual hubub takes up all their attention. . . . As for James, wee cannot keep him from amongst the hurly burly without I would chain him. Thers no getting them kept to their sett times of schooling, eating, goeing to bed, riseing in morning in the midst of this disorder and confusion."

Governor Bernard meanwhile met the crisis with his customary decisiveness by calling a meeting of the Council. Here it came out that McIntosh had led the assault on Hutchinson, and the Council ordered a warrant issued for his arrest. Sheriff Greenleaf found him on King Street and took him up without resistance. McIntosh was evidently so sure of himself that he felt no need to resist. It had already been rumored that the custom-house would be pulled down. Those who felt that the riots had gone far enough were ready to prevent this by use of the militia, but they were not ready to see McIntosh, who could name the instigators of both riots, tried in court. The word accordingly went around that unless McIntosh was released, not a man would appear to defend the custom-house. At this the officers of the customs went to the Sheriff and asked him to release his prisoner. Sheriff Greenleaf agreed and went to the Town House to tell the Governor and Council what he had done. "And did you discharge him?" asked Hutchinson.

"Yes," said Greenleaf.

"Then you have not done your duty."

"And this," Hutchinson wrote later, "was all the notice taken of the discharge."

McIntosh thus went free, and no one was ever punished for the destruction of Hutchinson's property. But from this time forward the persons directing the mob were careful to keep matters more firmly under control, an accomplishment made possible by the willingness of the militia and of McIntosh to cooperate. Further demonstrations of violence were in fact unnecessary, for the Loyal Nine had made it plain that they were not afraid to bring out the mob against anyone who dared oppose them. Governor Bernard, retired in the safety of Castle William, was ready to admit that he did not have the command of ten men and was governor only in name.

By the end of August, then, Boston was ready for the Stamp Act. With both the Stamp Distributor and the mob under control nothing remained to be done until the first of November, when it would be necessary to adopt a more vigilant watch to see that the Act should not be obeyed in any instance. A minor crisis occurred toward the end of September when the stamped papers arrived on a Boston merchantman. Governor Bernard was prepared for this and had announced earlier that he would lodge them in Castle William for safekeeping, since Oliver had disclaimed any responsibility. Fearing that Bernard would make an attempt to distribute them from the Castle, the Loyal Nine hinted that the people would storm the Castle the moment the papers were landed there and destroy them; but the Governor promptly stated in the newspapers that he was not authorized to distribute them and would make no attempt to do so. With this assurance the Loyal Nine were apparently satisfied, and when the papers arrived they were landed safely at the Castle under cover of the two men-of-war in the harbor.

In the ensuing weeks Boston waited uneasily for November first. Governor Bernard, brooding in Castle William over his grand scheme for reorganizing the empire, felt bitter about the mess which George Grenville had made of things. Although he had written to Richard Jackson on August 24, "to send hither Ordinances for Execution which the People have publickly protested against as illegal and not binding upon them, without first providing a power to enforce Obedience, is tempting them to revolt," yet he could not quite believe that the people of Massachusetts would be so foolish as to prevent the execution of the Act. At first he told himself that the rest of the province would disavow the hot-headed proceedings of the Bostonians. There had always been a split between the coast and the country, and the country had always been more moderate. Bernard had hopes of getting some backing for law and order from the sober farmers of the interior when the General Assembly should meet. "I depend upon the Assembly to set these Matters to right," he wrote to his friend John Pownall after the first riot, "as I really believe that there is not one out of twenty throughout the Province but what will disapprove the Proceedings of Boston."

When the Assembly came together on September 25, he pointed out to them that the doctrines of the *Boston Gazette*, however appealing they might be in Boston, would never find acceptance in Westminster. Though Parliament may have made a mistake in passing the Stamp Act, it was still an act of Parliament and the General Court of Massachusetts ought to see to its enforcement. When his speech was over, it appeared that the radicals had won over a majority of the farmers in the Assembly, and so, as they prepared to draw up an answer to the speech, Bernard adjourned them. Eventually he had to confess that the country people were even more violent in their opposition to the Stamp Act than the Bostonians: "They talk of revolting from Great Britain in the most familiar Manner, and declare that tho' the British Forces should possess themselves of the Coast and Maritime Towns, they never will subdue the inland."

When he became disillusioned about the interior sometime in September, Bernard still clung to the idea that economic necessity would force the people of Massachusetts to accept the Act. He understood well the dependence of Massachusetts on trade. After November first, no ships would be cleared until the Stamp Act was accepted. Then Massachusetts would repent of her folly:

> If the Ports and the Courts of Justice are shut up on the first of November, terrible will be the Anarchy and Confusion which will ensue; Necessity will soon oblige and justify an Insurrection of the Poor against the rich, those that want the necessaries of Life against those that have them; But this is not all, it is possible that, when all the Provision in the Province are divided amongst the People without regard to Property, they may be insufficient to carry them through the Winter, by cutting off the Resources from Pennsylvania and Maryland, upon which this Province has great dependance, a Famine may ensue. Less obvious causes, but very lately, were so near producing one, even with the help of the usual importations, that many perished for want: And who can say that the present internal stock of the Province, is sufficient, without importations to support the Inhabitants through the Winter only?

Bernard was shrewd enough to see that the men directing the opposition to the Stamp Act wanted no insurrection of the poor against the rich. What he did not see was that these men would be able to turn the hatred of the poor against the British government instead of against the rich. It was true that if the ports were closed, famine would be the result in Boston, but before the poor should rise against the rich their fury would be aimed against the men who had closed the ports. In the face of that fury the ports would not stay closed, and neither would the clearances be on stamped paper. Bernard knew how to analyse the difficulties in the British imperial system, but when it came to analysing the immediate political situation he was helpless. His opponents had taken his measure correctly in the last weeks of August, and they knew that when the crisis came, his way of meeting it would be to pass the buck.

As the first of November approached, and word spread that there would be a grand parade and pageant that day, Governor Bernard performed his usual gesture. He called the Council and pointed out the danger that such a parade would end in more violence. To make matters worse, November 5 (Pope's Day) would follow hard after and give fresh occasion for riot. In order to forestall both these outbreaks, Bernard and the Council decided that several companies of militia should guard the town from October 31 to November 6. On the thirty-first the officers of the militia came to the Council Chamber and, as might have been expected, announced that the militia could not be raised. The first drummer sent out had had his drum broken, and the others were bought off. If Bernard had chosen, he could have had 100 regulars on hand. On September 10, General Gage had sent his aide-de-camp to offer that many troops for the maintenance of order. Bernard refused them, because, as he said, things had quieted down then, and because he was afraid that so small a number would only irritate the people without providing adequate protection to the government. When November first came, then, Bernard was helpless. He was assured that his image would not be paraded, but nevertheless he retired to Castle William—not that he was afraid, he hastened to assure his correspondents, but he did not wish to be present when insults should be offered to His Majesty's government.

As if to demonstrate how well they had the situation in hand, the Loyal Nine—or the Sons of Liberty, as they now began to call themselves—maintained perfect order in Boston on November first. The day was ushered in by the mournful tolling of church bells. The images of George Grenville and John Huske (whom the Bostonians took to be an instigator of the Stamp Act) were hung on the tree which had held those of Oliver and Bute on August 14. The tree had since been named the Liberty Tree, and a copper plaque commemorating August 14 (but not August 26) hung around the trunk. At two o'clock in the afternoon the images were cut down, and a procession of "innumerable people from the Country as well as the Town," marching in exact order, carried them through the streets to the gallows, hung them again, and then cut them to pieces. On November 5, there was a similar orderly demonstration, in which the union of the South End and the North End was celebrated with all the decorum of a church supper.

No one in Boston supposed for a minute that these polite celebrations were the end of the Stamp Act troubles. The Sons of Liberty had begun to plan for the next step on their program as soon as they had forced Oliver to resign. On August 26, the day when Hutchinson's house was attacked, Benjamin Edes's paper had carried this item:

> Since the Resignation of the Stamp Officer, a Question has been thrown out—How shall we carry on Trade without the Stamp'd Papers? — Carry

on no Trade at all, say some, for who would desire to increase his Property, at the Expence of Liberty. — Others say, that in Case there shall be no Officer to distribute the Stampt Papers after the first of November, a regular Protest will justify any of his Majesty's Subjects, in any Court of Justice, who shall carry on Business *without* them?

Governor Bernard naively supposed that the colonists would attempt to defeat the Stamp Act by ceasing all activities which required the use of stamps, but the Sons of Liberty had the second alternative in view—to proceed as though the Stamp Act had never been passed. Before attempting to achieve this by direct action, they tried to persuade the Assembly to effect it by law, as the Rhode Island Assembly had done by their promise to indemnify anyone who suffered by disregarding the Act. When the Massachusetts Assembly convened again on October 23, a committee of both houses was appointed to consider a resolution declaring that since the Stamp Distributor had resigned, whereby the people were prevented from obtaining stamps, it should be lawful to do business without stamps, the Act of Parliament to the contrary notwithstanding. Governor Bernard, still not recognizing the boldness of the people with whom he was dealing, supposed that this was simply another means of harassing him. "It is true," he wrote to John Pownall, "that they who bring in this Bill know that I cannot and shall not pass it: But what of that? it will answer their purpose; which is to bring upon me all the odium of the inconveniences, losses and miseries which will follow the non-usage of Stamps. The People will be told that all these are owing to me, who refused passing an Act which would have prevented them, and no notice will be taken of my incapacity to pass such an Act: so that I shall be made to appear to bring on these Evils, which I have taken so much pains to prevent."

To Bernard's surprise the resolve did not pass the House, but the reasons for its failure were not calculated to reduce his uneasiness. The representatives rejected it, because they felt that it implied a right in Parliament to levy the tax. If the reason for ignoring the Act was simply that the stamp officer had resigned, the legality of the Act was admitted. If the resolution were adopted and a new Stamp Distributor should be appointed, it would be morally incumbent upon the Assembly to support him. These complex considerations could be avoided only by an open defiance of the Act, and this was more than the Assembly wished to put on its records. The matter was left therefore, for the Sons of Liberty to resolve in their own way.

The most pressing problem would be the opening of the ports so that the trade which was Boston's lifeblood might go on. By putting every possible vessel to sea before November first the merchants gained a little time in which to consider the risks of ignoring an act of Parliament. The risks seemed to diminish in importance as ships returned from voyages to lie dismally idle, accumulating wharf-charges instead of profits; and the conviction that the Stamp Act must be ignored grew stronger.

While the Sons of Liberty waited for public pressure to rise, the customs officers, the Attorney General, and the Governor engaged in an elaborate rigmarole, in which the question of clearing vessels without stamps was tossed from one to the other and back again with graceful and disgraceful gestures, each person trying to shift the unpleasant decision from himself. The whole procedure is only to be understood in the light of the personal feud which had been going on for over a year between the Governor and John Temple, Surveyor General of the Customs. Temple's headquarters were in Boston, but he supervised the collection of the customs in the entire Northern District from Nova Scotia to Connecticut. Bernard was jealous of Temple's power and did all he could to subordinate it to his own inside Massachusetts. Temple, on the other hand, regarded Bernard as a corrupt and grasping politician who had sabotaged the collection of the King's revenue (one example was the slowness with which he had moved to the support of John Robinson when Robinson had been put in the Taunton jail at the suit of Job Smith). Knowing that sooner or later either he or Bernard might have to take responsibility for clearing ships without stamps, Temple was anxious, if possible, to put the onus of the decision on Bernard.

The whole situation was further complicated by the fact that the only knowledge of the Stamp Act in Boston was hearsay. Two copies of the Act had come in private letters and from one of these the Act was printed in the newspapers, but Governor Bernard had received no official copy. From the newspapers he discovered that he was obliged by the terms of the Act to take an oath to support it, and accordingly he did so, but he naturally felt somewhat less responsible than he might have, had he known for certain what he was supposed to support. The same was true of Temple, and to a less degree of Oliver himself. Oliver received a notice of his appointment from the Secretary of the Stamp Office in England, but by November first he had not received his official commission as distributor. He surmised that this might be in the packet of stamped papers which was stored in Castle William, but neither he nor anyone else cared to break open the packet and find out.

Although everyone concerned with enforcing the Stamp Act could thus plead ignorance on November first, no one seriously doubted that the Act which had been printed in the newspapers was genuine, and it was plain that the customs officers whose duty it was to grant clearances would have to decide in the near future what course they should take. Accordingly on October 29 Benjamin Hallowell, Comptroller, who had already tasted the fury of the mob, and William Sheaffe, Collector, asked John Temple what they should do. He replied that "as I have nothing in Charge from my Superiors concerning the Stamp Act, I can give you no other Advice or direction, for your Conduct than that of strictly observing all Acts of Parliament that have any Relation to the Duty of your Office, and wherein you may be at a loss for the true meaning of any Act of Parliament, I recommend you to the Advocate and Attorney General for their Advice." No help there.

The next day, October 31, Sheaffe and Hallowell went through the formality of asking Oliver for the stamped papers needed in their office. Oliver replied the same day that he had no commission as distributor and even if he did would not be able to handle the stamps. The next step was to ask Governor Bernard what should be done. He replied as quickly as Oliver that he had no authority to appoint a distributor or to distribute them himself. Sheaffe and Hallowell accordingly sent copies of their correspondence with Bernard and Oliver to the Attorney General, Edmund Trowbridge, and to the Advocate General of the Admiralty Court, Robert Auchmuty, and asked for their advice—all this by the evening of October 31.

On November 1, while Boston was diverting itself with the effigies of Grenville and Huske, Trowbridge sent his answer: ask Mr. Temple, the Surveyor General. As Auchmuty did not choose to make any reply at this point, the Collector and Comptroller were now back where they had started from, and here a disturbing thought occurred to them. Suppose they should refuse to grant clearances on the ground that they had no stamped paper. To grant clearances was their job, and no one else could do it. If they refused would they not be liable to suits for damages from every individual who applied for a clearance and was refused? On the other hand, suppose they granted a clearance on unstamped paper, and suppose further that the ship proceeding under this clearance were seized by the British Navy and condemned for proceeding under improper clearance papers. Would they not be liable in such a case to a suit for the value of the ship? Whatever they did were they not thus liable to innumerable suits? And were not the New England merchants notoriously quick to sue customs officers whenever they could?

Hastily they put their questions to the Surveyor General. Without hesitation he replied, "With regard to the Queries you have put to me, as they are mere points of Law, I must refer you to the Advocate and Attorney General." To the Advocate and the Attorney General they went, and this time obtained a reluctant opinion, that the Comptroller and Collector would not be liable to damages if they cleared ships on unstamped paper, provided they certified that no stamped paper was available. Having received this opinion, which of course was only an opinion and not a guarantee, Sheaffe and Hallowell still hesitated to proceed without some authorization from either the Surveyor General or the Governor. Accordingly they told Temple of the legal advice they had received, and he of course referred them again to the Governor. The Governor gave them the same answer that Temple had previously: "It is the Business of the Attorney General and the Advocate General to advise you in matters of Law and not mine."

It was now the nineteenth of November, and the merchants were becoming restless. Temple still refused to take responsibility. On his advice Sheaffe and Hallowell approached Bernard again on November 22, saying that they were afraid he might not have read Auchmuty's opinion at the time when he told them to go to the Attorney General and Advocate General for advice. Bernard was not to be caught in this trap: "I must again repeat to you that it is not my business to advise you in matter of Law. . . . I have perused the opinion of the Attorney General and Advocate General but desire to be excused giving my opinion upon the case myself."

Sheaffe and Hallowell next pressed the Attorney and Advocate for more explicit instructions, about how the clearances should be drawn up, and whether bonds as well as clearances might be unstamped. The only result was that Trowbridge got cold feet and withdrew his former advice. On November 30 he wrote, "I do not look upon myself as the Proper Person by whose advise You (in an affair of such importance, and which seems to be at present a matter rather of prudence than of Law) are to govern yourselves and therefore must be excused advising you either to grant Cockets or Clearances upon unstamped Papers or to refuse to do it."

On this same day, November 30, Andrew Oliver's commission finally arrived. Sheaffe and Hallowell again hopefully applied for stamps, but Oliver replied quickly enough that though he had received his commission it was still impossible for him to exercise it. Sheaffe and Hallowell therefore went back to plying Auchmuty and Trowbridge with questions. This time Trowbridge folded up completely. They received an answer written by a friend of Trowbridge's who was directed "to inform you that last Monday night he was seized with the Rheumatism in his right Arm and Shoulder to such a degree, as that he hath not ever since been able, either to write as much as his Name or attend to any business, wherefore he must be excused considering or answering those Questions."

By now the pressure was acute, and the Sons of Liberty were almost ready to take action. On December 11 Sheaffe informed the Surveyor General "that the Town was in an uproar and that there was a meeting of the Merchants and that the Mob intended at night to storm the Customhouse." Temple promptly sent the news to Bernard, with the additional intelligence that there was over six thousand pounds sterling of the King's money in the custom-house. As it grew dark, and the King's customs officers listened for the approaching rumble of the mob, Bernard penned his answer: "I will call a Council tomorrow."

But December 17, not December 11, was the day which the Sons of Liberty had scheduled for opening the custom-house, and the night of December 11 passed calmly. On December 13 Sheaffe and Hallowell made one more nervous attempt to get the stamps out of Oliver or to put the blame more squarely upon him. This time they got a categorical response: "In answer to your Letter of this date demanding my determinate and absolute answer to this question, whether I will or will not deliver you any stamp'd papers after having answered it twice already: I say No."

This was plain enough as far as Sheaffe and Hallowell were concerned, but the Sons of Liberty wanted a public statement. Before they put the final pressure on Sheaffe and Hallowell, they wanted to be certain that there would be no stamped papers available. On December 16, therefore, Benjamin Edes published an anonymous letter in the *Gazette*, asking whether Oliver intended to execute the commission he had lately received. Before publishing the letter Edes secured an answer from Oliver, which he also published, stating "that altho' he had now received a Deputation to act as Distributor of the Stamps for the Province of the *Massachusetts*, He had taken no Measures to qualify himself for the Office, nor had he any Thoughts of doing it."

To the Sons of Liberty this did not appear to be a satisfactory answer. They met in their headquarters at the distillery on Hanover Square and wrote another letter to Oliver:

Hanover Square Dec. 16, 1765

Sir,

The respectable Inhabitants of the Town of Boston, observe your Answer to an anonymous Letter published in Messi'rs Edes and Gill's News-Paper of Today, which we don't think satisfactory; therefore desire that you would, To-morrow, appear under Liberty Tree, at 12 o'clock, to make a public Resignation. Your Non compliance, Sir, will incur the Displeasure of *The True-born Sons of Liberty*. N.B. Provided you comply with the above, you shall be treated with the greatest Politeness and Humanity. If not . . . .!

When a messenger knocked at Oliver's door and handed his servant this letter, it was too late in the evening and the weather too dirty for Oliver to consult the Governor. The next morning, the weather still stormy, notices were found posted up all over town, reading:

St-p! St-p! St-p! No.

Tuesday Morning, Dec. 17th, 1765

The true-born SONS of LIBERTY are desired to meet under Liberty Tree at XII o'Clock This Day, to hear the Public Resignation, under Oath, of Andrew Oliver, Esq; Distributor of Stamps for the Province of the *Massachusetts-Bay*. . . .

A Resignation? Yes.

Oliver realized that he had no way out. He sent for his friend John Avery, whose son was one of the Loyal Nine. The father, he surmised, would be able to act as an intermediary between himself and the Sons of Liberty. Avery came to him at nine o'clock and told him that effigies were already prepared as a signal for a riot in case he failed to appear at the Liberty Tree. In a last-minute attempt to save his dignity Oliver offered to make his resignation at the court house. This was not acceptable, and so at 12 o'clock noon, escorted by the redoubtable McIntosh himself, Oliver marched through the streets, the rain beating down tempestuously, and read his resignation from an upper window of the house which stood next to the Liberty Tree. In spite of the rain two thousand people had assembled, and when he was finished they gave three huzzas. Oliver replied with a polite, if somewhat bitter, statement that "I shall always think myself very happy when it shall be in my power to serve this people," upon which there were more cheers, and the crowd departed.

Meanwhile messengers had been hurrying back and forth through the rain from Sheaffe and Hallowell to Temple, Trowbridge, Auchmuty, and Bernard. Auchmuty alone seems to have had the courage to advise flatly that the clearances be issued without stamps. Trowbridge still had the rheumatism, and Temple and Bernard refused to offer any advice. Sheaffe and Hallowell were still afraid to take the responsibility themselves. But when two thousand people could assemble on a rainy day to watch Oliver resign for a second time, present danger loomed larger than future damage suits. On the afternoon of the seventeenth the custom-house opened for business, and in the evening the Sons of Liberty sat down in their headquarters to a dinner of celebration, to which they invited their good friend Sam Adams and spent the evening drinking healths.

With the ports open, the Sons of Liberty wasted no time in arranging for the opening of the courts. On the morning of the eighteenth the town of Boston, by petition of "a number of Inhabitants," held a special meeting in Faneuil Hall, at which a memorial to the Governor was drawn up. The memorial stated that "Law is the great rule of Right, the Security of our Lives and Propertys, and the best Birth right of Englishmen." By the closing of the courts the rule of law must cease; therefore the Governor was requested to order the opening of the courts. Since the memorial was addressed to the Governor in Council, Bernard gratefully seized upon this opportunity to avoid a decision and appointed the next morning, December 19, for a Council meeting. When the Council met, Bernard informed them that he would leave the matter entirely to them. Since most of the members present were no more anxious to face the question than Bernard himself, and since many were absent, the meeting broke up with a decision to call in all the Councillors who lived within twenty miles of Boston for another meeting the following afternoon. As the gentlemen descended from their chamber in the upper story of the Town House, they could find a hint of what was expected of them in a paper hung up in the room below:

Open your Courts and let Justice prevail
Open your Offices and let not Trade fail
For if these men in power will not act,
We'll get some that will, is actual Fact.

When the Councillors assembled the next day, the lawyers of the town of Boston presented them with a long harangue on the necessity of opening the courts. The arguments were by now familiar. John Adams told them that the Stamp Act was "utterly void, and of no binding Force upon us; for it is against our Rights as Men, and our Priviledges as Englishmen." Parliament, he said, could err, and when it did, need not be obeyed. "A Parliament of Great Britain can have no more Right to tax the Colonies than a Parliament of Paris." James Otis, moved to tears by his own eloquence, argued that "The shutting up of the Courts is an Abdication, a total Dissolution of Government," and he too affirmed, as a principle well known to lawyers, "that there are Limits, beyond which if Parliaments go, their Acts bind not."

Listening to these arguments, Governor Bernard perceived that the lawyers had given him another loophole. What they had said, he told them, "would be very pertinent to induce the Judges of the Superior Court to think the Act of no Validity, and that therefore they should pay no Regard to it; . . ." The question at issue was a matter of law, and it would not do for the executive branch of the government to determine a matter of law. In short the judges must decide the question. The Council welcomed this solution, and adopted a resolution to the effect that the memorial presented to them was none of their business. In order to appease, as they hoped, the wrath of Boston, they added a recommendation that the judges of the several courts determine the question as soon as possible. When the answer was delivered to the town meeting, on Saturday afternoon, December 21, the meeting considered the extraordinary question of whether the Council's reply was satisfactory, and came to the unanimous conclusion that it was not.

The Superior Court of the province was not scheduled to meet until March, so that there was no immediate necessity for the justices of this court to make a decision, but the Inferior Court of Common Pleas for Suffolk County was to meet in Boston during the second week in January, and the session of the Probate Court of Suffolk County was already overdue. In the Probate Court the obstinate figure of Thomas Hutchinson again appeared in the path of the Sons of Liberty. Hutchinson as Chief Justice of the Colony could postpone acting until March. Hutchinson as Judge of the Suffolk County Probate Court, would have to take his stand at once. His friends told him he must choose between four things: "to do business without stamps, to quit the country, to resign my office, or —" Here one may assume the friends supplied a significant gesture.

Hutchinson was not an easy man to scare, but his friends assured him that he had no time to deliberate. His brother, Foster Hutchinson, did not share his unwillingness to do business without stamps. Governor Bernard suggested therefore that Hutchinson deputize his brother to act for him, but Hutchinson could find no precedent for such a proceeding. The Governor then offered to appoint Foster Hutchinson as Judge of the Probate Court for one year only. Such a limited appointment, Governor Bernard persuaded himself, could be made without stamped paper. Hutchinson complied with this arrangement, and so the Probate Court opened.

Meanwhile the Boston town meeting had made inquiries—one suspects that the questions were heavily weighted—and discovered that the judges of the Inferior Court of Common Pleas in Suffolk County were ready to proceed without stamps. When the next town meeting was held on January sixteenth, both the Probate and the Inferior Courts in Suffolk County were open for business as usual, but the courts in the other counties of the province were still closed. Since the only way in which the Bostonians could bring pressure upon these courts was through the General Assembly, the town meeting instructed their representatives in the Assembly to use their influence "that Measures may be taken that Justice be also duly Administred in all the County's throughout the Province and that enquiry may be made into the Reasons why the course of Justice in the Province has been in any Measure obstructed."

The House of Representatives was by this time so thoroughly in accord with the town of Boston that on January 24, 1766, a resolution was passed by a vote of 81 to 5, stating that the courts of justice in the colony, and particularly the Superior Court, ought to be opened. When the resolution reached the Council, there again stood Thomas Hutchinson, prepared to block it. He wished the Council to reject it at once, but the other members postponed consideration until January 30. The *Boston Gazette* immediately went to work on Hutchinson with a highly colored story to the effect that he had said that the resolution was "Impertinent and beneath the Notice of the honorable Board, or to that effect." The *Gazette* had attained such a degree of power by this time that the Council thought it necessary to answer the charge. Governor Bernard, recognizing his old enemy Otis as the author, wanted the Council to have him arrested, but the Council was no more ready than Bernard himself to assume responsibility for so dangerous a move, and contented themselves with passing resolutions in which they denied that Hutchinson had ever said anything derogatory to the House of Representatives.

At the same time the Council thought proper to inquire of the judges of the Superior Court whether they would proceed with business when the next scheduled meeting should come up on March 11. The judges were as reluctant as everyone else to take a stand on the question but delivered their opinion that if the "Circumstances" of the colony remained in March what they were in January, and the lawyers should wish to proceed, they would be obliged to do so.

This report from the judges was published without any mention of the provision that made opening contingent upon the wishes of the lawyers. Actually the judges were shifting the responsibility back to the lawyers who had pleaded so eloquently before the Council for the opening of the courts. When March 11 rolled around, rumors of the repeal of the Stamp Act had already begun to arrive, and the revolutionary tension had relaxed to the point where the lawyers were dubious about risking their interests in an irregular procedure when a regular one might be obtained by waiting. Hutchinson, the Chief Justice, manufactured an excuse to be absent from the March session—much to the annoyance of John Adams, who found himself as a lawyer in the dilemma which Hutchinson had escaped as a judge. When the judges, perhaps perceiving the hesitation of the lawyers declared themselves ready to proceed, even James Otis, who had led the movement to force the opening, was unwilling to plead. Finally a case was dug up which had been continued from the previous session, and after disposing of this, the Court postponed other civil business until April and from then successively until June. The newspapers announced that "all the courts of Justice in this Province are not to all Intents and Purposes open." With this token victory, which everyone could hope was the prelude to a real victory in Parliament, the agitation for opening the courts subsided, and Massachusetts waited for the news of repeal.

6   Gordon S. Wood

A NOTE ON MOBS IN THE AMERICAN REVOLUTION

There used to be a time when we thought that mob violence in the preindustrial age of the eighteenth century was strictly a European phenomenon. In recent years, however, we have been made increasingly aware of how important and prevalent

Reprinted from *William and Mary Quarterly*, XXIII (October, 1966), pp. 635-42, and by permission of the publisher.

mob activity was in early American history. From the time of the first settlements on through the eighteenth century, social eruptions and popular disturbances were a recurrent event in the American colonies. Mob rioting at one time or another paralyzed all the major cities; and in the countryside violent uprisings of aggrieved farmers periodically destroyed property, closed courts, and brought government to a halt. With such a history of popular disturbances in the colonies it was not surprising then that mob action would become, as the Tories pointed out, "a necessary ingredient" in fomenting the American Revolution. "Mass violence," Arthur M. Schlesinger reminded us in 1955, "played a dominant role at every significant turning point of the events leading up to the War for Independence. Mobs terrified the stamp agents into resigning and forced a repeal of the tax. Mobs obstructed the execution of the Townshend Revenue Act and backed up the boy-cotts of British trade. Mobs triggered the Boston Massacre and later the famous Tea Party." And even after the Revolution had begun "civilian mobs behind the lines systematically intimidated Tory opponents, paralyzing their efforts or driving them into exile." In short, the American colonies were no more free of urban and rural riots and disturbances than eighteenth-century England and France.

Yet while recognizing that eighteenth-century crowd disturbances were as prev-alent in the colonies as in Europe, almost all historical accounts of American mob activity have suggested that the colonial mobs were fundamentally different from their European counterparts. True, the American Revolution produced mob vio-lence, but these crowd disturbances, most historians imply, were by no means comparable to the popular uprisings during the French Revolution, or even to the various English mob demonstrations during the same period. The American mobs seem to have behaved in a particularly unusual fashion, and in contrast to the violent uprisings of eighteenth-century Europe they appear to be hardly mobs at all.

Apparently in order to distinguish the American from the European crowds of the eighteenth century, historians have usually emphasized the middle-class charac-ter of the colonial mobs. "It is evident," Carl Bridenbaugh has written, "that in American cities those who constituted the mobs, so called, were far from being a mere 'rabble' seeking bread and an opportunity to release pent-up boorish boister-ousness by despoiling the Egyptians." Indeed, "the contrast with the still medieval English mob is striking in that the colonial variety had in them always a majority of middle-class citizens and the approval of many more." Bridenbaugh has concluded, however, as has Bernard Bailyn in a more recent note on American mobs, that the American crowds possessed many real "deeply rooted, popular grievances" which found expression in general political issues and principles, a conclusion which by itself has important and unsettling implications for our traditional assumption about the character of the American mob behavior. In his comprehensive account of the mob violence surrounding the Stamp Act and its marked effectiveness in presssuring the stamp distributors into resigning, Edmund S. Morgan has given us a somewhat different view, denying that the mobs were the "spontaneous outbursts of the rabble," and picturing them more as passive bodies of men manipulated by their socially superior leaders; indeed "the episodes of violence which defeated the

Stamp Act in America were planned and prepared by men who were recognized at the time as belonging to the better and wiser part." So extraordinary in fact were the mobs' discipline and discrimination in the destruction of property that Morgan was led into a noticeably sympathetic description ("the previous evening's entertainment") of the mob violence. The American Revolutionary mob, Lloyd Rudolph has concluded in a pointed comparison of eighteenth-century European and colonial mobs, demonstrated particular restraint "in confining its activities to specific and limited objectives. . . . In America, the mob stopped when it had attained what it set out to do." The rioters destroyed only property, and particularly selected property, and took no, or few, lives during the Revolution. "Heads did not roll in the American Revolution," wrote Bailyn; "mobs did not turn to butchery." "A singular self-restraint characterized the frenzies," declared Schlesinger, "for the participants invariably stopped short of death." In short, as Rudolph has summarized, the American mob, like the Revolution of which it was a part, was remarkably moderate and disciplined. It was "never swept up into an irrational destruction of lives and property." Thus America was "spared from the mob in the European sense of the word." Indeed, it seems to be the assumed conclusion of all historians of eighteenth-century American crowd disturbances that it was only "in Europe that the real mob existed."

But what actually is a "real mob," a mob "in the European sense of the word"? It would seem that our image of the eighteenth-century European mob has been very impressionistic and hazy, but understandably so, since only in recent years have scholars begun to study the preindustrial European crowds with care and sympathy, investigating them not as static abstractions but as concrete historical and social phenomena, seeing them not as the authorities saw them, but as they were to the participants. One of the boldest and most prolific of these scholars is George Rude, who has recently sought to bring together his several studies of the European crowd into a more general discussion, entitled *The Crowd in History: A Study of Popular Disturbances in France and England, 1730-1848*. Speculative as Rude's conclusions about the European crowd may be, they still have interest and significance for all historians; but they have a special relevance for students of the American Revolution, for in effect they call into question the assumptions about the unique quality of the American mobs in the eighteenth century.

Far from discovering the irrational, fickle, and destructive abstractions described by Gustave Le Bon, the father of modern crowd psychology, and others, Rude found the eighteenth-century English and French crowds to be unusually rational with a "remarkable single-mindedness and discriminating purposefulness." "In fact," he writes, "the study of the pre-industrial crowd suggests that it rioted for precise objects and rarely engaged in indiscriminate attacks on either properties or persons." The Gordon Riots of 1780, for example, were "directed against carefully selected targets," and "considerable care was taken to avoid damage to neighboring property." Moreover, those who assume that the mobs "have no worthwhile aspirations of their own and, being naturally venal, can be prodded into activity only by the promise of a reward by outside agents or 'conspirators' " are greatly mistaken. The crowd's motives were diverse and complicated, ranging from the seeking of "elementary social justice at the expense of the rich, *les grands*, and those in authority" to the devotion to political principles and generalized beliefs about man's place in society. Such complex goals reflected the varied composition of the crowds. For the crowds of eighteenth-century England and France, even the French Revolutionary mobs, were not composed of the riffraff of society, but rather represented a fair cross section of the working class together with some petty employees and craftsmen occasionally interspersed with men of "the better sort." Nor were the preindustrial crowds bloodthirsty. According to Rude the usually selective destruction of property was a constant characteristic, "but not the destruction of human lives." There were notably few fatalities among the rioters' victims. In the week-long Gordon Riots not a single person was killed by the mobs. And, in fact, "the French Revolution in Paris, for all the destructive violence that attended it, was not particularly marked by murderous violence on the part of crowds." Most of those who died during the European demonstrations were rioters killed by the magistracy or the army. "It was authority rather than the crowd," Rude concludes, "that was conspicuous for its violence to life and limb."

What is particularly striking about Professor Rude's analysis of the eighteenth-century European crowd is its resemblance to the description of the American Revolutionary mobs that we have been used to. When viewed in light of Rude's study, eighteenth-century American crowd behavior loses much of its distinctiveness. It now becomes more difficult to emphasize the peculiar rationality and discrimination of American mobs in their treatment of property. It is also hard to see how they were composed of more respectable, middle-class elements than their European counterparts. And it appears especially distorting to stress the unusual moderation and respect for lives displayed by American crowds. It seems misleading, in short, to conclude that during the American Revolutionary crisis "no mob action approached the mayhem and destruction of French and English mobs of roughly the same period."

Nevertheless the historical and social situation and the consequences of mob violence in America were very different from those in Europe, and it would be distorting the very basis of Rude's studies to ignore these differences. Eighteenth-century American society had neither the complexity nor the number of grievances possessed by eighteenth-century French society. In the colonies there were no bread riots, no uprisings of the destitute. Yet, as Rude has pointed out, it was not really poverty that precipitated rioting in Europe. Many of the disturbances occurred in times of greatest prosperity; even the food riots were not the product of long-suffering deprivation but of temporary price rises and shortages. Rude's study suggests that the preindustrual demonstrations represented not the anarchic uprisings of the poor and hopeless but rather a form of political protest made both necessary and possible by the increasing democratization of a society lacking the proper institutions for either the successful expression or the swift repression of that protest. It is perhaps in this context that the American mobs can most instructively be viewed and compared with the European crowds. What particularly seems to set mob violence in the colonies apart from the popular disturbances in England and France is not so much the character of the mob, the purposeful and limited nature of its goals, its consideration for human life, or even the felt intensity of its grievances; rather it is the almost total absence of resistance by the constituted authorities, with all that this absence may signify in explaining the nature of the society and the consequences of the outbursts. If the institutions of law and order were weak in eighteenth-century England and France, in America they were unusually ineffectual. Scholars have emphasized time and again the helplessness of the imperial government when confronted by a colonial mob reinforced by widespread sympathy in the community. It was apparently more the restraint and timidity of the British authorities, and less the moderation of the American crowds, that prevented a serious loss of lives during the American rioting. The nearly complete breakdown of the royal government's ability to command support in the society in the years before independence worked to retard an aggravation of colonial grievances and a rapid escalation of killing and violence, but it did not make the American mob any less a mob.

Moreover, the weakness of the legally constituted authority in America did not end with the Declaration of Independence and the formation of new popular governments. The Whig belief in the people's "right of resistance" (which had often hampered magistrates in England dealing with mobs) became a justification for continued disorder in the years after 1776. Serious rioting recurred in many of the major cities and formed the background for the incorporation movements in Boston, New Haven, Philadelphia, and Charleston in the 1780's. Extralegal groups and conventions repeatedly sprang up to take public action into their own hands, to intimidate voters, to regulate prices, or to close the courts. To some in the 1780's it seemed as though mobs were taking over the functions of government. This was not simply a chimerical fear, for the legislatures in the 1780's appeared to be extraordinarily susceptible to mass demonstrations and mob violence. The state governments were continually forced to submit to various kinds of popular pressures, often expressed outside the regular legal channels. In this atmosphere Shays's Rebellion represented something of an anomaly, largely because the farmers of western Massachusetts, unlike other groups in the 1780's, found no release for their pent-up grievances in legislative action but instead were forcefully resisted by the authorities. Connecticut had no violence like that of Massachusetts, said Noah Webster, "because the Legislature wear the complexion of the people." Only "the temporising of the legislatures in refusing legal protection to the prosecution of the just rights of creditors," remarked David Ramsay, freed the Southern states from similar disturbances. Within a few months, however, observers noted that the Shaysites were trying their strength in another way, "that is," said James Madison, "by endeavoring to give the elections such a turn as may promote their views under the auspices of Constitutional forms." With "a total change" of men in the legislature, wrote Webster, "there will be, therefore, no further insurrection, because the Legislature will represent the sentiments of the people." Some Americans in the 1780's could thus come to believe that "sedition itself will sometimes make law."

Hence, it might be argued that it was the very weakness of the constituted authorities, their very susceptibility to popular intimidation of various kinds, or, in other words, the very democratic character of legislative politics in the 1780's, rather than any particular self-restraint or temperance in the people, that prevented the eruption of more serious violence during the Confederation period. If this is the case then our current conception of the period and our understanding of the Federalist movement may have to be reexamined.

What Professor Rude's analysis of the eighteenth-century European crowd requires at the very least, it seems, is a new look at American mob violence during the Revolution focusing on the structure of the society which prompts popular demonstrations and on the nature of the institutions which are compelled to deal with them. If the conservatism of the American mobs is not as peculiar as we once assumed, if the crowds were not simply the passive instruments of outside agents, we must learn more about their composition, their goals, and the sources of their discontents. Particularly we need to know more about the circumstances and consequences of repression or the absence of it. In short, in light of Rude's finding the obvious differences between mob action in America and in Europe that do exist demand a broader and yet more precise explanation than we have had. It is not enough now to say that the nature of the American mob in and by itself was distinctive.

Moreover, if the mob is pictured as a kind of microcosm of the Revolution, Rude's studies may even have wider implications. Perhaps the American Revolution was as moderate as it seems, so lacking in the violence and ferocity of the French Revolution, not because it was inherently conservative and unrevolutionary, led by law-abiding men with limited objectives, but rather because it was so unrestrained, so lacking in strong resistance from counterrevolutionary and authoritarian elements, and consequently so successfully revolutionary. Unchecked by any serious internal opposition, unrestrained by any solid institutional bulwarks, the American Revolutionaries may have ultimately carried themselves further in the transformation of their society, although without the bloodshed or the terror, than even the French Revolutionaries were eventually able to do. For if the American mob was no less a mob because of the absence of effective resistance, was the Revolution any less a revolution?

IV

THE ANTE-BELLUM DECADES

Civil strife did not pass into history along with the Revolution and Independence. The crowds had helped end British rule, while at the same time they had also brought about changes in their societies. The theoretical right of revolution, which John Locke used to justify the Revolution of 1688 in England and which Thomas Jefferson, borrowing generously from Locke, used in the Declaration of Independence to justify the American Revolution, had become a part of our political heritage.

Now, no longer revolutionaries, the leaders of the new states were faced with the task of building a government while being frequently confronted by riots and mob action, which as rebels they had helped to inspire. The antagonism of the western frontiersmen for the seaboard upper classes continued to spawn violent clashes in Massachusetts and Pennsylvania. Of these, the Massachusetts uprising, known as Shays' Rebellion, was more important. Daniel Shays, a former captain in the Revolutionary Army, led the revolting western farmers in armed protest. The Shaysites were 4,000 militiamen.

In western Pennsylvania two years later John Fries led another group of armed men also in protest to what they felt were unjust taxes. They proceeded against the U.S. marshal in Bethlehem and forced him to release prisoners taken in earlier demonstrations. A more bizarre episode took place in New York City in 1788 when an outraged mob ransacked the Columbia Medical School and then continued to riot for several days against the doctors and students of the city. The "Doctor's Riot" was triggered by rumors of body snatching. The angered crowd eventually stormed the jail where some of the young students and doctors were being held; there they were met by the militia who stopped them with a volley fired point blank into their midst. still their underrepresentation in the legislature. In 1787, this movement was crushed by 4,000 militiamen.

The nineteenth century did not bring with it less tension; it portended much more. The year 1800 was a fateful one for America since it saw the birth of John Brown and Nat Turner, a slave and later leader of a black rebellion, Denmark Vesey purchase his freedom, and the fight for freedom of Gabriel Prosser and 1,000 Virginia slaves. The crowd was, by the time of Andrew Jackson, a commonplace factor in history. The hundreds that gathered in Washington to join in the inauguration of President Jackson seemed to symbolize this development.

The three decades leading up to the Civil War were scarred by civil strife. Richard Maxwell Brown in *Violence in America* notes that this period "may well have been the era of the greatest urban violence that America has ever experienced."[1] It was a period when extreme nativism led to attacks on immigrant groups, particularly the Irish Catholics in the cities. It was an era when abolitionists were for some fair game and always in season. This resulted in the killing of Elijah Lovejoy in Illinois, the attack upon Prudence Crandell in Connecticut, and the assault upon William Lloyd Garrison in Massachusetts. Almost every leading figure in the anti-slavery movement faced a hostile mob at one time or another. Later these same abolitionists turned from their non-violent approach and used force and violence themselves. With the passage of the Fugitive Slave Law in 1850, mobs gathered across the North in protest, and, as John Demos noted, "the great majority of Americans still believed in the 'right of revolution' when other avenues of redress were closed.[2] Some of the new recruits, indeed, may well have been among the mobs which attempted to use force *against* the abolitionists in the 1830's." In New York, the old colonial anti-rent conflict flared anew in 1844 and 1845. In Rhode Island, Thomas L. Dorr led a rebellion aimed at reforming the state constitution (1842). The Mormon leader, Joseph Smith, and his brother Hyrum were gunned down because of their Mormon religious beliefs in Carthage, Illinois (1844). Finally, there was a special form of political disorder, the slave rebellion. The most notable of these was the Nat Turner uprising of 1831.

Such a listing, brief as it is, gives some idea of the impact that violence and the crowd had on this period. The articles of this section discuss only abolitionists and their opponents. Nothing is said about lynchings, vigilante groups, or slave rebellions. In the 1830's, nativist mobs sacked monasteries and physically attacked Catholics. Throughout our history racist mobs have lynched black men, assaulted Chinese laborers, attacked Jews, Irishmen and other immigrants. Generally these mobs were nativist groups fearful of foreigners and their ideas. Often these mobs were organized to commit violence. They were politically motivated, frightened and alienated. They, too, felt the institutions of the state were unrepresentative, and did not express or protect their interests. They reacted in the only manner which appeared open to them. These riots stand out in our history for the violence and death they brought. Generally, they were directed at a particular group of people and were coupled with the hatred and passions of the time. These riotous crowds sought ends that would not improve or ameliorate the state of their lives but which would end another man's life or destroy his property.[3]

Though slave rebellions are clearly related to the subject of this book, for reasons of space they are not included. These were complex events that present incredible problems for analysis and interpretation. Many scholars, for instance, have emphasized the continuous struggle of black Americans for freedom as a consequence of the numerous uprisings that did occur. Others have raised the question of why there were so few revolts when compared to the large number of uprisings that took place in South America. That these interpretations are far apart may be seen by comparing Herbert Aptheker's account of some 250 slave revolts with the more recent statement of Winthrop Jordon in *White Over Black* wherein he estimated that "not more than a dozen" revolts actually took place. The impact of this heritage of violence on contemporary black movements is an aspect of this controversy too involved for one book.

It is the abolitionist crusade that precipitated the two essays reprinted here. Many of today's New Left demonstrators and revolutionaries find historical precedent for their acts in the anti-slavery movement. Truman Nelson's little volume, *The Right of Revolution*, confirms this line of radical thought, and Howard Zinn's book about the Student Nonviolent Coordinating Committee, *The New Abolitionists*, further emphasizes this point. To these writers and their adherents, William Lloyd Garrison, Frederick Douglass, Henry Highland Garnett, and John Brown are heroes. Their writings and philosophies are often quoted in the rhetoric of the radical movement. The violent reaction to the early anti-slavery movement appears capable of finding its modern analogy.

Howard Schwartz's, "Fugitive Slave Days in Boston", presents a clear account of the abolitionist protest against federal legislation providing for the return of escaped slaves. This is followed by a chapter from Leonard L. Richards' *Gentlemen of Property and Standing*, an exciting and important book about anti-abolitionist riots in the northern cities. Professor Richards tries to identify the participants and to determine why they opposed the movement. His views are a long way from those of Gustav Le Bon: Richards finds the mobs to be organized, their goals clear, with members representative of a town's leading citizens as well as the "very ordinary citizens who despised Negroes and dreaded the thought of miscegenation."

If there is a clear relationship between the abolitionists of the ante-bellum North and the protesters of today, there seems also to be a tie between the racism and violence of the anti-slavery opposition and their contemporary counterparts. The disorders of that bloody period preceding the Civil War bears obvious relevance for our contemplation.

Suggested Further Readings

Marion L. Starkey, *A Little Rebellion* (1955) is a delightful account of the Shays'

Rebellion of 1787. The Doctors' Riot in New York City is recounted in Joel Tyler Headley's *The Great Riots of New York* (1873, reprinted in 1970), a classic book on the crowd which, though written prior to LeBon's *The Crowd*, presents most of his biases. The best account of the nativist riots is found in Ray Allen Billington, *The Protestant Crusade* (1938). Although the author has modified many of his ideas, Eugene Genovese, "The Legacy of Slavery and the Roots of Black Nationalism," *Studies on the Left*, VI (1966), 3-26 is highly recommended. John Demos, "The Anti-Slavery Movement and the Problem of Violent 'Means'," *New England Quarterly*, XXXVII (1965), 501-26, is an interesting study which suggests that many persons opposed to Garrison in the 1830's may have supported him in later mob actions.

Footnotes

1   Richard Maxwell Brown, "Historical Patterns of Violence in America", Hugh Davis Graham and Ted Robert Gurr, (eds.), *Violence in America* Washington, D. C.: Government Printing Office, 1969), I, p. 40.

2   John Demos, "The Anti-Slavery Movement and the Problems of Violent Means," *New England Quarterly,* XXXVII (1965), pp. 501-526.

7   Leonard L. Richards

GENERATION OF ANTI-ABOLITIONIST VIOLENCE

Historians have rarely given much attention to the question of what triggered violent anti-abolitionism, but the traditional historical argument—or, to be more exact, the traditional assumption—is that the mobs were a reaction against "Garrisonism." Garrison's children, for example, took it for granted that their father's moral crusade touched the South where it hurt; and for this reason Southern "man-stealers" and their Northern lackeys responded with wrath and fury. Forty years later Gilbert Hobbes Barnes, who clearly disliked Garrison and enjoyed debunking his "legend," reversed the tone of the argument: Garrison's vitriolic pen, his visionary and reckless agitation, and his notoriety fostered hatred and violence not only toward himself and his "fanatics" but toward Theodore Dwight Weld and

From *"Gentlemen of Prosperity and Standing": Anti-Abolition Mobs in Jacksonian America* by Leonard L. Richards. Copyright © 1970 by Oxford University Press, Inc. Reprinted by permission. Certain footnotes omitted were informational rather than bibliographical.

"moderate" antislavery men as well. Thus Garrison's staunchest admirers and his foremost debunker have agreed that anti-abolitionist violence was largely a response to "Garrisonism."

There are ample grounds for partially accepting the traditional argument. The *Liberator* and its fiery editor undoubtedly contributed to tension in Northern society; the Garrisonians surely heightened the fears and anxieties that bred outbursts of anti-abolitionist violence. Any white friend of the Negro—any advocate of Negro uplift—probably would have inspired Northern racists to mob abolitionists and to terrorize Negroes. Yet neither Garrisonism nor Northern racism can account for the dramatic upsurge of anti-abolitionist violence in the summer of 1835.

2

Garrison's vehement denunciations of the South caused scarcely a ripple in the North. Even after the Nat Turner insurrection in Virginia in August 1831, when Southerners became alarmed and demanded that Garrison be silenced, Northerners expressed little concern. Most, in fact, were unaware of the *Liberator*'s existence. Even in Boston few men knew the *Liberator* or its editor. In October, 1831, the influential Washington *National Intelligencer* startled Boston's Mayor Harrison Gray Otis by demanding that he find some legal way of silencing the "incendiary" paper that was operating in his city. Otis made a few inquiries, but "no member of the city government, nor any person of my acquaintance, had ever heard of the publication." At Otis' orders city officers "ferreted out" Garrison in his "obscure hole" and reported that his only supporters were "a very few insignificant persons of all colors." The *Liberator*, concluded Otis, commanded "insignificant countenance and support."

It was Garrison's attack against the American Colonization Society that eventually commanded attention. Since 1817 this society had been trying without much success to promote the migration of free Negroes to Africa. Staunch colonizationists insisted that African colonization would rid the country of the poor and despised free blacks, encourage planters to emancipate their slaves, and provide a nucleus of black missionaries to carry the Gospel to the Dark Continent. Their plan had the support of such men as President James Monroe, Henry Clay, and Chief Justice John Marshall. Zealots claimed that it had the endorsement of God Himself. For years, however, Northern blacks had angrily denounced African colonization as forcible expulsion, and Garrison's *Liberator*, which was essentially a Negro newspaper, saved its sharpest barbs for the Colonization Society.

African colonization, said Garrison, was "a libel upon humanity and justice—a libel upon republicanism—a libel upon the Declaration of Independence—a libel upon Christianity." The colonizationists, said Garrison, were not simply misguided; they were evil, deceitful, hypocritical, anti-Christian, odious apologists for the crime of slavery. The American Colonization Society was a monster, a "creature without heart, without brains, eyeless, unnatural, hypocritical, relentless, unjust." It was essentially anti-Negro, rather than antislavery. It bolstered Southern slavery by the removal of free Negroes, by annually sending "hundreds of worn-out slaves . . . off to die, like old horses." Above all, its philanthropic facade dulled the nation's conscience concerning the sin of slavery and "shamefully duped" many men of good intention. It had to be destroyed. "I look upon the overthrow of the Colonization Society," Garrison told his future brother-in-law, "as the overthrow of slavery itself—they both stand or fall together."

It would be a mistake to assume—as many have—that Northern sensibilities were outraged by these epithets. Obviously colonizationists objected, and some abolitionists pleaded with Garrison to tone down his language. But rancorous journalism prevailed in the 1830's. Almost every town and village in the nation had at least one editor who in vileness and vulgarity approached James Fenimore Cooper's Steadfast Dodge. Not only the penny presses, but also the more "respectable" presses used with abandon words such as "cur," "fool," "knave," "scoundrel," "wretch." Newspaper editors, Tocqueville insisted, were generally vile and abusive, and American readers had conditioned themselves to read for facts, rather than for opinion. And at least one of Garrison's future enemies, a religious journal, even praised him for the "strength" of his language.

Whatever effect the *Liberator*'s denunciations had on Northern sensibilities, it is abundantly clear that Garrison's harangues did not drive men to violence. Some colonizationists fumed secretly, but outwardly they remained calm. It was not until Garrison and the New England Anti-Slavery Society proved that abolitionists had bite, as well as bark, that colonizationists became openly hostile.

From the beginning Garrison had been committed to organized agitation. Without a formal "concentration of moral strength," he insisted, little could be accomplished either for the slave or for the free Negro. In November, 1830, several months before the founding of the *Liberator*, he sought to establish an antislavery society. This attempt failed, but after numerous false starts and much constitutional quibbling, twelve men formed the New England Anti-Slavery Society in January, 1832.

Almost immediately the new society launched a campaign to destroy the American Colonization Society. In May, Garrison's materful polemic, *Thoughts on African Colonization*, came out. With a boost from Arthur Tappan's pocketbook it soon circulated widely. In June the New England Society instituted weekly anti-colonization forums in Boston, sent lecturers to nearby cities and towns, and planned special Fourth of July meetings to compete with traditional colonizationist exercises. Taking excerpts from the *African Repository* and other colonization publications, the Garrisonians relentlessly hammered readers and audiences with the theme that the Colonization Society out of its "own mouth" condemned itself; it clearly showed itself to be a moral cancer, and thus it must be destroyed.

Still colonizationists remained mute. Their press ignored Garrison's *Thought*, and their lecturers refused to rebut abolitionist attacks. So long as abolitionist audiences remained small or black and collections were meager, the Colonization Society held fast to its policy of not calling attention to the opposition. The society, after all, held a virtual monopoly in the antislavery field, and thus it had no reason to panic.

But reason was soon abandoned. As the New England Society's grass-roots operation expanded, as more whites began turning out to hear anticolonizationist arguments, as Providence and other cities showed signs of forming abolitionist societies, and as Garrison's *Thoughts* stunned colonizationists as far west as Hudson, Ohio, colonizationists became increasingly edgy. New England members, particularly, demanded action. In August 1832, the Colonization Society's principal New England agent, the Reverend Joshua Danforth, pounded the abolitionists with abuse. Finally in October, the Colonization Society's official organ mentioned the New England Anti-Slavery Society, but only in a footnote: "A few men in Boston (chiefly young, and of course ardent), with A. Buffum a Quaker, for their President, and Garrison for their Secretary, have associated and assumed this larger title, than which none could be more inappropriate. New England disavows them." In November, the same journal mildly denounced Garrison's *Thoughts*. And then, as if in response to a signal, Eastern colonizationists erupted with tirades against "amalgamationists," "fanatics," "lunatics," "reckless incendiaries," "cut-throats," and "firebrands." The self-imposed silence was over; war had been declared.

Declaring war on the Garrisonians did not bring the reversals that many colonizationists had expected. If 1832 had been a troublesome year for the Colonization Society, 1833 proved to be disastrous. From four local societies in two states, the antislavery movement expanded to forty-seven in ten states. Arthur Tappan, who had been secretly supplying the Garrisonians with funds, shocked colonizationist clergymen and temperance reformers by dramatically renouncing the Colonization Society and accusing it of drenching Africa with "liquid poison." British abolitionists—using Garrison as their main weapon—not only checkmated the Colonization Society's campaign for English largesse, but also maneuvered a large audience at Exeter Hall into censuring the Colonization Society and unanimously endorsing the New England abolitionists. Fortified with these victories and the famous "Wilberforce Protest"—a document in which some of England's leading philanthropists formally denounced colonization—Garrison returned to America in triumph.

Meanwhile the Colonization Society developed serious—and perhaps overwhelming—internal weaknesses. At the annual meeting in 1833 delegates became bitterly divided over a bold attempt to depose five managers and give Northerners more control of the society. The society's Fourth of July collections fell from $12,000 in 1832 to $4,000 in 1833; many donors failed to honor their pledges; and by the end of 1833 the society faced a $46,000 deficit. Thus, while the Garrisonians were apparently riding a wave of triumph, once-confident colonizationists were fighting to stay alive.

It was against this background that some colonizationists decided on mob action. On the evening of October 1, 1833, a group of active colonizationists and their sympathizers met in the office of James Watson Webb, the thirty-one-year-old editor of New York City's influential *Courier and Enquirer*. There they planned to pose as "Friends of Immediate Abolition in the United States" and invade the initial meeting of the New York City Anti-Slavery Society, which had been called for seven-thirty the following evening at Clinton Hall. Their object, John Neal informed the Colonization Society's secretary, was to put a stop to Garrison's "calumnies" and "misrepresentations." "For my own part," explained the thirty-six-year-old Portland Yankee, who eagerly sought the Colonization Society's agency in England, "I am for mild, firm and effectual measures—but it is not so with most who are opposed to Garrison."

Indeed not! Even the most naive of Neal's Quaker relatives would not have expected that evening's proceedings to be limited to "kind and temperate, but manly resolutions." That morning, as Neal knew, both Webb's *Courier and Enquirer* and Solomon Lang's *Gazette* had issued thinly veiled calls for a mob. "Are we tamely to look on," asked Webb, "and see this most dangerous species of fanaticism extending itself through society?" No, counseled Webb, the safe and proper course was for everyone to meet outside Clinton Hall a half-hour before the scheduled meeting and crush "this many-headed Hydra in the bud." Such fearless and prompt action, said Webb, would "expose the weakness as well as the folly, madness, and mischief of these bold and dangerous men." And that day posters were tacked up all over the city:

NOTICE
TO ALL PERSONS FROM THE SOUTH

All persons interested in the subject of a
meeting called by

J. Leavitt,   W. Goodell,
W. Green, Jr.,   J. Rankin,
Lewis Tappan,
At Clinton Hall,
This evening at 7 o'clock,
Are requested to attend at the same hour
and place.

Many Southerners
New-York, Oct. 2d, 1833.
N.B. All citizens who may feel disposed
to manifest the *true* feeling of the State on
this subject, are requested to attend.

That evening, as expected, some fifteen hundred New Yorkers—and perhaps a handful of Southerners—stood outside Clinton Hall yelling for the blood of Arthur Tappan and Garrison. Wandering amongst them was Garrison himself, who had arrived early only to find the hall locked. After learning of the proposed mob, the building's trustees had withdrawn permission to hold the meeting there; and Tappan and his friends—without notifying Garrison—had decided to meet uptown at Chatham Street Chapel.

The crowd soon adjourned to Tammany Hall for a meeting of their own. In the chair, cautioning moderation, was General Robert Bogardus, a sixty-two-year-old veteran of the War of 1812, a former state senator, and one of the city's leading lawyers. At his side were the meeting's secretaries, M. C. Patterson and P. P. Parsells, with whom Neal had previously planned the night's events. Also on the platform were the aristocratic-looking Colonel Webb, his former associate James Gordon Bennett, the prominent Whig and next state senator Frederick Tallmadge, the future postmaster James Lorimer Graham, and the "literary genius" John Neal. All were men of some prominence. All except Bogardus were young men—in their twenties or thirties. All except the Scotsman Bennett were Northeastern-born. And all except Bennett openly identified with African colonization.

The Tammany Hall audience had settled for speeches and resolutions, when suddenly news came that the abolitionists were meeting at Chatham Street Chapel. Quickly the crowd passed the resolutions and then proceeded to the chapel. Finding the iron gate locked, they milled about until a janitor came out and opened the gate. With a roar the mob stormed the chapel only to find it empty. The abolitionists had just slipped out the rear door after quickly organizing their society and electing Arthur Tappan president in a thirty-minute meeting. In frustration, the mob seized "a wretched looking old black," derisively dubbed him "Arthur Tappan," and forced him to preside over a mock meeting. Laughing and shouting, the rioters cheerfully agreed to resolutions favoring immediate emancipation and—significantly—"immediate amalgamation." An hour later, they dispersed. And thus, as the *Journal of Commerce* quipped the next day:

The King of France with 80,000 men,
Marched up the hill, and then marched down again.

In the next few years—when Arthur Tappan and his New York associates took over the reins of the antislavery movement and expanded both its operations and its campaign against African colonization, when prominent colonizationists such as James Gillespie Birney and Gerrit Smith defected to the American Anti-Slavery Society, when state and local auxiliaries openly or clandestinely seceded from the American Colonization Society, when Colonization society funds dropped disastrously—still other colonizationists resorted to mob violence. The New York City rioters of July, 1834, shouted colonization vows in Chatham Street Chapel. The Uitca mob of October, 1835, included leading local colonizationists. The Cincinnati mob of July, 1836, included most of the city's prominent colonizationists. The rioters who killed Elijah Lovejoy at Alton, Illinois, in November, 1837, identified openly with African colonization. Almost automatically, as antislavery organizers invaded one Northern community after another, zealous colonizationists became alarmed. They saw antislavery societies as menaces to their well-being, as threats to their holy cause, as killers of their sacred dream. Time and again they aroused their townsmen to violence and sought their enemy in battle.

3

In adopting the position of the free Negro and in waging war against the American Colonization Society, the abolitionists infuriated not only zealous colonizationists but Negrophobes as well. The antislavery alternative to African colonization—"immediate emancipation without expatriation"—accepted the proposition that some day the free Negro would be assimilated into American society. For most Northerners this proposition was anathema.

It was probably fear of racial assimilation that prompted the New York City mob of October, 1833, to discuss and to support mock resolutions favoring "immediate amalgamation." and it was certainly this fear that prompted men such as James Watson Webb, the key figure in the October mob and the North's most vehement anti-abolitionist spokesman, to support African colonization and to crusade against the abolitionists.

Webb supported African colonization, but he was never a "true believer." The thirty-one-year-old editor never believed that African colonization was God's plan for Christianizing Africa, aiding the free Negro, and eliminating Southern slavery. To Webb, an ardent Episcopalian, African colonization was not a holy cause; indeed, it was not even a practical one, for its cost would be twice that of the War of 1812. Nevertheless, he said it should be supported, for it was the "most effective barrier" against the abolitionists, and it served as a bulwark against the "heinous" and "pernicious" thought that some day the free Negro could become a vital and significant part of American society.

Webb was basically a traditionalist. In general he reflected many of the crass, self-seeking, speculative aspects of the Jacksonian period, but essentially he was loyal to an older America. Due to this loyalty, the former army officer refused to alter his newspaper's traditional fare, to aim at a mass audience, to report prize-fights or rape trials, to publish a Sunday edition, or to allow newsboys to hawk his paper on the streets; and eventually his newspapers folded when he clung to traditional ways in the face of the revolution in journalism. Fiercely proud of his lineage—which he could trace to early Puritan Massachusetts—Webb fancied himself as the staunch defender of country squires and gentlemen merchants, or ardent, brave, and magnanimous patricians, of superior breeding and of social deference. In particular he saw himself as the foremost protector of the interests and the traditions of New York City's gentlemen merchants. Accordingly, he shunned impersonal relations in business, cuffed and caned "inferior" rivals on the street, fought one duel and caused another.

For a man such as Webb, the question of future amalgamation was undoubtedly crucial. Webb's ideal America was not only traditional in its values, but was also of old American stock in its blood lines; the two, in his mind, stood or fell together. For this reason, he opposed vehemently any plan that promised the eventual assimilation of "inferior" breeds such as the Irish and the Latin-American into the mainstream of American society. Above all, he denounced any proposal that even hinted that the Negro might someday become a part of his America. The proposals of Arthur Tappan and other "amalgamators," thundered Webb, amounted to treason; they threatened not only slavery and African colonization, but the "very fabric" of Northern society as well. To preserve their heritage, their institutions, and themselves, Webb thus called on gentlemen of the "highest character" to crush the "amalgamists" in the bud.

This fear of assimilation, of being "mulattoized," of losing one's sense of identity, existed long before Webb and the New York mob expressed it. Indeed, it existed long before Northerners had ever heard of the *Liberator*. Everywhere in the North, as countless travelers noted, Negrophobia and racism flourished, and Northern whites—either legally or illegally—made the lot of the Negro miserable in "a thousand ways." Indeed, it was largely because Northern Negrophobia was so vicious and so pervasive that colonizationists insisted that their cause was holy. Anything as unyielding and malicious as Northern fear and hatred of the free Negro, they argued, was obviously "an ordination of Providence, and no more to be changed than the laws of nature." Northern thought was so permeated with racism, argues Leon Litwack, that even the abolitionists accepted many of its most pernicious tenets. Even the *Liberator* talked about the Negro as "branded by the hand of nature with a perpetual mark of disgrace."

Northern Negrophobia was not manifested merely in social and legal prescription, in barring Negroes from jury boxes and election polls, in excluding Negroes from white men's schools and railroad cars, in limiting Negroes to "Nigger work" and "Nigger pews." It hounded Northern Negroes from cradle to grave. Indicative was a potter's field in Cincinnati, where whites were buried east to west and blacks north to south. Among the dead, Northerners insisted that white supremacy must prevail.

This antipathy frequently expressed itself in violence. Often whites suffered from black felons, who apparently abounded under these circumstances. And in September, 1824, about 150 Philadelphia Negroes attacked white officials as they were taking a runaway to jail. But in nine instances out of ten, whites were the aggressors, and blacks the victims. Northern law and custom left Negroes unprotected, and they suffered continually at the hands of frustrated whites, practical jokers, and village sadists.

Occasionally whites tried to expel free Negroes forcibly from their communities. In Providence, where anti-Negro feeling was "very bitter," several attempts were made in the 1820's. On one occasion, respectable whites became alarmed about "Hardscrabble," a predominantly Negro slum which also harbored most of the city's drunkards, sailors, and prostitutes. The whites raised a mob which drove Negroes from their homes, tore down their houses and carried off their furniture and sold it at auction in Pawtucket. Another time, a brawl between blacks and whites broke out on Olney Street, another disreputable neighborhood. After the death of a white sailor, lower-class whites invaded the Negro quarter and began razing Negro homes. To stop the destruction, the Governor of Rhode Island called out the militia and finally ordered them to fire. This resulted in further destruction, and by the time peace was restored, Olney Street was virtually uninhabitable.

The most serious incident of this kind occurred in Cincinnati in August, 1829. For two decades the city fathers had ignored the provision of Ohio's infamous

Black Laws that compelled free Negroes entering the state to post a $500 bond as guarantee of their good behavior and providence. But between 1826 and 1829, which were the years of greatest Negro migration to the state, Cincinnati's Negro population suddenly jumped from about 4 to 10 percent of the total population. White citizens became alarmed. The Cincinnati Colonization Society, which had been formed in 1826 for the express purpose of "forwarding to Africa the free blacks of Cincinnati," received increasing support, and the number of local colonization societies in Ohio increased from one in late 1825 to forty-five by 1830. In 1828, the city council appointed a committee to consider a petition asking for measures to stop the inpouring of free blacks. In the spring of 1829, the Negrophobes scored heavily in a ward election that centered around the question of enforcing the Black Laws. And in July, the city fathers responded positively to this sentiment; in their role as Overseers of the Poor, the Trustees of Cincinnati announced that after thirty days they would enforce the $500 bond requirement.

Almost immediately, white bands began raiding Negro quarters. These assaults reached a climax on the weekend of August 22, when several hundred whites invaded "Bucktown," spreading terror and destruction. By the end of 1829, about half of the Negro population had left the city. Unfortunately, wrote the editor of the Cincinnati *Gazette*, the "sober, honest, industrious, and useful portion of the colored population" left, and thus the enforcement of the Black Laws, which he had supported, only served "to lessen much of the moral restraint, which the presence of respectable persons of their own color, imposed on the idle and indolent, as well as the profligate." But never again in the ante-bellum period did Cincinnati's Negro population exceed 5 percent of the total, and for many whites this fact alone justified the excesses.

It is clear, then, that violent antipathy toward the free Negro existed before the founding of the *Liberator* in January, 1831. It is also obvious that antislavery men did not cause Northern Negrophobia, as some of their opponents later argued; they merely inherited it. And it was this legacy of fear and hate—rather than any concern about the practicality or the impracticality of immediate emancipation—that caused many Northerners to side with the colonizationists in their war with the abolitionists. It was not the doctrine of immediatism, as Gilbert Hobbes Barnes insists, but the heritage of racism that generated much of the controversy in the North.

Anti-abolitionists, as Barnes and others maintain, invariably denounced immediatism as unsound doctrine. They always took advantage of the abolitionists' confusion of terms, the abolitionists' inability to define what immediate abolition really entailed. On those rare occasions when antislavery men actually spelled out a program, their opponents picked at details. And on those numerous occasions when antislavery men refused to make their position clear, their enemies chided them for vagueness and impracticality. If the abolitionists proposed that state legislatures immediately free the slaves, then anti-abolitionists denounced them for wanting to flood the country with millions of black paupers and vagabonds. If the abolitionists suggested that "immediate abolition" did not necessarily circumscribe all forms of compulsory labor, such as villeinage, copyhold, or apprenticeship for year, then anti-abolitionists reproached them for wishing the substitution of one kind of slavery for another.

But these attacks and denunciations were primarily parries and counterthrusts, rather than reflections of anxiety about immediatism. Anti-abolitionists rarely showed any interest in finding practical solutions to the slavery question. And they certainly did not offer any. With the notable exceptions of the New York *Herald* in the 1830's and the New York *Day Book* in the 1850's, both of which favored slavery, anti-abolition journals invariably supported ill-conceived plans for transporting millions of unwilling American Negroes to Africa, Brazil, or Central America. And mobs constantly thundered their approval of the same schemes. For most anti-abolitionists, it seems that a plan's practicality depended on whether it promised an all-white America.

It is also clear that before the New York philanthropists assumed control of the antislavery movement, a community's initial response to immediatism hinged largely on the race question. That is, it depended primarily on whether the doctrine was identified with Negro uplift or racial assimilation. Throughout New England, for example, there was almost no response—either positive or negative—to immediatism until the late summer of 1832, and then only a stirring until the summer of 1835. Even in Boston, we may recall, civic officials did not learn of the *Liberator* or its editor until October, 1831, and then Mayor Otis dismissed the whole operation as trifling. Indeed, it was not until 1835 that he really became alarmed. But there was a notable exception to this over-all tranquility, and that exception was Connecticut.

In Connecticut, the promotion of immediate abolition coincided with an attempt to establish a Negro college in New Haven. In June, 1831, Simeon S. Jocelyn, a white pastor of a New Haven Negro church, Arthur Tappan, and Garrison proposed such a college to a Negro national convention. The enterprise would "produce a band of educated men to take up the pen" for Negro rights. New Haven, they agreed, was an ideal site because of its location, its intellectual fame, and the "friendly, pious, generous, and humane" character of its inhabitants.

The friendly inhabitants disagreed. Almost immediately they became alarmed, and after the Nat Turner insurrection broke out in Virginia in August, their apprehension increased. In September, a month before Boston officials had heard of the *Liberator*, the mayor and aldermen of New Haven called a town meeting. And by a vote of approximately 700 to 4, the citizens of New Haven denounced the proposal for a Negro college and denounced Garrison and the abolitionists for "unwarrantable and dangerous interference with the concerns of other states." Calling "the institution a *College*," Jocelyn reported to Garrison, "touched the very *quick* of oppression," for "it carries the assurance of equality with it."

Although Jocelyn, Garrison, and the other abolitionists accepted defeat and abandoned the project, local newspapers continued to berate them for sponsoring amalgamation and causing New Haven Negroes to become "impudent and insolent." Several newspapers demanded the suppression of vice in "New Liberia," the Negro ghetto. Finally, in October, 1831, one mob stoned Arthur Tappan's house on Temple Street, another tore down a Negro shanty on "Sodom Hill," and still another invaded "New Liberia" and attacked amalgamation where it actually existed, capturing four white women and fourteen white men.

A year and one-half later, but still six months before the New York City mob of October, 1833, an almost identical reaction occurred in nearby Canterbury, Connecticut. This was the famous Prudence Crandall incident. In the spring of 1833, Miss Crandall, a young Quaker schoolmistress, who had just been publicly rebuked for admitting a Negro day student, decided to challenge the community's prejudice in a radical way. Securing the support of antislavery leaders, she opened her boarding school exclusively to black girls.

Immediately the townfolk, led by Andrew T. Judson, town selectman and later United States district judge, Democratic politician, and an officer of the local colonization society, called a town meeting and denounced the scheme. Ignoring this condemnation and pleas from angry citizens, Miss Crandall received between ten and twenty girls. To offset this devilish plot to make "New England . . . the Liberia of America," the town fathers called a second meeting, which condemned the school as a "rendezvous . . . designed by its projectors . . . to promulgate their disgusting doctrines of amalgamation and their pernicious sentiments of subverting the Union." The angry citizens drew up a petition to the General Assembly "deprecating the evil consequences of bringing from other states and towns, people of color for any purpose, and more especially for the purpose of disseminating the principles and doctrines opposed to the benevolent colonizing system." In May, the state legislature, responding to pressure, enacted a statute designed to outlaw Miss Crandall's boarding school.

Miss Crandall defied the law, was twice tried, and finally was found guilty. Throughout her ordeal, the abolitionists, with healthy stipends from Arthur Tappan, effectively used the trials for propaganda purposes. By declining to furnish bail, for example, they threw on the prosecution the responsibility for lodging the young Quakeress in a cell that had been previously occupied by a notorious wife-murderer. Subsequent woodcuts, prints, and calico kerchiefs of the delicate young lady in a murderer's cell provided organized antislavery with more dynamite than thousands of pages of argument. Eventually in late 1834, an appellate court quashed the case on a technicality.

Meanwhile, the exasperated citizens of Canterbury resorted to violence. Townfolk harassed Miss Crandall continuously. Vandals filled the school's well with manure, stoned the schoolhouse frequently, and even tried to burn it down. All these efforts, however, failed to stop Miss Crandall. Finally, in September, 1834, a band of men attacked her house at night and rendered it uninhabitable; Miss Crandall at last gave way and departed for Illinois.

Connecticut remained the most inhospitable of the New England states. From 1833 through 1837, antislavery journals reported 16 anti-abolition and anti-Negro mobs there. Of the New England states, only Massachusetts had not only a much larger population but also much more antislavery activity. Between 1833 and 1837, antislavery men organized 243 auxiliaries in Massachusetts and only 46 in Connecticut. If we regard the number of auxiliaries formed as a reasonable indicator of antislavery activity, then the relative hostility of Connecticut and the other New England states becomes clear. Connecticut, as the following table indicates, had a much higher percentage of mobs for auxiliaries organized than any of the other New England states:

Connecticut	34.8%	(46 auxiliaries—16 mobs)
New Hampshire	16.4%	(79–13)
Rhode Island	15.4%	(26–4)
Maine	8.3%	(48–4)
Massachusetts	7.0%	(243–17)
Vermont	6.7%	(104–7)

Even in Cincinnati, which bordered a slave state and depended heavily on the Southern trade, there was little reaction to immediatism until it became associated with amalgamation and Negro uplift. The earliest penetration of antislavery sentiment into the Queen City came in early 1834, when Theodore Dwight Weld and his fellow students at Lane Theological Seminary formed an antislavery society. Contrary to historical belief, their call for the "immediate emancipation of the whole colored race" met little resistance either at the seminary or in the city of Cincinnati. Only the *Cincinnati Journal* bothered to comment, and it found "nothing exceptionable" in the society's goal. Indeed, the editor of the *Journal* was happy that the antislavery movement was "falling into the hands of men, who express their views clearly and kindly.

It was not until the Lane students opened schools in "Little Africa" or "Bucktown" and associated publicly with Negroes, particularly "sable belles," that the editor of the *Journal* and other Cincinnatians expressed alarm. Weld often visited Negro homes, and August Wattles, the most zealous supporter of Negro education and uplift, boarded with a Negro family. One student, who had been seen leaving town with a black girl and returning with her a few hours later, caused a stir; few believed his claim that he was only giving directions. On another occasion, a carriage of Negro students visited Lane Seminary, and it soon became common gossip that the Lane students paid "marked attention" to the girls. And thus rumor followed rumor, and gossip became nastier and nastier.

In May, less than two months after he had praised the Lane students, the editor of the *Journal* reprimanded them for lacking common sense and being overzealous in their efforts. At the same time, the illustrious James Hall, editor and co-owner of the *Western Monthly Magazine* and an ardent supporter of African colonization, denounced the crusade for immediate emancipation, the activities of the students, and "the idea of inoculating . . . embryo clergymen" with radical political and social ideas and "thus *preparing* a trained band of missionaries to traverse the land and inoculate a particular creed." In August, the board of trustees of Lane Seminary, responding to numerous complaints, outlawed the antislavery society. In October, forty members of the society left Lane, many of them bound for newly established Oberlin College. Thus the first antislavery controversy in Cincinnati was short-lived.

But Cincinnati, which had anti-abolition and anti-Negro riots in 1836, 1841, and 1843, remained sensitive to questions of Negro uplift and racial assimilation. Repeatedly cries of "Amalgamationists! Amalgamationists! Amalgamationists!" rang through the Queen City. The "bugbear of 'amalgamation,' " reported one traveler, permeated southern Ohio. Even the notable Lyman Beecher was "so far jaundiced" that he supported African colonization, because "he considered it a salutary preventive of that amalgamation, which would confound the two races and obliterate the traces of their distinction." And after the riot of September, 1841, which was the most violent and destructive of Cincinnati's outbursts, zealous Negrophobes organized themselves into the Anti-Abolition Society of Cincinnati. The society's primary goal was to secure the expulsion of the Negro from Ohio, either by the enactment of harsher anti-Negro legislation or by enforcement of the Black Laws of 1804 and 1807. Its only enemies, the society declared, were those "white traitors" who favored a "mixture of races." After the same riot, Dr. Gamaliel Bailey, the editor of the *Philanthropist*, issued a public disclaimer. It began: "We are not *amalgamationists*."

Across the nation, abolitionists made the same disclaimer time and again, but to no avail. Throughout the ante-bellum period, anti-abolitionists repeated no charge with greater pertinacity than that of amalgamation, and none could more effectively stir up the rancor and the brutality of a mob. It was this charge—rather than any complaint about the technical difficulties of immediate emancipation or the future of the Southern trade—that generated the more savage anti-abolition mobs, such as those in New York City in July, 1834, and in Philadelphia in May, 1838.

4

It is difficult to avoid the conclusion that this charge of amalgamation touched the heart of what Tocqueville called the "all-pervading disquietude" about the future of the two races in America. Underlying anti-abolition pamphlets and harangues to mobs was the assumption that only miscegenation would solve the American race problem. Repeatedly, of course, anti-abolitionists denied the feasibility of miscegenation. They argued that the two races found one another physically repulsive—often in the face of overwhelming evidence to the contrary. At the same time, however, they assumed that miscegenation was the only practical answer to America's racial dilemma.

For many Northerners, the probable alternative to slavery and African colonization was *either* race war *or* miscegenation. For Northern anti-abolitionists, this alternative was as immutable as the law of gravity or the Ten Commandments: if slaves were freed, it followed that the two races must completely separate or wholly merge. To free millions of slaves and then leave them as a distinct race, to leave them in wretchedness and disgrace as the North had done with its few Negroes, was nothing less than to build a house with powder kegs. Destruction was certain.

The slave, as anti-abolitionists saw him, was contented and cowardly; he had been, as one ardent defender of the Lovejoy mob put it, "despoiled by Slavery." But once the spirit of freedom and hope revived his dormant passions, he would be a new creature. He would never be satisfied with a few limited freedoms. He would want more and more. He would, in fact, never be content until he had access to women of both races, as white men had had for centuries, and particularly until he married the master's daughter. Onto the Negro the anti-abolitionists projected their own view of the American way. Marrying "well," they assumed, was the only real sign that an "inferior" had arrived. And since all "inferior" nationalities and classes measured their standing on the basis of their access to a "superior's" women, it followed that the most "inferior" of all would do likewise.

Once the slave became a new creature, he would also wield the sword with all the terror and the ferocity of deep revenge. The anti-abolitionist imagery of racial war, of slaughter, or carnage rested on the foreboding that the Negro had a score to settle with the white American. With dread anti-abolitionists looked forward to the day when the white man stood before the judgment seat of the black man. When that day came, as the expression went, "Quaker hats would be in quick demand."

The only alternative to that day and the only penance for their sins, anti-abolitionists feared, was the horror of horrors—amalgamation. For most white Americans, such thoughts were undoubtedly painful. But for the James Watson Webbs—for Americans who desperately dreaded being cut off from deep and permanent ties of family, clan, class, community, and position—amalgamation touched the heart of their passions: their dread of sinking below their forefathers' station and their nightmare of becoming cogs in a mass society.

For such men, African colonization offered the happy illusion of excluding the Negro not only from "society" but from the country as well. By attacking the American Colonization Society and by closely identifying themselves with the free Negro, the abolitionists made it clear that they entertained a far different vision. They proposed to lift the Negro not only out of bondage but out of the gutter as well. They proposed to give the free Negro citizenship—second-class citizenship to be sure, but citizenship nevertheless. Many anti-abolitionists were thus alarmed, and some resorted to violence. It took, however, the sudden appearance of a "powerful combination" to heighten their fears into fury and to generate a general outburst of violence.

8   Harold Schwartz

FUGITIVE SLAVE DAYS IN BOSTON

Bostonians were never more conscious of their traditional position in the United States as a Cradle of Liberty than during the 1850's when the Fugitive Slave Law was in effect. Residents of the capital of a sovereign commonwealth in the fore-front of Revolutionary struggle, they absorbed history in their daily affairs. Wor-shipping in the same churches as the patriots, and walking the very streets they trod, the descendants of the Minute Men of '75 could never forget their heritage. Thus admonished to sacrifice their comfort for the liberties of others, they took the law into their own hands, and nullified the most hateful statute since the Alien and Sedition Laws.

1

In no city had fugitive slaves felt greater security than in Boston where they even had their own preacher and church. Massachusetts law protected them, when fol-lowing the United States Supreme Court's decision in the Prigg Case which pro-hibited states from legislating on fugitive slaves, the General Court passed a Personal Liberty Act to forbid judges and other law-enforcement officers from acting under the provisions of the national Constitution. To all intents and purposes, after 1843 there was no way of recovering a slave legally in the Bay State.

The Fugitive Slave Law changed all that by providing machinery to operate through the federal courts.

Cotton Whigs saw no cause for alarm over the act. The *Advertiser*, their leading journal, considered that the North had at last fulfilled a Constitutional requirement too long neglected. It was sure the South would have no further grounds for complaint, but it forgot that abolitionists threatened never to uphold the law. Apart from its constitutionality, Horace Mann charged that there was no legal protection to the 8,000 free Negroes in Massachusetts *"from being turned into slaves, on any day, by the easy, cheap, and short-hand kidnapping of a legislative act."*

Rumors and fears multiplied haphazardly. In mid-October it was whispered that the first slave-hunters were in town. Quick action was urgent. A "non-partisan" meeting in Faneuil Hall, the night of the fourteenth, attended by an estimated 3,500, over which Charles Francis Adams presided, urged repeal of the act. Frederick Douglass, the famous Negro spokesman, expressed the fears the new law had struck into his heart and the hearts of others of his race. Though he had bought himself and had his "free papers," some irregularity might yet be discovered, which

From *The New England Quarterly*, XXVII (1954), pp. 191-212. Reprinted by permission of the publisher.

would result in his return to bondage. Perhaps the hunters were after him even as he was speaking. Denouncing the law as contrary to the Declaration of Independence and the Constitution since it deprived men of liberty without due process of law, the assemblage

> *Resolved*, That we cannot believe that any citizen can be found in this city or vicinity, so destitute of love for his country and his race, and so devoid of all sense of justice, as to take part in returning a fugitive slave under the law.

A Vigilance Committee was instituted with the Reverend Theodore Parker, the intense leader of unorthodox thought, recently appointed chaplain to the fugitive slaves, as chairman of the executive committee. Abolitionists made elaborate preparations. In less than two days there were eighty members (at full strength there were 200), and a special Legal Committee to serve as counsel for fugitives was created, whose staff was to use all legal delays possible. Should a prisoner be adjudged a slave, they were to alarm the city.

Organization was completed none too soon. On the afternoon of October 25, Parker returned home to find one of his associates on the committee, Dr. Samuel Gridley Howe, the famous teacher of the blind, anxiously awaiting him with the disquieting news that warrants had been issued for the arrest of William and Ellen Craft, a young couple in Boston since 1848. The machinery now swung into action, thus setting a pattern that was to become familiar. By means of handbills scattered broadcast, the city was alerted to the presence of the two agents of the Crafts' owner, John Knight, and a man named Hughes, the jailer of Macon, Georgia. Parker directed a relentless campaign of intimidation against them. He had them arrested for slander, although they were shortly afterward released on bail. Crowds jeered at them so threateningly that they feared to appear in public. Through it all Hughes piously declared, "It isn't the niggers I care about, but it's the principle of the thing." Having decided that the game had gone on long enough, Parker decided to take the final step. In an interview in their hotel room, with guards posted in a hall outside, he told them that he could not guarantee their safety much longer. Hughes, thoroughly cowed, admitted he could not fulfill his task. A few hours later they slunk away secretly.

Though the Crafts were now safe, it was deemed wiser for them to leave the United States for Great Britain. Just before their departure, Parker married them legally in a solemn rite in a house on "Nigger Hill." At the conclusion of the ceremony, he put a Bible and a sword into William's hands and bade him use both with all his might. The liberated couple stayed in Britain where Parker saw them in 1859.

The shame Massachusetts men felt at the thought of Americans having to flee to England to gain freedom can only be imagined by a later generation. Parker expressed the feeling of all abolitionists as he wrote:

> I keep in my Study two trophies of the American Revolution, one is a musket which my Grandfather fought with at the Battle of Lexington . . .

against the "British" the other is a great gun which he captured in that battle. He was the Captain of the Lexington Soldiers; and took the first prisoners, and the first musket taken in [the] war for Independence and the Rights of man. But now I am obliged to look to "the British" for protection for the liberty of two of my own Parishioners who have committed no wrong against us! Well, so it is, and I thank God that Old England, with all her sins and shames, allows no Slave-Hunter to set foot on her soil.

2

Abolitionists did not feel they were subverting law. To them the Fugitive Slave Act was illegal, no matter how constitutional. The fiery Charles Sumner, shortly to enter the United States Senate, best expressed their view when he called it a "cruel devilish law," a heathen bill which "set at naught the best principles of the Constitution, and the very laws of God!" It is apparent that they considered America as much a society of men as of laws, while the Slavocracy were hiding behind the Constitution to enforce unjust demands. Even learned members of the bar supported this view. Richard Henry Dana, Jr., the author of *Two Years Before the Mast*, now a distinguished attorney, offered his services to the Legal Committee, as did Ellis Gray Loring and John Albion Andrew, the great Civil War Governor. These men were not rabble rousers nor demagogues, but charitable persons, to whom law and justice were synonymous. Slavery was illegal in Massachusetts, and no one could be enslaved from out of its territory, where the ground was hallowed by the blood of the mulatto "patriot," Crispus Attucks, "martyred" in an earlier defense of liberty (or that is what they were taught he died for). Parker, Dana, Andrew, and Howe were the sons of patriots who believed in freedom and fought for it. They would not be found wanting when their turns came.

The *Advertiser* might mumble about meeting the obligations due another section and partner in the Union, and that fugitives who had escaped their legal obligations elsewhere were not subject to Massachusetts law. "J" might even suggest that when cases arose, the populace might avert unpleasantness by buying the slave, but he was wrong in thinking anyone would take that proposal seriously. Certainly the slave-owners didn't.

3

In the months following the Crafts case, though there were several scares, not one slave was taken to court. The Vigilance Committee proved effective. But in the midst of a bitterly fought Senatorial election, which was to result in the choice of Charles Sumner, the forces of the law, descending on a Cornhill coffee house, apprehended Fred Wilkins, a devout Christian who preferred to be known as "Shadrach" for obvious reasons. He was alleged to be the property of John Debree, a purser in the Navy, who had ordered the contest only to see if the act would be enforced. A battery of respectable and ordinarily very expensive attorneys, Samuel E. Sewall, Ellis Gray Loring, Charles G. Davis, Charles List, and Dana, appeared as counsel for Shadrach, to hinder proceedings as much as possible. Shortly after noon, on Saturday, February 15, they wheedled an adjournment until the following Tuesday out of Commissioner George T. Curtis, who was determined to give the slave every opportunity to prove his claim to freedom.

The room began to empty. Suddenly, an armed mob led by a fugitive slave long-time resident in Boston, rushed in, enveloped the prisoner, and escaped with him into the throng. By nightfall Shadrach, rescued as it were from a second fiery furnace, was out of the law's reach. The authorities tracked him to Concord where they lost the trail. From there he was driven to Sudbury and to further stations on the Underground Railroad, until he reached Canada where he opened a barber shop.

Let the Whigs howl if they would that "such exhibitions of the impotence of the civil authorities" jeopardized life and property in addition to disgracing the community. The *Courier* declared that the real question was no longer confined to the enforcement of the Fugitive Slave Law. Rather, the "point to be determined now is, whether *any* law shall prevail in Boston."

Abolitionists scorned such mouthing. The important thing was that a man had been saved from Hell. What amazed Howe in the stand of the "decency & respectability" of Boston was that there was "not a blush of shame, not an expression of indignation at the thought that a man must fly *from* Massachusetts to the shelter of the red cross of England to save himself from the bloodhounds of slavery."

Shadrach's sensational rescue had kept the record clear. No slave had yet been returned from Boston, but the lesson of February 15 was clear to those who could see. For example, the editor of the *Atlas* warned of the danger of mob rule resulting from disregard of a statute, no matter how onerous. The Vigilance Committee was treading on dangerous ground. If it persisted in stirring up the city, inevitably there would be bloodshed.

Law enforcement having twice been thwarted, the government took measures to safeguard its judicial processes. Three days after Shadrach's escape, the Board of Aldermen ordered that the Mayor direct the city marshal to assist agents of the state and federal government in the execution of their duty when obstructed by a mob. The same day, President Fillmore ordered that prosecution proceedings be instituted against Shadrach's rescuers. Several persons were arrested, among them Elizur Wright of the *Commonwealth*.

Just as the government girded itself for the next trial which all knew would come when a determined slaveowner appeared, so the Vigilance Committee strengthened its resources, financially and otherwise. Success continued to crown its efforts throughout the rest of the winter when, by quick, decisive action, it frustrated attempts of slave catchers in New Bedford. Parker convened his associates daily during the crisis. As he put it, "Our eyes must be 'in every place beholding the evil and the good.'"

4

On the morning of April 3, a United States deputy marshal arrested Thomas Sims, a young mulatto, as a fugitive from the service of James Potter of Chatham, Georgia. Captured after a struggle in which he stabbed one officer, the prisoner was held at the Court House for a hearing. Though every effort was made not to arouse attention, within a few hours the Vigilance Committee learned of it. Parker and the others remained at their headquarters in Chauncy Place awaiting news, but all was quiet for the rest of the day.

The next morning a strange sight assailed the eyes of Bostonians when they reached the square. In addition to a company of 100 policemen who guarded the building, a great chain had been stretched around it on all four sides, three or four feet from the ground. The government was taking no chances. The truth was out; Massachusetts justice lay enchained at the mercy of Slavocracy. For years the abolitionists had said so, now they saw it. So that everyone might savor the disgrace, the *Commonwealth* published an engraving of the scene, the only time during its existence it ever ran a picture. Parker was glad of the symbol. He ostentatiously stepped over the chain, while he noted grimly that "old stiff-necked" Lemuel Shaw, Chief Justice, and the other judges grumblingly went under it, as subjects of slavery should.

The committee held frantic consultations, but all they agreed on was Howe's proposal to hold a meeting in the State House Yard that afternoon. Posters were quickly prepared to announce it, but the legislature refused permission. The rally began on the Common instead, and then shifted to the Tremont Temple, where those assembled resolved to hold a great mass meeting on April 8.

While a crowd of several hundred milled around outside waiting for news, Sims's lawyers stalled for time before Curtis, who again had been tapped for the unpleasant task of returning a slave. Sewall introduced an affidavit attesting to the prisoner's free status, and Robert Rantoul, Jr., questioned the commissioner's power to order an alleged slave remanded. Curtis, still making every effort to meet their demands, again withheld judgment after the second day's testimony, adjourning court over the week end to give the defense more time to prepare.

Abolitionists were desperate; the Vigilance Committee was in almost constant session. No case had ever gone so far as this. The wildest schemes were proposed, much to Parker's pain and surprise. Thomas Wentworth Higginson, then a young Unitarian minister of Newburyport, was shocked by the indecision among his colleagues on the committee. Summoned to Boston for the emergency, he arrived there on the fourth.

> It is worth coming to Boston occasionally to see that there are places worse than Newburyport [he wrote Samuel J. May]; there is neither organization, resolution, plan nor popular sentiment—the Negroes are cowed & the abolitionists irresolute & hopeless, with nothing better to do on Saturday than to send off circulars to clergymen!

Essentially men of peace, inexperienced in extra-legal work, there was little they could do. It would take many such incidents to educate them to an attitude of revolution. Even Higginson, ready for anything, found it strange to be on the outside of established institutions, to be obliged to lower his voice and conceal his purposes, to have to see law and order, police and military as the wrong side, good citizenship a sin, and bad citizenship a duty. The only thing they really knew how to do was to talk, to pass resolutions, and sign petitions in the hope of carrying their view by the weight of public opinion. But this time, all their legal efforts were beaten. They could not enforce a writ of replevin, and Chief Justice Shaw rejected their application for habeas corpus; he could not interfere in a federal matter. Abolitionists needed no further proof that Massachusetts justice, already enchained, wore its bonds willingly. The federal judiciary, rejecting another try for habeas corpus on April 11, proved no friendlier.

There was now no further hope. Curtis ordered Sims returned to his master. In a long decision in which he examined all sides of the question, he spoke bravely. Though he would have been glad to have been relieved of his responsibility, there was no tribunal competent to assume the burden. He could not avoid his duty. Legally, the hearing had not been a trial, but merely a proceeding to establish the right of removal. The Georgia courts had the final trial right if there were really any question. He thereupon gave the marshal a certificate attesting that Sims was the slave of James Potter.

To avoid disturbance, the authorities sought to keep their plans for the return secret, but Higginson, maintaining a ceaseless vigil, waited in the square for any indications. At dawn he watched the police drilling.

> They marched & countermarched, drew their cutlasses & went through various evolutions. Lastly they formed a hollow square & marched a little way up Court Street. It was a horrible thing, that hollow square.... Massachusetts ceased to exist & we seemed to stand in Vienna.... Yet I do not believe they will dare to carry out this plan; I do not think the blood even of Boston merchants could bear it.

At 3:15 a.m., April 13, Parker was summoned to the scene. The others were already there. For an hour they waited as preparations were completed. At last the prisoner emerged between two guards who placed him in the center of the formation. The march to Long Wharf began. The abolitionists could not control their feelings. As the company approached the site of the Boston Massacre, they pointed out the holy spot. "Gloomy and silent those wretched men passed on, sacrilegiously desecrating by their act this martyr stand of the Revolution," wrote Dr. Henry I. Bowditch. There was an impromptu prayer-meeting, the Rev. Daniel Foster leading the service on the wharf as the brig *Acorn* sailed into the dawn. At its conclusion they broke out spontaneously into Bishop Heber's "Missionary Hymn" ("From Greenland's Icy Mountains"), which they sang as they walked up State Street to the Anti-Slavery Office.

Sims was given up primarily because the city still respected the abstract principle of law, no matter how offensive it might be at times. Conservative classes were satisfied with the conclusion of the case. Abolitionists felt otherwise. They realized now that there was no use in appealing to the judiciary. The Court House stood as the "Bastille of the Slavocracy" and would sanction any enormity.

Feeling in Boston ran so high after the rendition of Sims that the Aldermen refused to rent Faneuil Hall to a committee of Webster supporters who wished to welcome him there. Much to the abolitionists' delight, the Secretary of State had to be received at the Revere House in Bowdoin Square.

5

In the years following the Sims case, opposition to the Fugitive Slave Law became more efficient. Freedom-loving men, spiriting hapless Negroes to liberty, grew used to furtive action, no doubt to Higginson's delight. Cities throughout the North organized their own vigilance committees. (New York and Philadelphia had them as early as 1838.) Routes of escape from the Mason-Dixon line to the Canadian border were skillfully maintained and patrolled. Though dating back to the 1790's, the "Underground Railroad" experienced a remarkable expansion after 1850, with the further establishment of way stations and alternate routes almost as if it were a regular line in legitimate operation.

While most fugitives escaped by way of the Ohio River tier of states, the relatively few who made their way by sea or land to Boston were assured of the most cordial reception possible. The Vigilance Committee kept up its work, meeting frequently, sometimes at Parker's house for dinner, or at Garrison's quarters, dubbed the "Anti-Slavery Office" at 21 Cornhill, or wherever they needed to. Funds continued to pour in to meet expenses for printing posters to advertise the presence of the slave-hunters during the Crafts and Sims cases, and for carfare and board bills for dozens of slaves, none of whom attracted attention. The rescue of Shadrach, for example, cost $1,820. Some of the most distinguished names are listed in the account book of the committee as contributors. In addition to Parker and Howe, there are references to Octavius Brooks Frothingham, James Rusell Lowell, Charles Francis Adams, and John G. Palfrey.

Austin Bearse was the jack-of-all-work for the committee. He notified the members of meetings, printed special tickets of admission, and guarded the doors. A native of Barnstable on the Cape, he had earlier made his living as the master of the yacht *Moby Dick*, in which he took pleasure parties on short trips. While he probably continued in this occupation, the committee bought him a new craft, the *Wild Pigeon*, specially designed for the transportation of fugitives. The ship appears to have been used frequently during these years.

The conspiracy to violate a duly enacted law was much more widespread than one might have thought. Even those who would not flout it themselves, became accessories after the fact by not betraying those who did. George S. Hillard, for example, Sumner's old law-partner, who had broken with his abolitionist friends, and was now a commissioner, would have been obliged to issue a warrant for the capture of a slave, had he been asked, yet his wife kept a room in readiness for any emergency without interference from him. The police followed their consciences too.

> When I was a marshal [one of them said later], and they tried to make me find their slaves, I would say, "I don't know where your niggers are, but I will see if I can find out." So I always went to Garrison's office and said, "I want you to find such and such a negro; tell me where he is." The next thing I knew, the fellow would be in Canada.

The sight of a fleeing slave softened the hearts of the most determined letter-of-the-law men. In Sudbury, Nathan Brooks, father-in-law of E. Rockwood Hoar, who had long remonstrated with his wife against her lawlessness, wilted when Shadrach stood hatless before him on the night of the rescue. Immediately crossing the road to his own home, he brought one of his old silk hats which the fugitive wore happily away.

The number of slave escapes mounted rapidly. By May 27, 1851, a little over a month after the Sims case, Parker estimated that 400 "citizens" of Massachusetts had fled as a consequence of the Fugitive Slave Law. He knew of one man who, besides having helped ninety-three to escape in the previous eight months, still had eight or ten more waiting. In 1853, Lewis Hayden, a member of the Vigilance Committee, and himself a fugitive, had as meny as thirteen in his house, "of all colors and sizes." Since there was no end in sight to the steady stream, the committee established an employment office under a paid agent to whom fugitives might apply for assistance. Parker felt confident that the people would never allow another slave to be returned.

6

For three years, not so much as one fugitive was arrested in Boston, but the law of averages eventually caught up with the abolitionists. One clever master succeeded where so many others had failed. Shortly after eight o'clock on the evening of May 24, 1854, Anthony Burns, aged about twenty-three, was arrested in Court Street on a warrant alleging him to be the slave of Col. Charles T. Suttle of Alexandria, Virginia. The next morning Edward Greeley Loring, a distinguished member of the bar, lecturer at Harvard Law School, and Judge of Probate for Suffolk County, began hearing the case in his capacity as commissioner. Richard Henry Dana, Jr., appeared as defense counsel.

Few had as yet heard of the arrest except the interested parties. Speed and secrecy were of the essence. The city was in an ugly mood for another slave rendition. Since 1851 the temper of the people had changed markedly against enforcement of the law. The Kansas-Nebraska Bill, then under debate in Congress, had convinced even the most law-respecting Whig that there could be no compromise with the South. Curtis, who had earlier ordered Sims remanded, refused to act now, although he had originally been approached.

Though there was no doubt of Burns's identity, Loring granted Dana's request for more time to prepare his brief. In the meantime the Vigilance Committee remained in constant session to prepare for the new threat. The seven-man executive committee took the invariable first move; it called a meeting at Faneuil Hall for Friday evening, May 26. So far everything had gone as usual, but now there came a profound change. Early on Friday morning Higginson urged an armed attack on the Court House, just as he had three years earlier, and just as before it was rejected. Young and impulsive (he was only thirty-two), he saw but one path open: forcible rescue. Precious hours were being wasted. Meetings and speeches were not going to free Burns. If necessary he would lead the assault himself. The Worcester clergyman (he moved there during the intervening years) saw his chance to play a combined St. George and Siegfried fading.

> The more I pondered . . . the more hopeless our position seemed, & mainly fr. the inexperience & want of organising faculty among our own men. But that something should, be done first or last, I was determined. Let another slave be carried off without the *attempt* at resistance, & we should become so tame that future cases would occur with less & less trace of manly feeling on our part.

Wasting no more time, he sent for his men to come into town from Worcester that evening. During the afternoon he purchased a dozen handaxes. He and Martin Stowell, another member of the executive committee, decided that an attack would have a better chance of success while the meeting was in progress, since they assumed the guards at the Court House would be unprepared for anything so early. Higginson hurried over to Faneuil Hall to tell his plan to the others. Howe and Parker, deeply involved in arrangements for the night's discussions, gave hasty approval, only half comprehending, as later events showed. Everything was done to make the maneuver look spontaneous, but Higginson always insisted that he had planned it carefully. At a conference with fifty or so of his company, he outlined the course of action. Only about half were willing to go along. Undaunted, Higginson was certain an adequate number of reinforcements to back up the initial assault would come running when the alarm was given.

At eight Sewall called the throng to order. Dr. Howe presented the inevitable resolutions. Parker was in rare form, addressing the audience as "Fellow subjects of Virginia." Both he and Wendell Phillips, who followed, urged peaceful methods. They did not speak as if they expected an attack. In the midst of discussion, shortly after nine, Higginson's agent planted in the audience cried out that a crowd was rushing the Court House. Immediately, so far as can be determined, pandemonium broke loose as all made for the exits. Higginson, waiting outside, realized at once that the effort would fail. The "froth and scum" of the meeting had come out first. Unfortunately the auditorium had no separate stage exit. The leaders were still on the platform unable to get out.

By the time Howe could get over to the scene, the issue had been decided. A few attackers, Higginson among them, had managed to squeeze inside the door, but were beaten off. A guard named Batchelder was killed, but it was impossible to say who had fired the shot. Higginson, the man of God, has become so hardened to thoughts of violence that though he regretted the bloodshed, he was relieved that none of his men had been injured seriously.

Loring's adjournment still in effect, the courts were closed the next day, Saturday. The city was quiet but tense. During the night army units were placed in and around the scene of the disturbance, and the streets leading to it were roped off. Attacks on the homes of Parker and Phillips, considered to be the ringleaders (although they had all along cautioned peace), were feared. The mayor, calling out the state militia, made what preparations he could to suppress disorder, but none was attempted. It was reported that federal marshal Asa Butman had received permission to send to New York for reinforcements.

Meanwhile poor Burns could be seen from time to time as he looked out of his cell window at the crowd gathered below. A quiet, devout Baptist, desirous of becoming a preacher to his people, he had captured the hearts of the populace as none of the earlier fugitives had. All grieved with him, including his captors. Boston was not the same city it had been during the Sims case. There had been a profound change. This time the *Advertiser* could understand why people should be tempted to violate a law. The repeal of the Missouri Compromise had incited public exasperation to such a pitch as to make execution of the Fugitive Slave Law more difficult than it had ever been. Sadly it acknowledged that the Compromise of 1850 was binding on one side only. The crowning touch to show the shift in attitude comes from the *Commonwealth*, which for the first time found its sister journal's remarks "sensible and judicious."

Parker's sermon on Sunday at the Music Hall was a masterpiece. In his "lesson for the day," he turned his fury on the distinguished jurist, Horace Mann's old law partner, Judge Loring, whom all had hitherto respected. The others were not far behind him. It was in such a mood of hatred, sullenness, and suppressed rage that Boston faced the new developments.

Over the week end frantic attempts were made to purchase Burns. On Saturday two dozen men raised $785 for his freedom. Samuel A. Eliot, who had voted for the passage of the Fugitive Slave Law, contributed $50. Late that evening Loring joyfully prepared the papers, but the arrival of the Sabbath delayed the conclusion of the deal. By Monday, Suttle refused to treat. He had not come to Boston to "sell niggers." It was said that Ben Hallett, the United States District Attorney, had brought about the change in his attitude by telling him that it was illegal to sell slaves in Massachusetts. The negotiations were broken off.

Abolitionists could find one satisfaction in all the disappointment and sleepless nights the case had caused them, the "wonderful" change in public opinion. Never had there been such agitation. Everett, the unshakable legalist, could neither approve nor resist the hostility to the law which he found strongest among the staunchest friends of the Compromise of 1850. "The *oldest* hunkers are among the saints," William Francis Channing wrote Higginson. ". . . John H. Pierson heads the petition in the Merchants Exchange for the repeal of the fugitive slave law; which has been rapidly filling up with the heaviest Boston names."

But it was all of no avail. Though Dana took four hours to sum up his case, Loring ordered Burns remanded. Replete with tones of revulsion, his decision showed the dilemma of nonabolitionists trained in the law and sworn to uphold it, without regard to personal feelings. To this author, the judge's words are a remarkable display of judicial integrity. It is apparent from his text, though the ever said so, that he would much have preferred to release Burns, but could not legally do so. The terrible vengeance an enraged public wreaked on Loring cannot compare to the agony he suffered as he sent the fugitive back into bondage. Wendell Phillips broke the news to the pathetic prisoner who plaintively asked if there was nothing more that could be done for him.

Boston mourned, as if for a great popular hero, when Burns left that afternoon, June 2. A great concourse waited in the square, showing every mark of hostility to the agents of the law, who had mounted a six-pound cannon to maintain order. At 2:15, Burns, clad in the new suit the marshal and other special officers had brought him, took his place in the hollow square of 120 men, all with drawn swords and revolvers. To the tolling of the Brattle Street Church bell, the march began down Court Street between dense crowds, who, lining the route with continual hissing and groaning, fell in behind as the column passed. Besides Burns's personal guard there were a detachment of National Lancers, a company of army artillery, two corps of Marines, the cannon with its staff, and assorted marshals. Such a desperate character as Burns, numbed by his grief, had brought out a greater display of American armed might than had been seen in Boston during the Mexican War. Down past the lawyers' building at 4 Court Street, draped in black, they marched, then across Washington Street where the *Commonwealth*'s offices were similarly decorated. From its windows, stretching to the opposite structure, a coffin was suspended on which was printed "Liberty." A shower of cayenne pepper greeted the conquering heroes as they passed under these emblems, but a bottle dropped at the same time, reputed to hold sulphuric acid, struck a protruding parapet. The procession swung into State Street, where it went before the Merchants Exchange in which the petition hung "in many long folds, & told by its signatures, that the most solid men of Boston . . . are fast falling into the ranks of freedom." Finally T Wharf was reached. At 3:20 the steamer *John Taylor* took Burns down the harbor to the revenue cutter *Morris*. The tragedy was over. *"He Has Gone!"* Samuel May despaired, "and Boston & Massachusetts lie, bound hand & foot, willing slaves, at the foot of the Slave Power, the most cruel & accursed despotism this poor world has ever been oppressed by."

Dr. Howe, who had seen everything from the attack of the week before to the final rendition, "wept for sorrow shame & indignation" as he stood on the street that frightful day. Had it not been for the city police, he felt the people would have disarmed and routed the troops, but the

> fear of *law*,—the *fetish* of law, disarmed & emasculated us.
>
> The most interesting thing I saw in the crowd was a comely coloured girl of eighteen who stood with clenched teeth & fists, & flashing eyes, & tears streaming down her cheeks,—the very picture of indignant despair.—I

could not help saying, "do not cry poor girl—he won't be hurt,"—"hurt"! said she, "I cry for shame that he will not kill himself! Oh! why is he not man enough to kill himself!"

To Howe, this was the intuition of genius. By martyrdom Burns would have "killed, outright, the fugitive slave law in New England & the North." The doctor, for one, felt that he would have to emigrate or "choke in this disgraced community." It was no longer a place for a civilized man.

Abolitionists rededicated themselves to the maintenance of the city's traditions. Wendell Phillips, as he told Burns the sad news, recalled the state's schools, colleges, churches, courts, benevolent and philanthropic institutions, but above all

her great names, her Puritans, her Pilgrims. . . . There [in Burns's cell] I vowed anew before the ever-living God I would consecrate all the powers He had given me to hasten the time when an innocent man should be safe on the sacred soil of the Puritans.

They were determined never again to let their community forget to stand firm for freedom. Not two hours after Burns's departure, Howe, though sick at heart and in body, began the preparation of a public statement to Loring telling him the people had lost confidence in him.

I have liked him surely; & am loth to lose the last of my old associates in that circle;—but I must;—if he is white, I am blacker than hell; if he is right, I am terribly wrong. . . . Good bye, my pleasant old friend;—if you are going up, I go down; & vice versa.

"Better be the Slave returned to bondage, than the unhappy commissioner," wrote Sumner from Washington. Perhaps Loring agreed. A few months later Howe reported, after a chance encounter, that the disgraced jurist had lost interest in life, and would have been glad to die but for his children. Passion against him never cooled. In February, 1855, though he had not a personal enemy in the state, according to Parker, he was dismissed from his Harvard lectureship. Efforts to remove him from his judgeship remained fruitless, however, until 1858.

Burns was not forgotten either. Within two years he was given his freedom, mostly through the kindness of Boston, including the marshals, who contributed to the fund raised for his purchase. He went to Oberlin to study for the Baptist ministry, in which calling he spent the few remaining years of his life, until his death in 1862. A number of the rioters, Higginson and Parker among them, were arrested, but their indictments were quashed.

7

There were no further slave renditions after the Burns case. In effect the Fugitive Slave Law was nullified in Boston. During the summer of 1854 Henry I. Bowditch organized the Anti-Man-Hunting League, a secret society "pledged to use all proper means for rendering difficult or impossible the coming or the remaining of the Manhunter amongst us." For over two years they practiced carrying persons out of crowded halls in anticipation of an actual necessity for their services. In February, 1855, the less violent James Freeman Clarke founded the Defensive League of Freedom to aid those suffering penalties for opposition to the law. Unlike Bowditch's organization, the league was peaceable and open. Its object was only to see "that no man is beaten down by the Slave Power, without an adequate defence. . . ." The members pledged themselves to build so strong a moral resistance "that it shall be impossible to arrest a fugitive in this part of the Union." Neither of these groups was ever called upon to act; there was never a need.

As the decade wore on, and the government winked indulgent eyes, the Vigilance Committee grew devilishly effective in spiriting fugitives out of the country. Hundreds passed through Boston without difficulty, although it is impossible to say just how many. Parker, Howe, and the others, especially Bearse, always stood ready to assist. They knew all the little tricks, the secret routes, the persons to see, the places to go. The story of the committee has never been written, perhaps it never can be, but if it ever should appear, it will show beyond all question why the South looked on Boston as its bitterest foe. The Vigilance Committee was proud of that enmity.

V

THE CIVIL WAR AND ITS RIOTOUS AFTERMATH

On December 2, 1859, the day of his execution, John Brown handed a note to one of his guards in which he wrote:

> I John Brown am now quite *certain* that the crimes of this *guilty land*; will never be purged away; but with Blood. I had as I now think vainly flattered myself that without verry much bloodshed; it might be done.[1]

This tragic decade with its "bleeding Kansas" and abolitionist struggles gave way to the violent act of revolution at Harper's Ferry, and culminated in civil war. The democratic processes of debate and politics, lobbying, and bargaining could not solve the problem of slavery without conflict. Old pacifists such as Henry David Thoreau and William Lloyd Garrison altered their views, and saw a Christ-like symbol in John Brown, a martyr for the cause of liberty and justice, who by his act of violence did, they felt, much to avoid even greater violence. Barrington Moore, Jr., a present-day historian, echoes this view noting that frequently in history "the costs of moderation have been at least as atrocious as those of revolution. . . ."

Others argue that any act of violence brings about worse violence: This is the central argument of Frederic Wertham's *A Sign For Cain.*[2] "All forms of human violence," he writes, "are in some way connected with one another." This thesis, tested in a period of civil war, helps to explain the violent nature of the riots that occurred during and after the war. In 1863, a riot led by the urban poor and triggered by the discriminatory draft law, exploded in New York City. Anti-Black and anti-abolitionist feeling, particularly among the city's Irish population, culminated in a week of disturbances which were both anti-"rich" and anti-Black. In the first article that follows, James McCague gives a graphic account of the mob's force and passion on the first day of the week-long rampage. Accurate figures on the price of this riot in lives and property have been hard to establish: The estimate of Police Commissioner Thomas Acton that twelve hundred persons were killed does seem reasonable; his estimate of five million dollars in property losses, McCague believes, is conservative.

The forced change in the status of the Negro was only one of the alterations in the social structure which produced violence in this period; the nation was becoming increasingly industrialized, and labor strife became common to the American scene. New social forces intensified feelings of class consciousness in a period which is historically noted for corruption and crassness. The ideas about *laissez faire* and Social Darwinism were used to justify man's inhumanity to his fellow man. The depression of 1873, more than any earlier depression, produced violent labor strikes. In that age of rapid industrial expansion, the government served and protected the masters of industry. Private armies, from such organizations as the Pinkerton Detective Agency, were for hire providing spies, agitators, and "finks" for use against working men. With the depression firmly settled upon the nation, large numbers of unemployed men took to the streets and roads of the nation, unwanted "tramps" in a society of plenty. The poor, the unemployed, the rootless, the nameless wanderers, the immigrants, and the blacks comprised a volatile element that made the year 1877 one of bloody upheaval. The cities, North, South, East and West, were rent by civil unrest. The rioters struck out at obvious targets which represented the industrialized society, such as the railroad companies, but frequently they also attacked minority groups, such as the Chinese. If racism seems the obvious cause of such assaults, it should also be remembered that the crowd's motives were mixed; many of its members saw the Chinese as low paid job competitors preventing "American" workingmen from getting a fair salary. This was a period in which the poverty of many stood starkly beside the wealth of a few. This raises an important question: To what extent is racism an emotion that serves the "ruling class?"

The section concludes with an excellent article on "The Tompkins Square 'Riot' in New York City." The questions raised by Professor Herbert Gutman in his article about riots and social change in a democratic society are especially relevant to the present. The economic disorders which he discusses, coming at the end of a war and in a period of tremendous technological change, do not seem far removed from similar situations today.

Suggested Further Readings

Headley's *The Great Riots of New York*, mentioned in the last chapter, views the New York Draft Riots from the perspective of a horrified onlooker, and is now available in a paperbound edition. Current interest in mob disorder has led to a reprinting of the official reports on the Memphis and New Orleans riots as a part of a series titled *Mass Violence in America* (1969). For an exciting account of the turmoil of the year 1877, see the excellent book by Robert V. Bruce, *1877: Year of Violence* (1959). Unfortunately, no good essay exists on the anti-Chinese riots in the West.

Footnotes

1 Quoted from Louis Ruchames, (ed.), *John Brown: The Making of a Revolutionary* (New York: Grossett & Dunlap, 1969), p. 167.

2 Fredric Wertham, *A Sign for Cain: An Exploration of Human Violence* (New York: Paperback Library, 1966), p. 20.

9   James McCague

"YOU MUST ORGANIZE!"

At central police headquarters, as the minutes ticked away after nine o'clock, the situation must have appeared somewhat clearer. Reports had been telegraphed in from every precinct by that time, and most of them were on the encouraging side. Captain Speight and the sixty-nine patrolmen assigned to the Broadway enrollment office had encountered a large, noisy crowd there but had been able to disperse it without difficulty. The drawing of names was proceeding in a normal, orderly manner. Elsewhere around the big Metropolitan Police District there were some signs of unrest—mostly crowds gathering and loitering—but no open disorders. It seemed that Third Avenue was the only trouble spot. But there conditions were plainly not improving.

About this time, too, the telegraph lines to most of the precincts in the northern sections of Manhattan went dead, thus verifying the word from James Crowley. For the moment it was not too serious, since all stationhouses already had been ordered to stand by. But Superintendent Kennedy grew more and more concerned for the safety of Captain Porter's detail. Presently he ordered Captain Speight's detail to Number 677 Third Avenue also. Some time later he ordered other captains to send additional detachments from their precincts. Then, apparently dissatisfied with the scanty information coming in, he decided to go out and make a personal inspection. He set out alone and unarmed, driving his own light one-horse carriage. It was the act of a brave man, which John A. Kennedy unquestionably was, and perhaps of a rash one as well. At that point, though, there probably seemed ample reason to believe that the mob soon would be brought under control.

The better part of an hour passed; perhaps a little more. Headquarters routine went on, no doubt. No one recalled later how the time passed or bothered to put it down on paper if he did. Presently a wagon pulled up in the street outside. In it were two men, with something under a pile of old sacks in the rear. One of the men was John Eagen, resident of a neighborhood to the north around Lexington Avenue, who may or may not have been prominent enough to be known to some there at headquarters. It appears that there was a little difficulty about his admittance, at any rate. He had brought back John A. Kennedy, or what was left of him, but it took a while before the fact sank in. The mob had got Kennedy.

So badly battered was he, so covered with mud and clotted blood, that his closest associates failed to recognize him at first. According to Charles Chapin, "It was difficult to believe that this could possibly be the body of the Supt. of Police and it was refused admission. Only certain jewellry [sic] which he was known to wear established the fact." As soon as it did, Kennedy was hurried off to Bellevue Hospital. Examining surgeons there found his body bruised from head to foot and stabbed or slashed in a score of places. It would be touch and go whether he lived or died.

In the meantime, the Metropolitan District was without a superintendent of police. And now fresh reports were coming in, telling of new defeats for the police—the mob triumphant everywhere.

Captain Speight and his men, heading up Third Avenue toward the beleaguered enrollment office, never had reached there. At Forty-fourth Street the advance guard of the mob had met them in overwhelming numbers and turned them back after a brief, brutal skirmish. A second squad of police, and then a third, had managed only to rescue several downed patrolmen before retreating south on Third Avenue with half their men wounded. Some of the rioters had muskets now, probably taken from the routed Invalid Corps detachment. Worse than that, though, were their massive numbers—a flood of angry humanity that simply could not be handled. A fourth police detail had arrived in Third Avenue, led by a Sergeant McCredie; and shortly afterward a fifth, under Sergeant Wolfe. McCredie, an aggressive, able officer known throughout the force as Fighting Mac, took command of the combined squads. Though totaling only forty-four unwounded men, they had counterattacked and driven the mob back as far as Forty-fifth Street. Then fresh masses roaring down the avenue and out of the streets on both sides had rolled over them, broken their ranks, and sent them stumbling south in another retreat. Not a man of the forty-four had come out of it without injuries. Sergeant McCredie, driven up the front steps of a Third Avenue residence, had been hammered so viciously that he was smashed bodily through the splintered panels of the door. Half-stunned, he had dragged himself up the stairs to a second-floor room, where a young German immigrant woman had just time to hide him on a bed between two feather mattresses. When she persuaded the mob that he had jumped from the window, they set fire to the house and left. The young woman, taking

McCredie on her back, somehow made her way over to Lexington Avenue and put him in a hansom cab, which eventually got him to the nearest precinct station. But his injuries were serious; Fighting Mac was out of it.

Such small personal details would not be known till a great deal later, of course. But the main facts were becoming all too plain—full-fledged riot, and no immediate prospect of its being mastered. Other police detachments, flung into the fighting after the rout of McCredie's force, had been chewed up and forced back also. The mob was surging southward almost to Thirty-fifth Street, now, starting to loot and destroy, leaving a trail of flaming buildings behind it. Long afterward Charles Chapin's memories remained vivid:

"The scene on 3rd Ave. at this time was appalling.

"It was now noon, but the hot July sun was obscured by heavy clouds which cast dark shadows over the city.

"From the Cooper Institute at 9th St. to 46th St. the avenue, house-tops, windows and steps were crowded with rioters, or spectators.

"As one glanced along the dense mass of men and women the eye rested upon huge columns of smoke rising from burning buildings—for the mob had now begun to plunder and burn—at the north, giving a wild and terrifying aspect to the scene.

"The number of people in the street at this time was roughly estimated to be 50,000. Here and there along the avenue could be seen street cars which had been overturned and thrown from the tracks. . . ."

Among the worst of the fires was the one at the Third Avenue enrollment office, now burning fiercely. The building was a tenement, its upper stories occupied by laboring-class families who should by any rule of reason have had the mob's sympathy. But there was little reason at work here anymore. The watching throng cheered with delight as the flames took hold and frightened tenants came tumbling out into the street. At first, efforts were even made to prevent their leaving the building, and a few men who tried to calm the mob were brutally beaten. One contingent was ordered, or took it upon itself, to hurry to the bell tower at Fifty-first Street and prevent the ringing of any alarm. Apparently this failed, for an engine company and a hose company soon came up. The mob cheered and parted to let them through, then closed in and blocked their every effort to get to work. Finally the crews could only stand helplessly by while the buildings at numbers 675 and 679 Third Avenue also blazed up. In the end most of the block was gutted.

"The rioters were composed of the employees of the several railroad companies; the employees of Brown's iron foundry in 61st St. [and] various factories and street contractors," wrote an eyewitness. But, he conceded, "many had been forced."

The *Tribune*'s reporter wrote that, "The vast crowd swayed to and fro, racing first in this direction, then in that, attacking indiscriminately every well-dressed man. The general cry was 'Down with the rich men!' "

Though the main body of the mob had swept on southward, several thousand still milled about in this section of Third Avenue, apparently at loose ends, their appetite for violence only whetted by the destruction of the enrollment office. And presently a man climbed onto the roof of a shanty at a construction site across from the burning buildings and addressed the crowd. Next day the *Tribune* would identify him as "Mr. Andrews of Virginia"—the first mention of the notorious John Andrews in connection with the actual rioting. But the *Tribune*'s man, who seems to have been the only journalist on hand at this particular spot, admitted in his story that he could hear very little of Andrews' speech. And he added that "any attempt to make a note might bring on . . . an assault from someone in the crowd." But it was obvious, he also added, that Andrews was making a violent attack on the Federal government and the draft and that the crowd listened to him with intense enthusiasm. Many of them, believing at first that he was Benjamin Wood of the New York *Daily News*, hurrahed lustily for Wood. Among some others ran a rumor that he was a reporter for the *Evening Standard*. This was received with less enthusiasm. There were cries of "Hang him! Hang him!" before the crowd realized its error.

Other witnesses, agreeing that the speaker was indeed John Andrews, later described him as about six feet tall, blond and good-looking, with a short beard, and well dressed in a blue coat and striped trousers. Several of them were able to hear somewhat more of what he said than the *Tribune* man.

"You have done nobly," they quoted him, "but I tell you what I want, and what you must do if you wish to be really successful. You must organize!"

"That's the talk," cried voices from the crowd. "You're the boy, my chicken!"

"You must organize and keep together and appoint leaders," Andrews went on, "and crush this damned Abolition draft into the dust."

There was "tremendous cheering" from the crowd.

"If you don't find anyone to lead you," Andrews shouted, "by Heaven! I will do it myself!"

This too drew a wild outburst. Apparently the harangue went on for some time in the same vein. Thereafter, for a while, Andrews dropped out of sight in the confusion. The mob, its fury rekindled, went stamping off on new adventures and allowed the firemen to move in and save what was left of the smoldering block.

Another newspaper reporter was recognized at the corner of Third Avenue and Forty-sixth Street. "Here's a damned Abolitionist," somebody yelled. "Let's hang him!" He was taken by the hair and dragged to a post supporting a store-front awning. But something else distracted the crowd for a moment and he broke away. As he ran down Third Avenue, a well-aimed brickbat struck him on the head; and while he lay stunned in the street, his pockets were rifled, his watch and all his money stolen. Later he was pursued and struck down again. But the men of a hook-and-ladder company beat his tormentors off and helped him into the firehouse at Fiftieth Street and Lexington Avenue. They barred the door, and the crowd, after some aimless threats, finally went off in search of other prey.

The great number of those who had listened to Andrews, however, probably made up the same mob which soon afterward stormed down on the Bull's Head Hotel on Forty-third Street near Lexington. Two or three men who appeared to be leaders sprang up the front stoop and beat down the door with axes. The others swept in, plundered and wrecked the place, set it on fire, and went on. More than once during these first hours of rioting it was noticed that the mob seemed to be well supplied with cans or bottles of turpentine. And this inevitably suggested to some observers that the burning was more than a mere destructive impulse. Too, there had been a branch office of the American Telegraph Company at the Bull's Head—the only apparent reason why it was singled out for attack. The mob's earlier efforts to cut the lines of communication in the city, and between the city and the outside world, still continued. Even as flames crackled through the Bull's Head, other rioters were ripping up the tracks of the New Haven Railroad for several blocks above Forty-second Street.

But, while this kind of purposeful destruction did argue the existence of a rough overall strategy by some leader or group of leaders, various motley bands and gangs now began to pour out of the Five Points, the Fourth Ward, and all the city's squalid shantytowns. As always, the grapevine seemed to rival the telegraph itself for speed. These gangs were made up of men and women—and children, as well— bent only on plunder and the venting of poverty's ancient grievances in whatever mischief they could find to do.

In most sections of Manhattan, in these early phases of the disorder, they met little or no police resistance. Off-duty patrolmen still were being mustered at stationhouses. The heavy fighting that raged southward along Third Avenue re-quired most of the forces that could be thrown together immediately, and there still was some confusion as to the nature of the mob outbreaks and their main objectives, if any. Lone patrolmen caught out on their beats were fair game for the rioters. One, chased by a crowd on Lexington Avenue, tried to take refuge in the basement of a fine, large mansion at Number 44. But the door was locked, and as he pounded on it in desperation, the lady of the house appeared at an upstairs window and screamed, "For God's sake don't open the door, the house will be destroyed." Her cry, commented the anonymous witness who told the story, "seemed to give the mob the idea to do it." Windows were smashed, the door battered down. The mob swarmed in. Furniture was tossed out into the street and either set on fire or carried off. A valuable library of books and paintings was wantonly torn to pieces, silverware and other valuables stolen, the house itself finally set alight. In the midst of it all the lady of the house with her children and servants fled to the precinct police station, where they were given shelter. The patrolman's fate was not recorded; he too is thought to have escaped in the mob's preoccupation with its loot.

As a gesture of conciliation, Provost Marshal Nugent had ordered the Broadway enrollment office closed at eleven-fifteen, thus effectively putting the draft out of business in New York City. But the crowd dispersed by Captain Speight that morning, or another one, was back by early afternoon. Not all of its members were toughs, apparently. One man was heard to speak out boldly. "This is an unspeak-able outrage," he is supposed to have cried. "As an American citizen, I am ashamed." He got a bloody head for his trouble. The office was broken open, its furniture and equipment smashed, and the building fired. By this time other gangs, perhaps split off from the victorious mob in Third Avenue, were roaming up and down Broadway unchecked. A whole block of buildings between Twenty-fourth and Twenty-fifth streets was burning fiercely. More and more stores, here and in other parts of the city too, were being attacked and plundered now. And, ominously, a great many of them were hardware or sporting-goods establishments, in which the looters were concentrating on guns and other weapons.

Early in the afternoon, also, another large crowd appeared at Mayor George Opdyke's home on Fifth Avenue. No one had thought to provide a police guard for it. But a neighbor, a Colonel B. F. Manierre, called out forty or fifty other residents of the area and organized a hasty defense force. Many of them owned firearms. Stationing themselves about the premises, they met the crowd with such a show of determination that it drew back after a brief, bloodless encounter. A few police detectives had contrived to attach themselves to the fringes of this group without exciting suspicion, and they recognized one of its leaders as a minor underworld character by the name of Peter Dolan. They seized him as the crowd withdrew—probably the first arrest of any rioter that day. Most of these would-be attackers, they reported later, were mere teenage boys. Balked at the mayor's house, a large group of them straggled aimlessly south down Fifth Avenue and presently joined a great throng massing in front of the Colored Orphan Asylum between Forty-third and Forty-fourth streets. From the very beginning, of course, much of the antidraft resentment had been tangled inextricably with latent racial hatreds. Now they were flaring up, naked and vicious. Mr. Chapin expressed the mob's warped logic about as well as anyone: "There would have been no draft but for the war—there would have been no war but for Slavery—the Slaves were black—*ergo*, all blacks were responsible. . . ."

The orphanage was a handsome brick building set in its own spacious grounds. It housed two hundred Negro children, none of them more than twelve years old, attended by a staff of fifty adults. Fortunately the superintendent, one William Davis, kept his head when the mob began to show signs of ugliness. Bolting the front door and barricading it with chairs and tables, he and his assistants hurriedly assembled the children and marched them out through a rear exit. By the time the mob had nerved itself to the point of attacking, they were across the grounds and aboard omnibuses on Madison Avenue, bound for the Twenty-second precinct police station. Bursting in belatedly, the rioters raced through the building venting their frustration on everything in sight. Furniture was hacked apart with axes, draperies torn down, even the few cheap toys left behind by the children carried off or smashed to bits. One frightened little colored girl, somehow overlooked in the exodus, had hidden under a bed. They found her and they killed her. And the rest of it went according to the now familiar pattern—fires set throughout the building, mobsters howling exultantly in the street outside, others fanning out to pillage shops and homes nearby. When two volunteer fire companies answered the alarm, the mob massed to drive them back. Nevertheless, Chief Engineer John Decker and fifteen of his firemen fought their way through, connected up their hoses, and made their way into the burning orphanage. A brave try, but fruitless; the mob rallied, plunged in after them, and threw them into the street again. The orphanage burned to the ground, and three other buildings in the block along with it, while Decker was twice knocked off his feet and dragged to a lamppost amid furious cries of "Hang him! Hang him!" In the confusion and the heady flush of victory, they finally lost interest and let him go, but it was a near thing for several minutes.

"They had not yet begun to wantonly destroy life," commented Chapin wryly and not altogether accurately.

That would come. For the moment these roaming mobs were aimless, yet moved by resentful strivings after form and purpose. Already groups of rioters had begun to descend on railroad yards and depots in many localities, ordering the service stopped, the workmen enlisted in the cause. Horse barns of the omnibus companies and street-railway lines were visited too; Managers and foremen had no choice but to obey. It appears that much of this was less a matter of plan than of some vast, angry urge to bring all orderly life in the city to a standstill. Here and there even well-dressed passersby were seized and hustled along with the mobs. Clubs were brandished over their heads, wrote one witness, and they were "frequently kept encouraged by clouts on the sides of their heads."

Wrote another: "About 4 o'clock p.m., the rioters, perfectly frenzied with liquor, roamed about in every direction attacking people and burning every house in which they thought a policeman had taken refuge. . . ."

And still another: "Boys went through the streets, flourishing and firing off pistols, men brandished guns, and mad and hoarse with passion and bad spirits, cursed and swore and threatened every one disagreeing with them in their excesses. Some threatened to kill every 'Black-Republican-nigger-worshipping s-- of a b----' "and burn their houses."

Caught up in scenes like this, fleeing the streets to wait in dread and uncertainty behind barred doors—some feeling a great, slowly growing anger, too—respectable citizens could only wonder: where were the police?

10   Herbert G. Gutman

TOMPKINS SQUARE RIOT

The 1873 depression caused workers in many large cities—among them, New York, Chicago, Cincinnati, and Philadelphia—to press for government intervention and enlarged programs of public works to aid the increasing number of jobless workers. By January 1, 1874, the movement had died out in all cities except New York, where the Committee of Safety, set up by several thousand workers at a meeting in Cooper Institute on December 11, continued pressuring the city government for public works. The Committee included socialists, anti-monopolist reformers, and trade unionists among its fifty members. Efforts by the committee to meet with city authorities in late December failed. The press everywhere attacked the unemployed and their leaders.

These efforts came to a dramatic and unexpected climax on January 13, 1874, when police and workers battled furiously in the New York streets for several hours. Often called the Tompkins Square Riot, the event is mentioned by most labor historians, but its background and its aftermath have never been carefully studied. For this reason, the "riot" which revealed so much about the post-Civil War urban labor scene has not merited more than a passing reference in traditional labor histories. Contemporaries felt more strongly about it, for it shed light on the demise of the public-works movement, on contemporary attitudes toward socialists and radicals, and on the relationship between labor reform and civil liberties.

After the New York authorities refused to meet with the Committee of Safety, it asked "all those . . . in sympathy with the suffering poor" to gather in Tompkins Square and march to City Hall on January 13. The Committee also demanded that the city authorities turn over $100,000 to a Labor Relief Bureau made up of its own members and some aldermen to aid the unemployed. German and English handbills announced: "We have laid before the City authorities the demands you requested us to make . . . No answer. They ignore your Committee! Will they ignore you?" The Committee urged a large turnout on January 13 to show the public both the strength and seriousness of the movement.

No sooner did the Committee announce its plans than it ran into difficulty. A rival organization led by a bricklayer, Patrick Dunn, claimed to represent workers "in every ward," denounced the Committee as "humbug," called its leaders "Communists," and urged the unemployed to gather in Union Square on January 5 and march to City Hall. Dunn minced few words: unless the city officials gave jobs to the unemployed, they would "help themselves to whatever they could." Contempories disputed Dunn's motives. Samual Gompers called him and his followers

From "The Tompkins Square 'Riot' in New York City on January 13, 1874: A Re-Examination of Its Causes and Its Aftermath," *Labor History*, 6 (Winter, 1965), pp. 44-70. Reprinted by permission.

"honest" labor leaders protesting "against demagogic methods" and urging that "relief for human beings was the real thing." Others took a dimmer view. The United Order of Bricklayers said Dunn lied in claiming membership in that union, and the secretary of the Laborer's Union and Benevolent Association insisted that Dunn and his associates could not be called "laborers in the true sense of the term" since "most of them" had been "already provided with political situations." The socialists fumed at Dunn, calling him a "liar" and "a miserable instrument of the police" who "purposely" used inflammatory language to "discredit" the public works movement.

Accepting his challenge, the Committee of Safety wrangled with Dunn for nearly a week. Several hundred workers turned up in Union Square on January 5 and found two Committee leaders there, Theodore Banks and Peter J. McGuire, the latter a young socialist carpenter. Banks advised the men not to parade, but the workers instead selected a committee—including Dunn, McGuire, and Banks—to lead them to City Hall. They sought out Mayor William Havemeyer but, according to the *New York Herald*, "he was not in—at least to Banks." They pleaded unsuccessfully with the Board of Aldermen for enlarged public works and, afterward, outside City Hall, Banks and McGuire warned that "if the officials do not do anything, they must get out of the way and let the workingmen rule the city." They asked the workers to support the January 13 parade, but the workers expressed impatience. Feeling they would not wait a full week, Banks shifted his tactics and announced an earlier parade for January 8.

Careful palnning made it possible for the Committee of Safety to outflank Dunn and his followers. Urging its followers to turn out on January 8, the Committee assured itself of control of the demonstration. More than 1,000 workers gathered in the rain in Union Square on January 8 and rejected an appeal by Dunn for a second march to City Hall. They paraded instead to Tompkins Square to meet McGuire and 200 others. "Without music and in a rain that served to muffle their tread," as the *New York Sun* described it, "their approach was not in any way heralded. They made no noise . . . and were well-behaved in every respect." McGuire told the workers in Tompkins Square to support the Committee, join its ward organizations, and parade on the thirteenth when they would have "a permit from the police" and would "conduct themselves as orderly, decent, law-abiding citizens." At one point, McGuire's words became less tempered:

> If relief is not vouchsafed . . . a provisional committee in each ward will take food to help keep you from starving and send the bills to the city for collection . . . We'll see if we cannot impress these people with the idea that we are in earnest, and that they have got to do something for us.

Loud applause greeted McGuire when he restated the Cooper Institute demands for public aid and a suspension of evictions of the unemployed in the winter months. After rejecting another plea by Dunn to march to City Hall, the throng quietly dispersed. Dunn had failed, and the Committee boasted of preventing "small, unorganized, and uncontrollable" groups from taking violent action.

Yet, in spite of its surface moderation, the Committee of Safety found itself widely condemned. Its program was genuinely radical and aroused fears. Advising the unemployed to take food and charge the cost to the city, if an extensive public-relief program did not develop, was enough to frighten a great many people. The parades only added to whatever anxiety the speeches incurred. Gompers called the January 5 and 8 demonstrations "a folk movement of primitive need." He insisted that "something about a marching folk-group . . . rouses dread," and "those in authority do not rest comfortably." Police officials were among those who worried about the demonstrations. On January 5, more than 150 police and the entire Sanitation Squad guarded City Hall; and after the parade started, more than 400 police entered Union Square and chased away the remaining workers. On January 8, the press reported that 30,000 cartridges had arrived at the Thirty-fifth Street Armory. The entire city police force was mobilized; large numbers of blue-coats patrolled Union Square, Tompkins Square, and City Hall. Mayor Havemeyer and Thurlow Weed held "a great council of war" with the Police Commissioners, and the Commissioners promised to arrest workers using "inflammatory language." The police would not let the Committee of Safety "coerce" city officials and would "quell any disturbance within thirty minutes." The daily newspapers supported the police and attacked the Committee, calling its leaders "enemies of society" and "loud-mouthed demagogues" who taught American workers "the favorite tactics of the worst class of European socialists" and who admired "the extreme red repub-lic." McGuire and the others could not be argued with and had to be "handed over to the police" for abusing "liberty of speech and discussion." The unemployed, the press explained, included "the least capable, the laziest, and, by inference, the most thriftless and improvident" New Yorkers and had no right to "bully" the "better deserving." "He shares in prosperity," an editorial said of the jobless worker, "and when a season of difficulty arrives he must be prepared to bear patiently the suffering incidental to hard times."

The New York newspapers saw no reason to criticize the excessive numbers of police that surrounded the meetings. At best, the *New York Sun* published a letter from the recently arrived Joseph P. McDonnell, the exiled Irish Fenian and socialist, which warned that the police took orders from corrupted public officials and asked: "Casting aside all questions of approval or sympathy with the proceed-ings . . . does the right of public meeting exist? Is the Square private, police, or public property? . . . Has martial law been proclaimed?" These questions were not finally answered until January 13.

Public meetings and parades needed approval by the Department of Parks and the Police Board. The Department of Parks granted the Committee of Safety a permit to meet in Tompkins Square on the 13th, but the Police Board turned down its proposed parade route. The Committee asked to march from Tompkins Square to City Hall to present its "demands . . . for work and quietly disperse," but the police prohibited demonstrations near City Hall, limited the parade to the tenement districts, and suggested that it start in Tompkins Square, end in Union Square, and avoid City Hall by more than a mile. At the same time, the Police Board ordered its men to "arrest anyone intimidating or trying to persuade workingmen from laboring . . . for the purpose of making a demonstration in the public streets." Police officials turned away protesting members of the Committee of Safety. "You have the same rights as any body of men," they told McGuire, "but we want to avoid . . . annoyance to the business community and the public." When McGuire complained of the suffering among the immigrant poor, Police Commissioner Oliver Gardner cut him short to remind him that, "The sooner you gentlemen represent the American citizen the better." The police assured McGuire that if workers paraded near City Hall they would arrest the Committee's leaders. McGuire asked what statute gave the police such power, and Gardner replied: "Never mind the law."

The motives of the Police Board remain obscure. Several Board members were either wealthy entrepreneurs of a sort or powerful political figures. Oliver Gardner served as chairman of the Central Committee of the city Republican Party, and Abraham Duryee owned some tenements. Possibly, the police genuinely feared or misunderstood the unemployed and expected violence. They called the ward organizations of the jobless workers "revolutionary," and claimed that paid informers and detectives—who had joined these organizations—found the unemployed had "perfected a military organization" with the motto "Bread or Blood!" Still, genuine fear may have been less important than other considerations. Charging that a former associate of William Tweed dominated the Police Board, Gompers accused the police of making an issue of the unemployed to hide their corrupt dealings. Newspapers reported that certain commissioners protected gamblers and extorted money from the owners of houses of assignation. Sanitation workers, supervised by the Police Board, complained it misused its powers for political purposes. John Swinton, then editor of the *New York Sun*, called it "an abomination in the eyes and nostrils of all decent citizens." He found its members "incompetent and immoral" and "greedy for personal aggrandizement at any hazard."

Whatever its motives, the Police Board effectively thwarted the Committee of Safety. The Committee therefore asked Governor John A. Dix to restore the original parade route. It also announced to the public that workers would not break "police lines," condemned Mayor Havemeyer for ignoring its earlier pleas and "erecting . . . ramparts and barricades within a mile of City Hall," and again asked the right to parade to City Hall so the mayor could "see their number and their misery":

> Will the Mayor, who speaks of his good will, state what his good will has amounted to? . . . Is it true that men are starving in the midst of plenty? . . . Have we, the Committee for Safety, or any member of our body committed or advocated any violence? . . . Is it true that, instead of buying food for the poor, the authorities buy guns and cartridges to shoot them down if asked for work?

Urging public employment or increased public relief, the Committee concluded: "Let the public officials do their duty and there will be no riot."

Frustrated by the Police Board, the Committee also faced serious internal difficulties. Although he remained a member of a local ward organization, George Blair, its president since mid-December, resigned from the Committee on January 9. That same day the New York local of the Iron Molder's International Union attacked the Committee as a group of "Communists, Internationalists, and other social disturbers" bent on causing "social anarchy." And the Spring Street radical faction again condemned the Committee. Exaggerated newspaper stories told of even greater troubles: the German workers would not parade; every trade union had repudiated the Committee; the entire movement soon would collapse.

Nevertheless the Committee of Safety held many ward meetings and perfected its organization. The *Societe de la Commune*, a small radical French group, offered its support. And the Committee printed circulars urging workers to gather in Tompkins Square on the thirteenth:

> Winter is upon us, and nearly all employment has been suspended. Cold and hunger are staring in our faces. Nobody can tell how long the misery will last. Nobody will attempt to help if we don't do something ourselves. Now is the time to meet and consider how we are to get work, food, clothing, and shelter . . .

Anxious to keep "noisy rowdies, thieves, [and] detectives who pose as working-men" from parading, seventeen ward organization leaders agreed that only workers with "proper credentials" would be permitted to join in the demonstration.

At best, workers interested in the unemployed movement were confused by what took place the day before the parade, a day on which both the Police Board and the Committee of Safety shifted plans. After Governor Dix refused to inter-cede, the Committee accepted the Police Board route. While McGuire pleaded with the Board for the City Hall route, other Committee members called on Mayor Havemeyer and invited him to address the unemployed in Union Square. The Police Board denounced the Committee and told the press that McGuire was "a miserable loafer who prefers living on his family to working," but Havemeyer agreed to speak at Union Square. Adding to the confusion, the Committee met in secret that night and cancelled the parade to Union Square. McGuire announced a "mass indignation meeting" in Thompkins Square the next morning, and the Committee proclaimed:

> We advised a procession to the City Hall, not for the purpose of rioting but for the purpose of appealing to the authorities. . . . The Constitution of the United States guarantees to the people the right to peaceably assemble. The community is under apprehension and alarm that action of the Police Commissioner may lead to a disturbance of the public peace. . . . We . . . give up for the present all procession and line of march.

The Committee again appealed to Governor Dix against "this outrage upon the rights and liberties of American citizens."

Although the Committee had given up the parade, the Police Board still re-mained dissatisfied. Meeting that same night, it advised the Department of Parks to cancel the permit to meet in Tompkins Square to protect "public order and

safety." The President of the Department of Parks quickly revoked the permit.
Soon after Patrick Dunn and several supporters appeared before the Board and,
after charging that the Committee included "Communists, Internationalists, demagogues, and evil-disposed persons," urged it to ban the meeting. A police official
assured Dunn: "The police will see to it that no meeting is held there." Later, the
Police Board insisted it informed the Committee through McGuire of its last minute
decision. McGuire, however, denied receiving any such message from the Board the
night of the twelfth, said he was at a Committee meeting when it arrived at his
home, and therefore saw it for the first time the next morning. Independent evidence supports McGuire's claim.

Considerable misapprehension and confusion existed in New York that night.
The ward organizations, unaware of the last minute shifts by the police and the
Committee, met and planned to parade from Tompkins Square to Union Square.
Arthur Laurell, a Dunn supporter and a close friend to Samuel Gompers, went to
several meetings to tell the workers of the police decision. But, as Gompers remembered many years later, "it was not generally known that the permit had been
withdrawn" and Laurell was "unjustly denounced as a renegade." As if these incidents were not enough, rump meetings of the Workingman's Central Council and
the Workingman's Union convened on the same night and condemned the Committee of Safety, calling its leaders "the worst enemies of the trade and labor
organizations." Most participants in the movement knew little of the last minute
changes and, no doubt, planned to gather in Tompkins Square the next morning.

Located in the heart of the seventeenth ward, Tompkins Square was a gift to
the city from John Jacob Astor. It covered ten acres. It had served as a drill field
for Union soldiers, but now filled a recreational need for the 200,000 persons,
mostly poor immigrants, who lived in nearby tenements. It functioned as an arena
for grimmer doings on January 13.

The thermometer read below freezing that morning, but between four and six
thousand people had already gathered on the square at ten o'clock, an hour before
the scheduled start of the meeting. Few knew of the police decision, for the Police
Board posted no placards in the area and chased no one from the square. The
morning newspapers applauded Dunn and advised readers to stay home, but did not
emphasize the police edict. When the park filled up, people jammed into surrounding streets. Mostly foreign born, the crowd included many women and children.
Twelve hundred members of the German Tenth Ward Workingmen's Association
packed into a corner of the square, and Lucien Saniel and McGuire distributed a
Committee of Safety news sheet. "Everything was quiet with the exception of a
good bit of laughing and skylarking," said one eye witness. By ten-thirty, a great
human mass covered the square, and "everybody talked and wondered whether
there would be a disturbance." Fearful neighborhood storekeepers closed their
shops, but there was no sign of trouble. "Any riotous situation," observed the *New
York Herald*, "seemed to be exceedingly remote."

Meanwhile, the Mulberry Street Police Board central office appeared as "a
scene of hustle and bustle." The First Mounted Squad waited on call in front of the

building, and state militia General Alexander Shaler offered the Commissioners his services. The police, it seemed, needed little help. They had the situation well in hand. Local precinct captains held orders to suppress all meetings that day. At six in the morning, the Board mobilized the entire city police force; no less than 1,600 men, almost two-thirds of the total police, covered the area between Tompkins Square and City Hall. Nor was this all. Mounted police served as "scouts," a number of detectives lingered in and about Tompkins Square to arrest thieves and persons "showing symptoms of seditious intent," and still more detectives guarded public buildings, major banks, and other financial institutions. Ready for any emergency, including the possibility of "an uprising," police officials asserted that "Communists" had smuggled diamonds and precious gems (stolen from churches by leaders of the defeated Paris Commune) into New York to buy ammunition and bombs.

Shortly before eleven o'clock, a detective reported to Police Superintendent George Matsell that the Committee of Safety had formed a procession and was marching toward Tompkins Square. Matsell ordered the First Mounted Squad to follow the workers. Within an hour a special edition of the *New York Graphic* appeared, its headline reading: "A RIOT IS NOW IN PROGRESS IN TOMPKINS SQUARE."

The police acted swiftly. More than 7,000 persons had gathered in the square when Commissioner Abram Duryee, surrounded by detectives and accompanied by a number of patrolmen with drawn sticks, marched into the center of the crowd. "The hitherto peaceful and monotonous tone of affairs," wrote the *Herald*, " . . . suddenly changed." Looking into the crowd, Duryee ordered: "Now, you all go home, right away!" Without waiting, the police made "an onslaught on the crowd, using their clubs indiscriminately." Men, women, and children scattered "like wild birds." In the northeast corner, however, the tenth ward German workers held fast and battled the police. Joseph Hoefflicher, a wood turner, struck an officer with his cane and when another policeman, William Berghold, intervened, Christian Mayer, a second German worker, hit him with a hammer. At this moment, Captain Francis Speight led thirty mounted police into the square and drove the remaining workers from the area. Standing in the middle of the square, Duryee ordered the police to seal off every entrance. Within a matter of minutes the police had cleared the entire square.

But the battle between the police and the crowd had hardly started. Duryee ordered the streets nearby emptied of thousands of persons. What followed defied description, but a *New York Sun* reporter did his best:

> The rapidly moving crowd did not look behind. They simply yelled and moved as fast as their legs would carry them. Captain Speight's [mounted] men were close at their heels, their horses galloping full speed on the sidewalks. Men tumbled over each other . . . into the gutter or clambered up high steps to get out of the way of the chargers. The horsemen beat the air with their batons and many persons were laid low. . . . One policeman actually rode into a grocery and scattered the terrified inmates. The men

who tumbled into out of the way places gathered themselves up and as the horsemen passed hooted and jeered them.

When a zealous young German socialist named Justus Schwab marched toward the square carrying a red flag of the Commune, police attacked and arrested him. Arthur Laurell, Gompers' friend, felt a police club across his back; and Gompers himself, who saved his head "from being cracked by jumping into a cellarway," remembered the police action as "an orgy of brutality." The fighting continued for a few more hours. Gompers insisted the police beat any "group of poorly dressed persons standing or moving together." When large crowds gathered around the Fifth Street Police Station and called for the release of imprisoned workers, the police charged them again and again. A reporter described the police as "seized with a fit of St. Vitus' dance. It was only a question of luck who was clubbed and who was not."

Excitement swept through other parts of the city. Police squads dispersed crowds along the anticipated parade route and arrested those refusing to move. After an anonymous caller warned of a Hungarian immigrant "plot" to burn a schoolhouse, the building was put under police guard. Leaders of the Committee of Safety visited Mayor Havemeyer at City Hall and pleaded with him to address the workers at Tompkins Square. But Havemeyer refused to talk to "a body of crazy men" and insisted that public works belonged "to other countries, not ours." When the Committee leaders urged protection from the police, Havemeyer sent them to the Central Police office where Superintendent Matsell turned them away and, according to the *Herald*, treated "the whole affair as a joke."

By late afternoon, Tompkins Square and the area nearby were peaceful. Rumors that state militia would occupy the area proved false. The police made a few more stray arrests, jailing, among others, a small boy and his friend for pelting a police officer with stones. In all, forty-six workers, mostly under forty-years old, ended up in jail. Twenty-four were Germans and ten native born. The others included French, Polish, Italian, Irish, and Swedish immigrants. Five were shoemakers and three tailors. All but three of forty-six were charged with disorderly conduct. Hoefflicher and Mayer were accused of assault and battery, and Schwab was indicted for inciting to riot and "waving a red flag." None of the workers could raise the required $1,000 bail that day and therefore remained in the city prison. During the evening, several women who called to see relatives learned that visitors could not come until the next morning. Later that night, the commissioners questioned Mayer and examined his hammer and Schwab's flag. While they surveyed their day's work, a flurry of snow fell and by midnight four inches of fresh snow fall covered Tompkins Square. "The untrodden snow," observed the *New York Graphic* the next day, "lay all bloodless on yesterday's battlefield."

City authorities strongly defended their actions. Mayor Havemeyer said simply: "Nothing better could have happened . . . It is often easier to cure an evil than to arrest its progress when it is under way." Police Board members called the unemployed "a parcel of vagabonds of the worst stamp" who deserved "a sound flogging." Commissioner Duryee expressed elation over the prowess and discipline of his men: "It was the most glorious sight I ever saw the way the police broke and drove that crowd. Their order was perfect as they charged with their clubs uplifted."

Others extolled the police. "A rabble of blackguards, mostly foreigners," hoping to "rule the city by riot and terror" had been put down. The *New York Independent*, a religious weekly, called the unemployed "fools" and their leaders "idlers . . . and ruffians." Their behavior revealed "nothing more conspicuous than their unfitness to share the privileges and immunities of a free government." The *Independent* found them "public enemies" and advised: "There is always a great mass of idleness, ignorance, and vice in great cities which cares but little for any other logic but that of force, and when a crisis comes it should be this logic and plenty of it." *Harper's Weekly* rejoiced because labor had learned the "follies and ferocities of the Commune are alien to American thought and methods." A prominent clergyman supported the police for teaching the workers that "if they lift their hands against law, order, and good government, they will be mowed down like grass before a scythe." The "American Commune" had met its master, boasted the *Philadelphia Inquirer*, and should a similar "spirit" again emerge the *Inquirer* advised public officials to "club it to death at the hands of the police or shoot it to death at the hands of the militia."

Criticism of the unemployed and the Committee of Safety accompanied support of the police. The *New York Herald*, for example, accused those who believed that unemployment and poverty were "the direct and regular product of the present state of society" of lacking "morale" and of supporting "any theorist who denounces the restraints that keep the baker's window sacred from a hungry passer-by." The *Herald* feared that "noisy conspirators," financed by the "booty of the plundered churches of Paris" and desirous of "the apportionment of 'good things' and 'free love'," could easily influence such workers. "Force" alone would teach disaffected workers to "respect the rights of those who have plenty when [they] have nothing."

Only a few newspapers expressed concern over the police action. The *New York Sun* and the *New York Graphic*, while hostile to the unemployed and their leaders, nonetheless condemned the police for their "hurried, ill-considered use of authority," their "clubbing of innocent and peaceful men," and their violation of "a principle which Americans regard as sacred." "There is no law," argued the *Graphic*, "that forbids people from making foolish speeches." The *Graphic* cared "infinitely less for the riches of any than for the rights which are the property of all." Outside New York City, the only large urban newspaper found that condemned the police was the *Cincinnati Enquirer*, which mocked the Committee of Safety but defended its right to "let off surplus gas in public squares," because free speech was "the corner-stone upon which the safety of our government . . . rests."

Organized labor and its spokesmen joined radical groups in bitterly attacking the New York police. Organizations as varied as the Tailor's Union, the United Cigar-makers Union, the United Order of American Bricklayers, the *Societie de la*

Commune, and the Committee of Safety found the police action symbolic of monarchical despotism. Sympathetic to labor reform, the *New York Irish World* called the police officials "Grand Bashaws" who exhibited "a brutal contempt for law." The Committee of Safety even accused the police of "setting a trap to catch and destroy innocent victims." Complaints also came from Chicago's German socialists, labor reformers like Boston's Edward H. Chamberlain, and such trade unionists as John Fehrenbatch, the president of the International Machinist's and Blacksmith's Union. They compared the police to the men who dragged William Lloyd Garrison through the Boston streets and to the Virginia Governor who dealt with John Brown. The Tompkins Square "riot" symbolized the disintegration of popular republican political institutions to many labor reformers. "We inform the capitalists," said a group of Boston laborers, "that their system of first cheating the laborer out of his fruits of industry and then punishing him when he demands redress is surely bringing about the destruction of the Republic and their own ruin." "A model republic!" scoffed the *Workingman's Advocate*. Some labor radicals believed the "riot" to be "a precedent . . . to terrorize the people" and, according to John F. Bray, the old English Chartist living in Pontiac, the start of "a new era of force." Bray explained: "It was meant to give the workingmen a taste of the 'wholesale discipline' in store for them, if they persist in their trade unions and other contrivances to resist the authority of their 'masters'." Even the *Iron Molder's Journal*, which earlier had attacked the Committee of Safety, insisted that "the cry of Communism is 'too thin,' " and that "every protest, petition, or demand of labor is met with the cry of 'Commune'." Bray believed that "if the word had been in use among us a few years since, every anti-slavery man would have been denounced as a 'Communist'. " The *Irish World* dismissed the issue of radicalism:

> Suppose it was a Know-Nothing meeting? Suppose it was a meeting of monopolists or of stock gamblers? . . . Would such a meeting be prohibited? Would not the police and military be called out in force to protect them? It is not necessary that the composition of an association should command the respect of all classes to enable it to hold a meeting . . . When organized labor asks for bread, or rather a means to make its bread, you must not offer it a stone. Or if you do, it will take the stone only to hurl it back to destroy you.

The intensity of feeling could not hide the fact that critics of the police action numbered only a tiny portion of the urban population, and their complaints fell mostly on deaf ears.

Despite the efforts of the Committee of Safety to hold its own after January 13th the unemployed movement quickly fell apart. It claimed 20,000 followers and talked of forming "one grand union of workingmen," but fewer and fewer persons attended its meetings. A proposed second mass meeting and parade never came off, and a relief ball for the victims of the police attack attracted little support. Innocence about local New York politics helped wreck the movement. Since most of the Committee's leaders believed that political machinations "caused" depressions, and since they rejected the idea of permanently applying pressure from outside the political framework through powerful non-political organizations, they viewed the ward organizations of the unemployed as stepping stones toward independent reform politics and in late January turned the Committee of Safety into the Industrial Political Party to "save our sinking ship of the Republic . . . from political gamblers." According to the new party, the "time of humble petitions or of energetic protest to which our rulers answer only with silent disregard or violent clubbing is now gone forever." The party denounced the Police Board as "barbarous" and "law-breaking." It supported a platform that opposed child labor, contract labor, and government aid to railroads and corporations and favored a referendum on all national legislation, a flexible circulating medium, government ownership of railroads, mines, telegraph, and public utilities, reduction of public salaries, suffrage for all citizens, free secular education through college, and free legal counsel for everyone. McGuire and other party spokesmen believed the "people . . . strong enough to remedy their evils through the ballot box," but the new party foundered from the start. Factionalism plagued it. The German socialists scorned it and repudiated all "reformist" agitation. Trade unionists affiliated with the New York State Workingman's Assembly and the Workingman's Central Council rejected it and formed their own party. Some Tammany Democrats and "reform" Republicans joined both groups in order to bore from within. Eventually, both parties disintegrated and, when a labor ticket quickly was put up in the fall 1874 municipal elections headed by *New York Sun* editor John Swinton as its mayoralty candidate, it had only nominal ties with these earlier efforts and received few votes.

Attacks by the Police Board continued after January 13, and also weakened the Committee of Safety. The Board assigned special detectives, including women, to spy on labor and socialist meetings. Fearing police raids, workers stayed away from some meetings. The police successfully pressured a landlord to evict the *Societe de la Commune* from his premises. Police Board President Henry Smith warned that dangerous agitators kept workers from "their labor," and other police officials accused "radicals" of storing arms and ammunition and of setting fire to churches. Superintendent Matsell stationed officers at all churches to deter radical "incendiaries," and, after an accidental and harmless fire started in a Catholic Church, its priest blamed "the Communists." In what was an early example of a classic "red scare," the police released "documents" filled with "evidence" that Parisian "Communists," "heavily-armed German revolutionaries," "atheists," and "drunkards" planned to heave Mayor Havemeyer from a City Hall window and "burn down . . . buildings where gold was stored." The discovery of a worthless pile of hand grenades, purchased by a Frenchman for his government during the Franco-Prussian War but never shipped to Paris, provided the police with another opportunity. They arrested the purchaser, and Matsell offered fresh evidence of the close tie between "hand grenades and Communism." But after a judge dismissed the charges against the French patriot, the *New York Graphic* mocked the police for continually "calling wolf." The police nevertheless insisted that dangerous foreign agitators egged on immigrant and American workers "to the commission of acts of outrage and violence."

In part, the post-"riot" activities of the police can be explained as an effort to justify their performance on January 13 because a group of trade unionists, socialists, labor reformers, and prominent German immigrant leaders launched a vigorous campaign against the Police Board. Leaders of such unions as the United Cabinetmaker's Union, the United Cigarmaker's Union, and the Journeymen Tailor's Protective Union joined with the socialists, officials of the German Free Thinker's Association, and the *Turnverein* (a large and popular German mutual aid society) to urge its impeachment. They contributed funds to defend the arrested workers; the tailors, for example, raised more than $500. And these groups received encouragement from a few respectable New Yorkers, including editor John Swinton, the *New York Evening Post*, the *New York Graphic*, and two Congressmen, S. S. Cox and former Mayor Fernando Wood, who responded to pressure from labor and immigrant groups. Swinton said the German immigrants showed native Americans "what freedom really is," and Cox insisted that "no local government should purposely help capital and greed in place of labor and honesty." Wood spoke in a more forthright manner: "The police authorities have no right to break up a public meeting called for any purpose by the people."

But the city courts disagreed and rejected efforts by lawyers for the arrested workers to raise constitutional questions. The lawyers charged that the police acted "without the authority of law" in Tompkins Square, and claimed that the workers therefore "had a right to resist the force . . . used against them by the police, using no more violence than was necessary to overcome that used by the police." The courts unhesitatingly turned aside these arguments and insisted the workers had "to obey the officers and to assist them" in clearing the square. Guilt turned on specific acts of violence directed against the police. Two German workers, Joseph Hoefflicher and Christian Mayer, went to prison. Sentencing Mayer to six months, the trial judge warned "members of his class that there are certain laws in this country which they must respect." The *New York Herald* applauded him and hoped that immigrant radicals had learned finally that "America, while the land of liberty, is not a safe place for the mischievous advocates of communism."

The vigorous campaign to oust the Police Board failed, largely through public apathy outside the immigrant and labor communities. The Free Thinker's Association called a protest meeting in the New York Assembly Halls for January 23, but after pressure from the police the owners cancelled the rental agreement. Swinton attacked the police for denying "popular rights and the liberty of opinion," but the Assembly Halls remained closed to several hundred Germans and others who jammed the streets nearby on the twenty-third. While a few hundred police waited in station-houses nearby, cigarmaker Conrad Kuhn, a prominent German trade unionist, and Dr. Frederick Lilienthal, head of the small Free Thinker's Association, spoke in the streets. "We came to this country thinking it a land of free speech," Lilienthal angrily declared. "Our experience tonight shows us how much we have been deluded. . . . This outrage would never have been tolerated in monarchial

Europe. What shall we say when in free America our own rights to assemble are disputed?" Lilienthal said another protest meeting would be held in Cooper Institute. Its trustees rented the hall to the Free Thinker's Association after it posted a $2,000 bond to cover possible property damages. Trustee and iron manufacturer Abram Hewitt explained: "No one will dispute the right of good citizens to meet and to protest against the action of any body of men on any subject." The Germans printed handbills inviting all citizens to support the January 30 Cooper Institute meeting: "Whatever your view of the recent attempted workingmen's demonstration in Tompkins Square, it is your duty . . . to protest against a violation of one of our fundamental rights, for what was once tried against one class might soon be repeated against another class."

A large crowd jammed in Cooper Institute on January 30 to make the protest meeting a notable success. Hundreds were turned away. Although a number of detectives and plainclothesmen sat in the hall and policemen packed station houses nearby, no uniformed police attended and *Turnverein* members served as ushers. Except for John Swinton's speech, the entire meeting was conducted in German, and, according to the *New York Sun*, "a more intelligent or better behaved audience was never seen before in . . . Cooper Institute." Swinton, cigarmaker Kuhn, *Turnverein* leader Julius Kaufmann, and Dr. and Mrs. Frederick Lilienthal, the leaders of the Free Thinker's Association, defended the right of workers to petition for public aid and rebuked the police attack. Mrs. Lilienthal asked: "Suppose A. T. Stewart, John Jacob Astor, or William Dodge should assemble? Would the police interfere? No!" The police found "the most excellent means to frighten quiet citizens out of their purpose." Other speakers declaimed the "second-class" status of immigrants and American workers. Kaufmann even feared that immigrants soon might become "subjects," and Conrad Kuhn, a socialist, called for extensive labor organization to end the national "orgy of corruption, extortion, and monopoly." John Swinton commanded more eloquence. He related free speech to labor reform but also worried that if the police "can resist orderly freedom of speech in any direction whatever, they can by the same token interfere with every meeting and all freedom of speech." The police action outraged "liberty, order, decency, and human misery." Swinton demanded the immediate dissolution of the Police Board and explained:

> Those who suppressed the attempted meeting were catering to the prejudices of what are called the moneyed classes, who have become alarmed at the moral uprising of those whom they call the lower classes. The power of money has become supreme over everything. It has secured for the class who control it all the special privileges and special legislation which it needs to secure its complete and absolute domination. . . . This Power must be kept in check. It must be broken or it will utterly crush the people. . . .

And the thousands packed into Cooper Institute critized the "wholly unjustifiable and brutal proceedings of the police" and demanded that Mayor Havemeyer and Governor Dix abolish the Police Board.

But the success of the January 30 meeting meant little. Swinton's demand hardly caused more than a ripple outside immigrant and labor circles. The *New York Herald* attacked him, and the *Evening Post* and the *Graphic* had friendly words for him. The *Graphic* explained:

> If the rights of the people in this country are ever invaded and their liberties are ever infringed, it will be by attacks on people who are obnoxious or parties that are despised. . . . To defend a great principle in spite of . . . [the] unpopularities of the men who are momentarily associated with its expression is a service as important as it is thankless.

The *Graphic*s response was unusual. Most New Yorkers, especially those in positions of power and public esteem, gave little thought to Swinton's proposal. In mid-February, therefore, the Workingman's Central Council and at least ten trade unions—including the cabinet makers, iron molders, paper hangers, tailors, carpenters, and bakers—agreed to circulate a petition against the police. Discord, however, developed at once over cooperating with the socialists and the Free Thinker's Association. Several unions and the German socialists nevertheless finally collected affidavits from victims of the attack and circulated a petition charging the Police Board with "incapacity and malfeasance in office" and "trampling upon the law and the privileges of the people." The persons engaged in the riot," said the petitioners, "were the police, and those who incited the same were the Police Commissioners." Calling the police action "cruel perfidy on the part of unworthy servants of the people," the petitioners urged the State Legislature to guarantee citizens the right to use all public places for free discussion and to investigate the entire Tompkins Square affair. No record has been found of the number of persons signing the petition, but it is entirely probable that little support came from outside the German and labor communities.

Representing the petitioners, John Swinton and two German radicals appeared before the New York State Assembly's Committee on Grievances in Albany on March 25 and attacked the Police Board. The Germans submitted affidavits describing the police action and Swinton, dressed in swallowtail coat and white necktie, urged a thorough investigation, abolition of the Police Board, and popular election of municipal police officials. Later printed as a pamphlet entitled *The Tompkins Square Outrage*, Swinton's appeal bristled with indignation. Because the Police Board was steeped in corruption, jobbery, and graft, it "got up the cry that the unemployed complainants were revolutionists, destructionists, anarchists, communists, enemies of religion, property, and poverty." In a democratic society, workers had "peaceful means of righting every wrong, redressing every grievance," and public officials dared not "look on the commonality as *a dangerous mass*." The police wrongly applied notions of "constructive treason" to municipal affairs:

> *Riot* should consist only in *rioting*—in actual resistance to authority. It should not be considered riot when some man of a multitude threatens to become *riotous*. . . . If we so consider it, we thereby give a power to our rulers dangerous to public liberties which may be wantonly used to suppress the popular right of meeting or of speech.

"Even communistic ideas" could not be "scribbled out of heads . . . or clubbed out of . . . hearts." "You owe even such people justice," Swinton insisted. "It is not *right* to *wrong* even them." Labor reform could not be suppressed by "the old way of force—powerless, helpless force." To fear radical and socialist ideas meant "to doubt the very foundations of our republican democratic system . . . to deny the possibility of popular government . . . [and] to fall into the wilted methods of despotism." Neither Swinton's eloquent plea nor subsequent protest by small numbers of German and labor radicals stirred the legislators. Renewed efforts to convince Mayor Havemeyer to dismiss the Police Board also failed, and by the end of March most New Yorkers remembered little about Tompkins Square on January 13.

In the early summer, a few months later, *The Toiler*, a New York socialist weekly of short life, started a campaign to free Christian Mayer, who had been in jail since January. A socialist petition urged Governor Dix to pardon him and it was supported by the *New York Sun*. In order to attract attention to Mayer's incarceration and to test the right of free assembly, a "Committee of Citizens," including Swinton, McGuire, Jacob Morstadt (the president of the Journeymen Tailor's International Union), and other German immigrant leaders, trade unionists, and socialists, organized another Tompkins Square meeting for August 31. No group had met in the square for political purposes since the January melee. Some newspapers again warned of the revival of the "dangerous" Committee of Safety, but the meeting's sponsors appointed a "Police Committee" of 200 to maintain order. The *New York Evening Telegram* warned the police not to repeat their earlier "clumsy knavery and trickery." Though the fate of the August 31 meeting rested with the men responsible for the January "riot," it was different this time. The Police Board and the Department of Parks permitted the meeting. "The people," declared the President of the Department of Parks, "have a right to gather at any park set aside for meetings and to pass resolutions and make speeches to their heart's content." Governor Dix chose the occasion to pardon Christian Mayer, an action called "just and wise" by the *New York Sun*. The *Toiler*, however, accused Dix of making "another bid . . . for the votes of workingmen."

A vindication of the right of free assembly, the August 31 meeting was nonetheless anti-climactic. It attracted little attention and lacked the drama of the earlier January events. Uniformed police stayed away from the square and only fifty waited on call in station houses nearby as a crowd of between two and three thousand persons resolved that Tompkins Square always remain "open to the people for their free assembly." Christian Mayer sat on the speaker's stand and heard Francis Beck extol the new Social-Democratic Workingmen's Party. John McMackin, an early leader of the unemployed (and many years later New York State Commissioner of Labor), admitted that the failure to remove the Police Board revealed the weakness of organized labor in New York. John Swinton, greeted with great applause, spoke last and defended freedom of speech and assembly, attacked the "police infantry and dragoons," and called Tompkins Square a "sacrificial ground on which the victims of municipal diabolism" had been "immolated."

Swinton urged his listeners to commemorate the "riot" until "those who govern ... have learned that the liberties of the people cannot be trifled with." The evening passed without further incident, and *The Toiler* celebrated the "immense victory ... [for] the principle of free speech." Some New Yorkers drew another conclusion from the proceedings, for to them Swinton sounded like "a crazy spouter" and "an exasperating lunatic" pandering "to the passions of an ignorant mob" that deserved to be "met with clubs and answered with blows."

The extreme reaction against the concept of public responsibility for the unemployed in New York City should not be isolated and simply blamed on overly zealous or corrupt police officials. Even if accurate, such an explanation is too simple, for similar attitudes toward the unemployed existed in other large cities. Shortly before the New York radicals celebrated their second Tompkins Square meeting, fear of renewed agitation by the socialists and the unemployed swept Chicago. The *Chicago Times* pleaded for a stronger police force in the coming winter and warned:

> During last winter the city escaped a bloody riot only through the merest accident ... by assuring the mob of abundant support. ... The mob has become a terror viewed in any light, and the question arises, "How can any outbreaks be efficiently met and handled?" Already a number of business men have discussed this subject. ... Their property is in jeopardy so long as the communists are tolerated and they are anxious to know how it can be properly protected in case of a riot. Is the city prepared for an emergency where arms are required, or can communes by a sudden uprising pounce upon and take possession of our police stations ... ?

The *Chicago Tribune* feared the police force inadequate and urged a revitalized militia. "The State must furnish guns and accoutrements," advised the *Tribune*. "The city must rent an armory. The wealthy must subscribe to help defray the cost of uniforms, etc. And rich and poor must volunteer. Every large city needs a military force." Plainly worried, the *Tribune* concluded: "All law rests on force. Let us see to it in time that our force is strong enough to make our law respected at any and all times. When clubs are in vain, bullets are potent." In October 1874, the Chicago militia appealed to the business community for money for uniforms and other necessities. At that moment, Cyrus Hall McCormick became an honorary member of the First Regiment of the Illinois National Guard.

It cannot be argued, finally, that the bitter feeling toward the unemployed and the successful violation of traditional political rights by the New York police resulted only from the "radical" character of the Committee of Safety and its demands. The attitude toward the unemployed in 1873-74 reflected a much broader and more encompassing attitude toward urban workers. By this time, contact between the urban workers and the middle and upper classes had become casual and at best indirect. Trade unions and other efforts at self-improvement had become abstract movements separated from the human beings involved in them. The propertied urban classes already viewed the worker as little more than a factor of production. Organized criticism of the "free market" was interpreted as impertinent and irresponsible denial of certain immutable economic and moral "laws" and, therefore, a deterrent to economic development, capital accumulation, and even personal improvement. In explaining to its readers why workers refused to accept the *status quo* the *Chicago Times* put it this way:

> They are . . . vagabonds because they are very hard at work preaching the gospel of vagabondism, which says it is wrong to postpone the present to the future, and that those who do so ought to be compelled to reverse their life-habit and divide what they have laid up for the future with those who subscribe to the gospel of vagabondism and live only in the present . . . The man who lays up not for the morrow, perishes on the morrow. It is the inevitable law of God, which neither legislatures nor communistic blatherskites can repeal. The fittest survive, and those are fittest, as the result always proves, who provide for their own survival.

A Chicago worker responded to this crude Social Darwinist explanation of labor reform by questioning its relevance to the new social and economic order created by industrial technology:

> As a reward for our fidelity, we are considered vagabonds for not being at work when there is no work that we can procure. There are millions of acres of land lying untilled throughout our country that might afford a means of supplying many of our wants, were we allowed to cultivate them as nature would indicate we have a right to do, but "law and order" allows the fortunate to withhold all the land they can acquire for speculative purposes. . . . If we dare meet in council to resolve upon some future action for our future welfare, we are branded "communists." . . . When we condole with each other, it is "Chicago needs cannon." . . . Now do you seek by insidious devices to "palaver" at our determination to assert our rights as citizens of this Republic to discuss our grievances in public assemblages? If so, bring your cannon. You will need them. . . .,We have listened to your scorian ideas from childhood. Your gentle cooing we now find too tinctured with "self" to work anything but our ruin. And while we envied you in your ease, we little thought that in those social gatherings where the fumes of your choicest "Havanas" tended to portray your opulence, that you were concocting schemes to make yourself the "constituted authority" to which we must forever yield obedience. How long can we subsist on a "character as honest workingmen"? . . .

Most well-to-do urban residents did not understand this plea in 1873 and 1874. To them, men rose or fell solely through individual effort. Sufficiently alienated from the urban poor and assured by the real if uneven blessings of industrial development, they could join the *New York Graphic* in celebrating the nation in which republican equality, free public schools, and cheap western lands allowed "intelligent working people" to "have anything they all want." How could they permit the government to interfere in the economy, redistribute wealth, shift even slightly the burden of unregulated industrial development, and thereby thwart individual initiative and equal opportunity? In western Maryland, a sensitive and disturbed local citizen speculated on the import of the Tompkins Square "riot." He asked questions that remained unanswered but became even more relevant during the next forty years. "Haven't these men a right to demand bread and warmth for their wives and little ones, while many of their fellow citizens revel in luxury and have more of the good things of this life than they can possibly make use of? If not, what is the definition of humanity? . . . One fact is apparent: . . . in a land where there is more than enough for all, all should have at least enough."

VI

THE BEGINNING OF THE TWENTIETH CENTURY

In 1903, the Government Printing Office published a Senate document, "Federal Aid in Domestic Disturbances, 1787-1903," that had been prepared under the direction of the Adjutant-General.[1] This document is an historical account describing riots in which federal troops were engaged from Shays' Rebellion in 1787 to the "Coeur d'Alene troubles" of 1899. The volume's purpose was not public education, but rather was part of the plea for greater military expenditures for handling future disturbances. Evidently, in many minds the old fear of a standing army in a democratic society existed:

> It is a favorite argument of the opponents of a military system, since the beginning of history, that the existence of organized troops is, in itself, a temptation to use them. In the face of our compilation, one cannot but wonder what would have been the course of our history without them.

In 1922, this report was up-dated to include riots of the twentieth century. Both of these documents were all but ignored for fifty years. Then the National Commission on the Causes and Prevention of Violence prepared *The History of Violence in America.* The opinion expressed in 1903 for greater military appropriations differed little from that expressed a half century later: The best way to end mob disturbances is by increasing military force.

Underlying most riots are deeply felt grievances for which no redress is apparent. In the twentieth century, most strife has resulted from labor discontent and racial prejudice against blacks. This judgement does not make this a particularly different period. In Colorado, thirty years of labor unrest (1884-1914) did little to improve the living standards of the miners. The early years of the twentieth century were also the years of the Industrial Workers of the World (I.W.W.), a radical labor organization, itself violent and itself a victim of official violence.

In the South, there was always open season on blacks: Over 1500 people were lynched there between the years 1886-1900. In the next decade, about 100 people per year were hung. In 1906, Atlanta, Georgia was the scene of a bloody race riot. Springfield, Illinois kept pace and exploded in a race riot in 1908; and in 1917 East St. Louis, Illinois followed suit. These disturbances were not out of the ordinary inasmuch as similar outbreaks occurred across the country, reaching their peak in 1919 with race riots in twenty-five cities including Charleston, South Carolina; Boston, Massachusetts; Detroit, Michigan; Washington, D.C.; and Chicago, Illinois. The Chicago Race Riot of 1919 has been the subject of many studies. At the time, the Chicago Commission on Race Relations made a report and, like earlier reports on riots in New Orleans and Memphis, it proved of little use in preventing future incidents.

With World War II came another period of unrest. The causes are both simple and complex: the promise of America's ideals were held out to the blacks and then removed; white prejudice against black G.I.'s returning from Europe and Asia and expecting to be treated like human beings; fear of labor competition; shortage of adequate housing; and police forces of the major cities dominated by Southern whites who were anti-black. These all played a contributing role in the disorders of the 1940's.

The articles that follow concern some of these points. The first is a partisan account of the Ludlow Massacre (Colorado, 1914) written by Max Eastman. The Ludlow Massacre is one incident in the labor struggles that shook Colorado for thirty years, during which the anti-strike activities of the state are clear to see. Time and time again, the National Guard was used against labor, and when it was not available, private police forces did an equally violent job.

John Reed's account of the war in Paterson, New Jersey, the scene of an I.W.W. strike in 1913, could make the point just as well:

> There's war in Paterson. But it's a curious kind of war. All the violence is the work of one side—the Mill Owners. Their servants, the police, club unresisting men and women and ride down law abiding crowds on horseback. Their paid mercenaries, the armed detectives, shoot and kill innocent people. Their newspapers, the Paterson *Press* and the Paterson *Call*, publish incendiary and crime-inciting appeals to mob-violence against the strike leaders. Their tool, Recorder Carroll, deals out heavy sentences to peaceful pickets that the police-net gathers up. They control absolutely the Police, the Press, the Courts.[2]

To the public, however, the source of violence was the strikers, the I.W.W., or the Communists.

The second essay in this section concerns the Chicago Race Riot of 1919. Its author, William V. Tuttle, Jr., tried to unravel a few of the complexities of that event revealing a relationship between labor unrest and racism. He has expanded this into a book length study entitled *Race Riot: Chicago in the Red Summer of 1919* (1970). Finally, to demonstrate that no sectional or exclusive prejudice exists, a narrative of the 1943 zoot-suit riots in Los Angeles is included. When the role of the police in that outbreak, as seen through the eyes of Carey McWilliams, is read, the meaning of official violence is clear.

Suggested Further Readings

The availability of excellent materials on these years far surpasses that of earlier periods. On race riots Elliott M. Rudwick, *Race Riot at East St. Louis July 2, 1917* (1964); Arthur I. Waskow, *From Race Riot to Sit-In, 1919 and the 1960's* (1966); Alfred McClung Lee, *Race Riot* (1943) (on the Detroit Race Riots of 1943); and the official report by the Chicago Commission on Race Relations on the 1919 riot, *The Negro in Chicago: A Study of Race Relations and a Race Riot*, are all superb. James L. Crouthamel, "The Springfield Riot of 1908," *The Journal of Negro History* XLV (1960), 164-81 is just one of many articles on the riots of this period in this important journal. A classic study on labor violence is Louis Adamic, *Dynamite: The Story of Class Violence in America* (1934), but Graham Adams, Jr., *The Age of Industrial Violence, 1910-1915* is more valuable. Howard Zinn has an interesting essay on "The Ludlow Massacre," in his *The Politics of History* (1970).

Footnotes

1 Frederick T. Wilson, "Federal Aid in Domestic Disturbances, 1787-1903," Senate Document No. 209, 57th Congress, 2d. Session (Washington, D. C.: Government Printing Office, 1903), p. 260.

2 John Reed, "War in Paterson," in William O'Neill, (ed.), *Echoes of Revolt: The Masses, 1911-1917* (Chicago: Quadrangle Books, 1966), pp. 143-47.

11   Max Eastman

CLASS WAR IN COLORADO

"For eight days it was a reign of terror. Armed miners swarmed into the city like soldiers of a revolution. They tramped the streets with rifles, and the red handkerchiefs around their necks, singing their war-songs. The Mayor and the sheriff fled, and we simply cowered in our houses waiting. No one was injured here—they policed the streets day and night. But destruction swept like a flame over the mines." These are the words of a Catholic priest of Trinidad.

"But, father," I said, "where is it all going to end?" He sat forward with a radient smile.

"War!" he answered. "Civil war between labor and capital!' His gesture was beatific.

"And the church—will the church do nothing to save us from this?"

"The church can do nothing—absolutely nothing!"

"Yes, this is Colorado," he said. "Colorado is 'disgraced in the eyes of the nation'—but *soon it will be the Nation!"*

I have thought often of that opinion. And I have felt that soon it will, indeed, unless men of strength and understanding, seeing this fight is to be fought, determine it shall be fought by the principals with economic and political arms, and not by professional gunmen and detectives.

Many reproaches will fall on the heads of the Rockefeller interests for acts of tyranny, exploitation, and contempt of the labor laws of Colorado—acts which are only human at human's worst. They have gone out to drive back their cattle with a lash. For them that is natural. But I think the cool collecting for this purpose of hundreds of degenerate adventurers in blood from all the slums and vice camps of the earth, arming them with high power rifles, explosive and soft-nosed bullets, and putting them beyond the law in uniforms of the national army, is not natural. It is not human. It is lower, because colder, than the blood-lust of the gunmen themselves.

I put the ravages of that black orgy of April 20th, when a frail fluttering tent city in the meadow, the dwelling place of 120 women and 273 children, was riddled to shreds without a second's warning, and then fired by coal-oil torches with the bullets still raining and the victims screaming in their shallow holes of refuge, or crawling away on their bellies through the fields—I put that crime, not upon its perpetrators, who are savage, but upon the gentlemen of noble leisure who hired them to this service. Flags of truce were shot out of hands; women running in the sunlight to rescue their children were whipped back with the hail of a machine gun; little girls who plunged into a shed for shelter were followed there with forty-eight

From "Class War in Colorado," in William O'Neill, (ed.) *Echoes of Revolt: The Masses, 1911-1917* (Chicago: Quadrangle Books, Inc., 1966), pp. 149-54.

calibre bullets; a gentle Greek, never armed, was captured running to the rescue of those women and children dying in a hole, was captured without resistance, and after five minutes lay dead under a broken rifle, his skull crushed and three bullet holes in his back, and the women and children still dying in the hole.

It is no pleasure to tell—but if the public does not learn the lesson of this massacre, there will be massacres of bloodier number in the towns.

For you need not deceive your hearts merely with the distance of it. This is no local brawl in the foothills of the Rockies. The commanding generals are not here, the armies are not here—only the outposts. A temporary skirmish here of that conflict which is drawing up on two sides the greatest forces of the republic—those same "money interests" that have crushed and abolished organized labor in the steel industry on one side, and upon the other the United Mine Workers of America, the men who stand at the source of power. This strike in Colorado does not pay—in Colorado. It is a deliberately extravagant campaign to kill down the Mine Workers' Union, kill it here and drain and damage it all over the country. And you will neither know nor imagine what happened at Trinidad, until you can see hanging above it the shadows of these national powers contending.

It is not local, and moreover it is not "western." You cannot dismiss the bleeding here with that old bogus about the wild and woolly west. Fifty-seven languages and dialects are spoken in these two mining counties. The typical wage-laborers of America—most of them brought here as strike-breakers themselves ten years ago—are the body of the strike. Trinidad with its fifteen thousand has more of the modern shine, more ease and metropolitan sophistication than your eastern city of fifty thousand. It is just a little America. And what happened here is the most significant, as it is the most devastating human thing that has happened in America since Sherman marched to the sea.

Between one hundred and fifty and two hundred men, women, and children have been shot, burned, or clubbed to death in these two counties in six months. Over three hundred thousand dollars' worth of property has been destroyed. And the cause of this high record of devastation, in a strike so much smaller than many, appears bodily in the very first killing that occurred. On the 6th day of last August, Gerald Lippiat, a union organizer, was shot dead on the main street of Trinidad by Belcher and Belk, two Baldwin-Feltz detectives, one of whom was at that time out on bail under a murder charge in his home state of West Virginia. That was three months before the strike, and for three months before that these two detectives and others had been in this district engaged in the business of *spotting union members for discharge from the mines*—a fact which illumines Rockefeller's statement that only ten per cent of his employees were union men.

"Just let them find out you were a union *sympathizer*," I was told by a railroad man, "and that was enough to run you down the canon with a gun in the middle of your back. It was an open shop for scabs—that's the kind of an open shop it was."

And this fact, verified on all sides, is not only sufficient ground for a strike, but it is ground for a criminal indictment under the laws of Colorado. So indeed are most of the complaints of the miners, for Colorado has a set of excellent mining laws stored away at the capitol. Five out of the seven demands of the strikers were demands that their employers should obey the laws of the State—an incident which shows more plainly than usual what the State is in essence, an excellent instrument for those who have the economic power to use it.

"What was the complaint? Well, it was everything. They kept everybody in debt all the time. Lupi was fired and compelled to pick up his own house and move it off the property, because he wouldn't trade at the company store. Why, I says, if the Board o' Health even, would come up here and take a look at the water out o' this boarding-house—show me any human being that'll drink refuse from a coal mine! It was hay, alfalfa, manure-everything come right through the pipes fer the men to drink—and if that ain't enough to make a camp strike, I'd like to know what *ain't!* It was black an' dirty an' green an' any color you want to call it—and when I'd enter a complaint they'd say, 'Who's kickin'?' An' I'd tell 'em the man's name, an' they'd say, 'Give him his time! Let him get to hell out o' here, if he don't like it!'

"I give 'em a bit o' their own medicine, too. They had a couple o' these millionaire clerks down here from Denver oncet, an' they didn't have enough of the La Veta water brought down for their own table. I heard these fellers ask for a drink, an' I took in a little of this warm stuff right out o' the mine. Do you suppose they touched it? 'What's good enough for a miner,' I says, 'is good enough for you.' I wanted to tell that before the Congress committee so bad I was just bustin', an' you can say it's the truth from me, an' I don't care what happens to me so long as I'm tellin' the truth." She doesn't care what happens to her, Mrs. Suttles doesn't, but she cares what happens to other people, and I'm happy to be her mouthpiece.

You will know from her that there is nothing we are accustomed to call "revolutionary" in the local aspect of this strike. One sees here only an uprising of gentle and sweet-mannered people in favor of the laws they live under. In the mines they had learned to endure, and in the tents they surely did endure, smilingly as I have it from those who know, without impetuous retaliations, more hardship and continuous provocation than you could imagine of yourself—if indeed you can imagine yourself tenting four months in the winter snow for any cause. Patient and persistent and naturally genial—yet the militia, and the mine operators, and all the little priests of respectability of Trinidad are full of the tale of those "blood-thirsty foreigners," "ignorant," "lawless," "unacquainted with the principles of American Liberty."

As a pure matter of fact, so long as those foreigners remained "ignorant" and "lawless," their employers were highly well pleased with them. But when they began to learn English, and acquire an interest in the laws, and also in the "principles of American liberty," straightway they became a sore and a trouble to their employers—because their employers were daily violating these laws and these principles at the expense of *their* lives and *their* happiness, and they knew it. That was the trouble. And their employers, from Rockefeller down to the mine boss, are perfectly well aware of this, having brought them here in the first place for the express purpose of supplanting English-speaking Americans who knew their rights and had rebelled.

When you hear a man talking about "bloodthirsty foreigners," you can be perfectly sure there is one thing in his heart he would like to do, and that is drink the blood of those foreigners—especially if he happens to be one of these hatchet-faced Yankees.

The strike was declared on September 23, and the companies, having imported guards for about two weeks before that, were ready for it. They were ready to evict the miners from their houses, dumping their families and furniture into the snow, and in many of the mines they did this. Those miners who owned the houses from which they were evicted, having paid for them although they were built upon the company's land, must have received at this point a peculiarly fine taste of "American Liberty." That is almost as fine as having a tax deducted from your wages, to pay for a public school privately owned and situated upon private property, or being compelled to pay fifty cents toward the salary of a Protestant town minister when you are a Roman Catholic. Miners in one case were not allowed to pass through the gate of the mining camp, in order to get their mail from a United States Post Office located within the gate called "Private Property"—another sweet taste of "American Liberty." Was it such fortunes as this, I wonder, that led one of the strikers to run back among the blazing tents in order to rescue an American flag, "because he just couldn't see that burn up"?

Early in October, say the strikers, an automobile containing Baldwin-Feltz gunmen stopped under the hills and fired into the Ludlow tent colony in the plain.

Early in October, says the superintendent of the Hastings mine, an automobile containing men coming to work in the mines was fired on from the vicinity of the tent colony. The reader may solve this problem for himself. I can only picture the location of the mines and the colony, and let it stand that guerrilla warfare between the strikers and those men imported for their shooting ability, was frequent and was inevitable.

The mining camps are in little canons, running up into a range of hills that extends due north and south, and the Ludlow tent colony was out on the wide plain to the east of these hills by the railroad track. It stood just north of the junction of the main line of the Colorado & Southern with branch lines running up to the mines. In short, it held the strategic point *for warning strike-breakers on incoming trains*. And to those who cannot believe the story of its destruction for the sheer wantonness of it, that little fact will be of interest. The tent colony at Holly Grove, West Virginia, shot up in the same wantonness by the same gunmen last year, was similarly situated. These tent colonies are white flags on the gatepost, flashing the signal "Quarantine" to the initiated, and it is very important for the unsanitary business within that they be removed.

So the gunmen would issue down the canons, or shoot from the hills, and the strikers would sally out to each side of the colony, and shoot into the canon or the hills. And this occurred often in the days of October, leading up to the pitched battle on the 28th, when the people in that vicinity seemed to be breathing bullets, and Governor Ammons ordered John Chase into the field with the militia.

The militia came avowedly to disarm both sides, and prevent the illegal importation of strike-breakers, and they were received with cheers by the "lawless" strikers, who surrendered to them a great many if not all of their arms. For a week or two, in fact, the militia did impartially keep the peace. And the reason for this is that it had been asserted by the mine-owners, and believed by the Governor, that that famous "ten percent of union men" were forcibly detaining the rest of the strikers in the colonies, and that as soon as the ninety percent had the protection of the militia they would return to work.

In the course of the two weeks it became evident, however, that this happy thought was founded upon a wish, and that something else would have to be done to get the men back into the mines. Therefore the guns surrendered by the strikers were turned over to the new gunmen, and the protection of illegally imported strike-breakers began again. Began also the enrolling of Baldwin-Feltz gunmen in the Colorado militia; the secret meetings of a military court; the arresting and jailing by the hundred of "military prisoners"; the search and looting of tent colonies under color of military authority; and the forcible deportation of citizens. By such means and many others John Chase, riding about in the automobiles of the companies, made his alliance with invested capital perfectly clear to the most "ignorant" foreigner in the course of less than a month.

Thence forward we have to lay aside and forget the distinction between the private gunmen of the mine owners, and the state militia of Colorado—a fact which reveals more plainly than usual what the army is in essence, a splendid weapon for those who have the economic power to use it.

On November 25th, the strikers for the second time asked the operators to confer, and the operators refused.

On November 26th, Baldwin-Feltz Belcher was shot on the streets of Trinidad, not two blocks from where he had shot Lippiat in August. The militia cleared the streets, and indiscriminate arrests followed, strikers even being taken to jail, I am assured, in the automobiles of their employers. *Habeas corpus* proceedings were laughed at. Personal liberty. the rights of a householder, of free speech, of assemblage, of trial bv jury—all these old fashioned things dropped quietly out of sight, not only in the case of Mother Jones, which is notorious, but also in the case of the striking miners one and all. The State and organized capital were married together before the eyes of men so amiably and naturally that, except in retrospect, one hardly was able to be surprised.

Sunday, April 19th, was Easter Sunday for the Greeks, and they celebrated that day in the happy and melodious manner of their country, dancing out of doors in the sunlight all morning with the songs of the larks. In the afternoon they played baseball in a meadow, two hundred yards from the tents, the women playing against the married men, and making them hustle, too. It was a gay day for the tent colony, because all the strikers loved the Greeks and were borne along by their happy spirits. Especially they loved Louis Tikas for his fineness and his gentle and strong way of commanding them. To all of them he seemed to give the courage that was necessary in order to celebrate a holiday with merriment under the pointed shadows of two machine guns.

But in the very midst of that celebration eight armed soldiers came down from these shadows into the field. Standing about, they managed to place themselves exactly on the line between the home-plate and first base, and during a remonstrance from the players, one of them said to another, "It wouldn't take me and four men to wipe that bunch off the earth." After some discussion among themselves, the players finally altered the position of their bases, and the soldiers decided not to interfere again. One of them said, "All right, Girlie, you have your big time today, and we'll have ours tomorrow!"

On Monday morning, at about 8:30, Major Hamrock called the tent colony on the telephone, and asked Louis Tikas to surrender a mine-worker who, he asserted, was being held in the colony against his will. The person in question was not in the colony, and Tikas said so. But the major insisted, so Tikas arranged to meet him on the railroad track, half way between the two encampments, and discuss their disagreement. Tikas went to the meeting place, and the major was not there. He returned, called him on the telephone, and again agreed to meet him alone at the railroad station.

They met and continued their discussion, but while they were talking a troop of reinforcements appeared over the hill at one of the military camps. The machine-gun at the other camp was already trained upon the colony, and a trainman tells me that at that time he saw militia-men running down the track, ready to shoot.

"My God, Major, what does this mean?" said Tikas.

"You stop your men, and I'll stop mine," is the major's answer as reported. But before Tikas got back to the colony, the strikers had left in a body, armed. Three bombs were fired off in the major's camp—a prearranged signal to the mines to send down all the guards, officers, and strike-breakers they were able to arm. And immediately after the sounding of this signal, at the order of Lieutenant Linderfelt, the first shot was fired by the militia.

It is incredible, but it is true that they trained their machine guns, not on the miners who had left their families and made for a railroad cut to the southeast, but on their families in the tent colony itself. Women and children fled from the tents under fire, seeking shelter in a creek-bed, climbing down a well, racing across the plain to a ranchhouse. "Mamma tried to protect us from the bullets with her apron," said Anna Carich to me—a little girl of twelve years.

She herself plunged down the ladder-stair into the well—but no sooner arrived there than she had to go back and call her dog. "I says to him, 'Come on, Princie. Come on in!' but he was afraid or something, and when I stuck my head out, the bullets came as though you took a mule-whip and hit it on the floor. Papa pulled me back in, and Princie was killed. Maybe he wanted to go back after his puppy." I guess that was it, for it was way off at the rear of the colony that I saw him lying in the grass.

There were women and children too that did not leave their homes in this volley, but simply lay flat or crawled into the earth-holes under the tents. And to these Tikas returned, and he spent the day there, caring for them, or cheering them, or lying flat with a telephone begging reinforcements for the little army of forty that was trying to fight back two or three hundred—rifles against machine guns. But reinforcements came only to the militia, for they controlled the railroad, and in the evening, after a day's shooting, they took courage under their uniforms, and crept into the tent-colony with cans of coal-oil, and set torches to the tents. I quote here the verdict of the Coroner's jury: "We find that [here follow twelve names of women and children] came to their death by asphyxiation, or fire, or both, caused by the burning of the tents of the Ludlow Tent Colony, and that the fire on the tents was started by militia-men, under Major Hamrock and Lieutenant Linderfelt, or mine guards, or both."

When that blaze appeared, Louis Tikas, who had left the tent colony for a moment, started back to the rescue of those women and children who would be suffocated in the hole. He knew they were there. He was captured by the soldiers then. It is likely he did not tell his captors where he was going and what for? The women and children were left dying, and Louis Tikas was taken to the track and murdered by K. E. Linderfelt or his subordinates.

Linderfelt is a man who had his taste of blood in the Philippines, in the Boer War, and with Madero in Mexico. He was second in command of this gang—a lieutenant. "Shoot every son-of-a-bitchin' thing you see moving!" is what a train-inspector heard him shout at the station. And in that command from that man, brought here by the Rockefeller interests as an expert in human slaughter, you have the whole story of this carnage and its cause.

Is it a thing to regret or rejoice in that Civil War followed, that unions all over the state voted rifles and ammunition, that militia-men mutinied, that train-men refused to move reinforcements, that armed miners flocked into Trinidad, supplanted the government there, and with that town as a base, issued into the hills destroying? For once in this country, middle ground was abolished. Philanthropy burned up in rage. Charity could wipe up the blood. Mediation, Legislation, Social-Consciousness expired like memories of a foolish age. And once again, since the days of Paris of '71, an army of the working class fought the military to a shivering standstill, and let them beg for truce. It would have been a sad world had that not happened.

I think the palest lover of "peace," after viewing the flattened ruins of that little colony of homes, the open death-hole, the shattered bedsteads, the stoves, the household trinkets broken and black—and the larks still singing over them in the sun—the most bloodless would find joy in going up the valleys to feed his eyesight upon tangles of gigantic machinery and ashes that had been the operating capital of the mines. It is no retribution, it is no remedy, but it proves that the power and the courage of action is here.

12   William M. Tuttle, Jr.

LABOR CONFLICT AND RACIAL VIOLENCE

On a crowded South Side Chicago beach on the afternoon of Sunday, July 27, 1919, white and black swimmers clashed in savage combat. Sparked by this clash during which a Negro youth drowned, the inter-racial resentment that had been smoldering in Chicago for the past few years exploded in furious rioting. The violence raged uncontrolled for five days, as whites mauled Negroes and Negroes in turn assaulted white peddlers and merchants in the "black belt." Members of both races craved vengeance as stories of atrocities, both real and rumored, rapidly spread throughout the city. White gunmen in automobiles sped through the ghetto shooting indiscriminately as they passed, and black snipers fired back. Roaming mobs shot, beat, and stabbed their victims to death. The undermanned Chicago police force was an ineffectual deterrent to the waves of violence that soon over-flowed the environs of the black belt and flooded the North and West Sides as well as the Loop, the city's downtown business district. Only six regiments of state militiamen and a cooling rain finally quenched the passions of the rioters, but by then thirty-eight lay dead, twenty-three Negroes and fifteen whites, and well over 500 others had sustained injuries.

There were several factors precipitating this riot. From July 1917 to the erup-tion of the disorders two years later, for example, no less than twenty-six bombs were hurled at isolated Negro residences in once all-white neighborhoods and at the offices of certain realtors who had sold to blacks. Well over half these bombings occurred during the six tense months leading up to the riot. Politics, too, were important. Chicago's notoriously corrupt Republican mayor, William H. ("Big Bill") Thompson, was anathema to reformers and Democrats alike. Many of these Democrats, moreover, were blue-collar workers who lived in neighborhoods con-tiguous to the black belt and who felt threatened, politically and economically, by the "invading" Negroes. Yet Thompson was a favorite of the predominantly Repub-lican black electorate, some of whose leaders had been rewarded with posts in his administration. The mayor was re-elected in April 1919, after a bitter campaign which had racial overtones, and the Democratic organ, the *Chicago Daily Journal*, boomed out at dusk on election day in bold front-page headlines: "NEGROES ELECT BIG BILL." As racial friction mounted with the heat in the spring and summer of 1919, whites and blacks battled on the city's streetcars and in its parks and schools. Several Negroes were murdered in mob assaults, and both blacks and whites armed themselves for the riot that numerous Chicagoans feared would erupt at any moment.

This riot was also the result of longstanding discord between white and black job competitors in the Chicago labor market. Several contemporaries claimed that

From "Labor Conflict and Racial Violence: The Black Worker in Chicago, 1894-1919," *Labor History*, No. 10 (Summer, 1969), pp. 408-32. Reprinted by permission.

job competition was not only a cause but perhaps the most significant one. Later students of the riot, however, while admitting that interracial labor friction might have precipitated some bloodshed, have listed it as merely a minor cause. The most exhaustive study, *The Negro in Chicago*, by the Chicago Commission on Race Relations, for example, concluded that it was relatively unimportant since "race friction" was "not pronounced in Chicago industries." Recently Allan H. Spear in *Black Chicago* has similarly asserted that the riot "had little to do with labor conditions. . . ."

Both the Chicago Commission and Spear support this contention by pointing out that during the riot there was an almost total absence of violence in the stockyards, which was by far the largest single area of employment for black Chicagoans. And, indeed, there was far less bloodshed there than knowledgable observers had feared. But does this negative evidence prove anything other than that black workers did not dare return to the stockyards until after the militia had been ordered out of the armories to protect them? The absence of violence in the stockyards in the early days of the riot was, as Negro Alderman Louis B. Anderson explained, simply the result of fear of attack. "Colored men," Anderson said, "have refused to go to the stockyards to get paid even though their families were starving. . . ." And what happened when Negroes returned to work? Even under military and police protection, on the first day back, one worker was savagely struck with a hammer wielded by a white man. A mob then chased the dazed Negro through the sheep pens and finally killed him with shovels and brooms. When police rescued a second black man after a severe beating, white workers retaliated, and a vicious battle against police and soldiers ensued. Several days later the packers notified non-union black workers that order had been restored to the yards, and that additional police and soldiers armed with rifles and machine guns would be there to insure their safe return to work. Organized labor disagreed, arguing that the situation was still volatile. The packers "thought that if they would be able to jamb [*sic*] the colored laborers," charged President John Fitzpatrick of the Chicago Federation of Labor, "that is, the great body of colored laborers, and the white union men in the stock yards . . . that there would be murder there, and that they would destroy our organization. There was no other purpose in it, absolutely no other purpose in it. . . ."

Herbert Gutman has recently made a plea to labor historians "to explore in detail the confrontation of the black worker and industrial American in particular settings." The history of the black worker in Chicago from the Pullman strike of 1894 to the race riot of 1919 provides such an opportunity—in large part because the race riot was in many ways the tragic culmination of this twenty-five years of conflict between blacks and whites in the labor market.

The seeds of discord between white and Negro job competitors in the Chicago labor market had been planted in the stockyards in 1894, when masses of packing and slaughterhouse workers had conducted a sympathetic strike with Eugene V. Debs' American Railway Union. Violence marked this strike; and, in the midst of it, Negro strikebreakers were hired for the first time in the history of the meat packing industry. Although the packers initially disclaimed any intention of adopting this practice, less than a week later Negro strikebreakers were working, eating, and sleeping in the stockyards, and their presence fired racial animosities. "Cases of attacks on colored men were numerous yesterday," the *Chicago Record* reported on July 19. "Swinging from the cross tree of a telegraph pole . . . near the entrance to the yards, the effigy of a negro roustabout was suspended. A black false face of hideous expression had been fixed upon the head of straw, and a placard pinned upon the breast of the figure bore the skull and crossbones with the word 'nigger-scab' above and below in bold letters. . . ."

The strike ended in August, and the Negro strikebreakers were intimately associated with the defeat. The workers had been thoroughly vanquished. They seemed "unmanly and without self-respect," recalled Mary McDowell of the settlement house "back-of-the-yards." "A community cowed is a sad sight to one who has been used to freemen."

Gradually, the workers built a new union—the Amalgamated Meat Cutters and Butcher Workmen (A.M.C.B.W.). Chicago was its target, for "if a start could be made in Chicago," the center of the industry, the A.M.C.B.W.'s president Michael Donnelly wrote Samuel Gompers, "our success nationally would be virtually established." Success was slow in coming, but by 1902 Donnelly could proudly announce that twenty-one locals had been chartered in Chicago and that the union rolls had burgeoned to 4,000. Accompanying organizing successes were concrete gains in wages and hours.

Yet these benefits went only to skilled workers, and at the turn of the century less and less skill was required in the meat packing industry because of the minute subdivision of labor. The "facts are these," Homer D. Call, the A.M.C.B.W.'s secretary treasurer, explained to Frank Morrison of the A.F.L., "twenty years ago the trade of the butchers was one of the best in the country." Then, after the consolidation of smaller packing houses into a handful of "large packing houses . . . they began a system to crowd out the expert butchers and replace them by cheaper men in every way. . . ." The owners "divided the business up into gangs consisting of enough to dress the bullock, one man doing only one thing . . . , which makes it possible for the proprietor to take a man in off from the street . . . and to day [*sic*] the expert workers are, in many cases crowded out and cheap Polackers and Hungarians put in their places. . . ." The skilled worker realized that this specialization enabled unskilled workers with "muscle" to replace him; it appeared inevitable that unless a minimum wage were obtained from the unskilled, cut-throat job competition would drive all wages down. The unskilled were "the club held above our heads at all times," a skilled butcher complained. "If the packers refuse to agree to any minimum wage for the unskilled," asked Call, "how long will it be before they attempt to reduce the wages of the skilled men?" The skilled workers thus championed the demand for a minimum wage of 20 cents an hour.

This minimum was the union's objective, but it still faced an obstacle that had perpetually plagued unionization of the stockyards—the vast heterogeneity of races and nationalities that competed for jobs. No other divisive force more ominously threatened the union's goal of solidarity. Racial jealousies and antagonisms crumbled, however, as the unskilled enthusiastically joined the union because of dissatisfaction with the prevailing wage of 15 to 18 1/2 cents an hour, and Negroes joined as well as whites. Many of the 500 black workers in the Chicago yards had become members, U.S. Labor Commissioner Carroll D. Wright reported to President Theodore Roosevelt. The women's local reportedly greeted its black applicants with "a hearty welcome," and Mary McDowell noted that "black men sat with their white comrades" at union meetings. This fellowship extended beyond the confines of the the the meeting room. The A.M.C.B.W., for example, held a funeral for "Bro. Wm. Sims (colored) tail sawyer at Swift's east house," with sixty-eight whites and seven Negroes attending these last rites.

Negotiations with the packers over the minimum wage were fruitless, breaking down in late June 1904, and when the packers announced a wage reduction, 23,000 packing house workers struck. Seven thousand mechanical tradesmen later joined the strike, which dragged on for ten weeks before the workers sporadically drifted back to work. The A.M.C.B.W. had launched its strike in the face of a depression. Outside the stockyards each morning as many as 5,000 men stood lined up to replace the strikers. The strike was further doomed because the strikers' resources were so paltry compared to the combined assets of the packers. Moreover, the heterogeous nationalities, races, and foreign languages, which had united confidently in 1903 and 1904, were in the final analysis divided and weak.

Despite the hopelessness of the strike, the arch villains to emerge from the defeat were the packers and their black strikebreakers. One observer estimated that upwards of 10,000 Negroes served as strikebreakers, with almost 1,400 arriving in one trainload. To white workers their disturbing presence seemed to be ubiquitous. Five white women strikebreakers described the prevalence of Negroes in the yards. These women, who had been hired by a black man representing Armour, worked in the canning room, ate their meals in a massive improvised dining hall one floor below, and at night slept in the canning room which "had 40 cots arranged as close together as possible." They reported seeing many Negro strikebreakers, including thirteen- and fourteen-year-old boys.

Since the violence of the 1894 strike had alienated public opinion, in 1904 the union posted notices on trees and fences which admonished the strikers "to molest no person or property, and abide strictly by the laws of this country." Non-violence was also the theme of union meetings. These exhortations notwithstanding, the strikers' animosities frequently boiled over. A mob of 500 mauled a black laborer and his 10-year-old son, and in another skirmish white strikers stabbed both eyes of a Negro strikebreaker. Other black people were hauled off streetcars. A full-scale riot threatened to erupt when 2,000 angry strikers hurled brickbats and other missiles at 200 Negro strikebreakers and their police escorts. Harry Rosenberg, a worker at Mary McDowell's settlement house, reported witnessing a mob of women and children chasing a Negro down the street, crying "kill the fink," and in late August union pickets fatally stabbed a Negro suspected of strikebreaking.

Their fortunes waning in late August, union leaders desperately wired Booker

T. Washington. "Hundreds of Negroes are acting as strikebreakers," they informed Washington, as they begged him to come to Chicago to lecture on the subject, "Should Negroes Become Strike Breakers?" Washington, however, declined the offer.

The words "Negro" and "scab" were now synonymous in the minds of numerous white stockyards workers; and, lest they forget, anti-Negro labor officials and politicians were present to remind them. The strike, one union official wrote, was broken "by such horrid means that a revelation of them makes the soul sicken and the heart beat faint with an awful fear." If was broken by Negroes, most of them "huge strapping fellows, ignorant and vicious, whose predominating trait was animalism." South Carolina's Senator Ben Tillman traveled to Chicago a month after the end of the strike. "It was the niggers that whipped you in line," he told a group from the stockyards district. "They were the club with which your brains were beaten out."

It was not mere words, however, but another strike, the bloody teamsters' strike of 1905, that made the image of Negroes as a "scab race" even more indelible. Just days after the teamsters struck in April, trainloads of Negroes began streaming into Chicago. Shootings, knifings, and stonings soon paralyzed the city's commerce. Showers of bricks and stones greeted the black drivers as they attempted to deliver milk, coal, and other merchandise; and the injuries inflicted were recorded in the box scores of "strike victims" that Chicago's newspapers printed as front-page news. Pummeled with brass knuckles, "right ear almost torn off"; "injured by bricks, severely bruised and cut, struck on head and left leg with clubs during riot at Rush and Michigan"; struck on the head by a brick "said to have been thrown from the tenth floor"; beaten into unconsciousness, "three shovels broken over his head"—these were but a few of the injuries.

Fearing that such acts of violence would erupt into full-scale rioting, the city council enacted an order requesting the corporation counsel to file an opinion "as to whether the importation of hundreds of Negro workers is not a menace to the community and should not be restricted." The employers' association responded by consenting not to import any more Negroes, though it refused to discharge any of its black drivers.

Not only was the employers' gesture futile, but its very futility indicated that new elements had entered into the relationship between labor conflict and racial violence in Chicago. In this dispute, unlike the stockyards strike of eight months before, the hostility of striking whites toward strikebreaking Negroes had been generalized into hatred for the black race as a whole; any Negro was a potential target. Now, no longer were mob assaults limited to just one district; presaging the 1919 riot, racial violence had spread throughout the city but it was especially prevalent in the blue-collar neighborhood to the west of the black belt. "You have the Negroes in here to fight us," the teamsters' president told the employers' association, "and we answer that we have the right to attack them wherever found." Moreover, as Graham Taylor of the Chicago Commons settlement house observed, the "great intensity of class consciousness" in the teamsters' strike forged a firm bond between strikers and their families, neighbors, other wage-earners, and even the little children who supported them by hurling rocks at the strikebreakers. The focus of their violence was facilitated by the distinguishing physical character-istic of the Negroes—the black skin that represented so many varieties of evil and danger to them. Finally, the besieged Negroes were determined to defend them-selves, unlike 1904 when, unarmed, they had generally fled.

Some of the non-strikebreaking black victims were mistaken for non-union drivers. One of these was a dishwasher, who was kicked and beaten and his head smashed through a car window; when policemen came to his aid, the crowd began to yell: "That's what they will all get." Another was a porter who was attacked by a crowd that ran after him screaming that he was a scab; beaten into unconscious-ness, the porter died several days later of a fractured skull. The only offense committed by other Negroes, however, was that their color was "black and dis-pleasing." A Negro medical student, for example, was pummeled to the ground. Even a black union member was pelted with rocks; when he called out to his attackers that his employer was not involved in the strike, one of them replied that being a "nigger" he deserved a beating anyhow.

Perhaps there was no better example of white solidarity during these turbulent weeks than the sympathy strike conducted by hundreds of grade-school students. Protesting the delivery of coal at school buildings by black strikebreakers employed by the Peabody Coal Company, the students not only hurled missiles at the drivers but organized a "skilled pupils' " union with a kindergarten local affiliated. "We are on strike. Hurrah for the unions," read the paper badges of the students who threw bricks, stones, and pieces of wood at those classmates refusing to join the picket line. Many parents supported the strike, some asserting that they would never permit their children to return so long as scabs continued to deliver coal. They also sanctioned violence. One father, for example, told a judge that his son was "amply justified" in flinging coal at Negro drivers because these men were "black" and "nonunion." Even teachers encouraged the strikers. "I will invite the pupils to strike," one principal allegedly said, "if the dirty 'niggers' deliver coal at this school."

Negroes appeared resolved to defend themselves. When a white man made a crude remark about a black strikebreaker who was standing at the rear of a custom house, the Negro leaped down from the platform and leveled a revolver at the white. "Why, I was only joking," the white man quickly said. "You're just white trash and I ought to shoot you anyhow," replied the Negro.

It was this resolve that helped to precipitate unrestrained violence in mid-May. An 11-year-old boy died on May 16, after two Negro strikebreakers, leaving work at the Peabody Coal Company, had fired into a group of jeering children. Hysteria swept the neighborhood as enraged mobs hunted for Negroes. White anger swelled menacingly, so that black people feared to appear in the streets. Then, on the evening of May 20, rioting surged out of control. Parading down the streets and proclaiming their intention of "driving the blacks off the face of the earth," whites met armed resistance. Surrounded by attackers, another strikebreaker from

Peabody fired and fatally wounded a white man. The next day, as the rioting spread to other districts, police were unable to prevent the outbreaks and disturbances that grew bloodier as night approached. That evening a Negro was murdered by a white bartender in a saloon brawl, and other black men were dragged off streetcars. In the black belt, where Negroes marched the streets crying for "justice" and "down with the white trash," white men were chased and beaten. When the violence subsided on May 22, two people were dead and a dozen severely injured. It had been, as Allan Spear has written, "the bloodiest racial conflict in the city before the riot of 1919." Labor conflict, it was readily apparent, could easily escalate into racial violence.

The image of black people as a scab race no doubt continued to fester in the minds of white workers, even though Negroes did not reinforce it again until 1916. Pullman car porters and other black men and women replaced striking railroad car cleaners in the spring of that year. Fed in dining cars and sleeping in the Pullmans, the Negroes, according to the employer, were hired "not as strikebreakers, but with the understanding that their positions would be permanent," and they were "proving themselves much more efficient in every way than the cleaners who left. . . ." Most of these workers stayed on the job after breaking the strike.

In 1916, too, as a result of increased meat production to feed Europe's armies and a sharp decline in immigration, the lines of men waiting outside the stockyards each morning evaporated. "In the past years," Mary McDowell wrote a friend, "we have seen three to five thousand men and women waiting every morning for work and have been told that while there was such a surplus of labor a raise in wages could not be given to the unskilled workers." Surely, this must change.

Union leaders realized not only that the moment was propitious to organize all the stockyards workers, but that in this mass-production and minutely specialized industry some sort of industrial unionism would be required to do it. Under the leadership of John Fitzpatrick, president of the Chicago Federation of Labor (C.F.L.), and William Z. Foster, an organizer for the railway carmen's union, all the trade unions in the yards, with the exception of the A.M.C.B.W., united in July 1917 to form the Stockyards Labor Council (S.L.C.).

Next to persuading the nationals to lay aside jurisdictional jealousies for the benefit of central organization, the S.L.C.'s most formidable problem was that of unionizing Negro workers, of whom there were between 10,000 and 12,000 in the yards, or about one-quarter of the total laboring force. The C.F.L. asked Samuel Gompers to provide a method by which the S.L.C. could grant membership to Negroes without violating the constitutions, rituals, and other color bars of the nationals. Gompers' solution was that the A.F.L. would award federal charters to all-Negro locals, if no serious objections were raised by the nationals. Despite the established unworkability of federal locals, and the cries of "Jim Crow" that they would arouse, the S.L.C. confidently embarked on its campaign to organize Negroes. To assist in the drive, the Illinois coal miners donated two black organizers, and others later joined the team.

The yards, rather than the steel mills or other mass-production industries, were the focus of the unions' efforts to solicit Negro membership. Not only were the packers by far the major employers of Negro labor but, nearly as significant, success in organizing Negroes in the yards was generally considered a gauge of the unions' ability to organize them in any of Chicago's industries. Moreover, the slaughtering and meat-packing industry was the city's largest, employing over one-eighth of Chicago's wage-earners and ranking first in value added by manufacture and total value of its products.

A mass organization drive began in September 1917, with parades, smokers, hall and street meetings, and the distribution of 50,000 pieces of literature in various languages. "Brother's [sic] in all the Packing Houses. . . . BE MEN—JOIN THE UNION" read the handbills summoning black workers to a union meeting. The strike failures of 1894 and 1904 haunted union members, and it was rumored that the packers wanted a strike and had imported an enormous labor reserve of Negroes to break it and crush unionization. And, indeed, it seemed to be a fact, though a much disputed one, that employers were importing black laborers from the rural South.

On March 30, 1918, however, through the intervention of the federal government, Judge Samuel Alschuler, who had been appointed U.S. Administrator for Adjustment of Labor Differences in Certain Packing House Industries, awarded the eight-hour day and other benefits to workers in the yards. Such gains, the workers felt, were a tremendous union victory. Fitzpatrick jubilantly proclaimed to an excited crowd of thousands assembled in a Chicago public park: "It's a new day, and out in God's sunshine, you men and you women, black and white, have not only an eight-hour day but you are on an equality." Union membership soared in the weeks following these awards.

"I suppose you have heard from official sources that the Stockyards will soon be a hundred percent organized," Ida Glatt, an officer of the Women's Trade Union League, happily recounted to Agnes Nestor, former president of the League. "From intimate connection with the white and colored English-speaking women workers I can tell you firsthand that the women are just rolling into the organization." The unions' secretaries "do nothing but take in applications from morning to midnight." Negro men and women were also participating in the meetings of the S.L.C.

Not everybody shared Miss Glatt's optimism. Irene Goins, a Negro who was actively organizing in the yards, expressed her disappointment: "My people . . . know so little about organized labor that they have had a great fear of it, and for that reason the work of organizing has proceeded more slowly than I anticipated." Another black organizer, John Riley, echoed her disappointment.

The urgent need to organize black workers increased in the fall of 1918. The war was drawing to a close, and accompanying demobilization would be the termination not only of government contracts but of the federal wartime agencies which had supported union recognition, collective bargaining, and non-discrimination against union members. It was imperative for labor to meet with greater solidarity the employers' efforts to re-establish the pre-war pattern of industrial relations. Unorganized Negroes, union leaders feared, would be pawns of the employers in the future struggle. Southern Negroes continued to pour into the city; in recent years the Negro population in Chicago had more than doubled, increasing from 50,000 to over 100,000 while the Negro industrial force had risen from 27,000 to almost 70,000. In 1910, black men comprised just 6 percent of the laboring force in the yards; ten years later, they comprised 32 percent. The black laboring force of every packing house, reported Dr. George E. Haynes of the Labor Department's Division of Negro Economics, had increased rapidly from three to five times over the level of January 1916.

In addition, the image of Negro strikebreakers had not dimmed during the war. Hotel keepers, for example, locked out waiters in April 1918, hiring Negroes in their place. "This is a deliberate attempt to start a race war," Fitzpatrick wrote Secretary of Labor William B. Wilson. Wilson's conciliator in Chicago agreed that the dispute was "full of danger because of the Race problem." Negroes also broke strikes of egg candlers and garment workers.

With the Armistice, as the forces of demobilization touched all levels of the economy, the battle lines between employers and workers hardened. But the peace was also portentous to black Chicagoans whose employment security was in large measure attributable to the government's demands for war products. That spring, the prospect of a peacetime labor market disturbed people who were usually the first to feel the effects of the immediate postwar unemployment. Negro women were the first to be discharged; Negro men and white women soon followed. At the stockyards' National Box Company, where half of the workers and almost all the unskilled workers were black, Negro women were discharged after a pay raise for women workers. "After they gave that," a black woman complained, "there came a whole lot of white ladies." This woman, who wanted to remain at National Box, was told she could stay if she were willing to do the gruelling work of loading trucks formerly done by men. "If you don't want to do that," her foremen told her, "you will have to go home, because they are going to have all whites."

Upwards of 10,000 Negroes were unemployed in early May 1919. Employment in the sotckyards had fallen from over 65,000 in January to 50,000. Returning soldiers aggravated this situation, and thousands of black troops were mustered out in or near Chicago, many of them southerners who had little desire to return home. A. L. Jackson of the Wabash Avenue YMCA pleaded with the Chicago industrialists to hire these veterans; and in boosting their qualifications he even invoked the nativism so prevalent in 1919: "These boys are all good Americans. There are no slackers, no hyphens among them." To alleviate this distress, the Chicago Urban League distributed portions of the labor surplus to Battle Creek, Flint, and Detroit, and to areas of Wisconsin and Illinois, but it could place only a few hundred compared to the many thousands of placements it had made during the war. Even during the prosperous summer months of 1919, black Chicagoans doubtless realized that during a labor depression they were the most expendable, and many did not want to jeopardize their tenuous positions by unionizing.

In early June the stockyards unions kicked off their most spirited organization drive since 1917. Following a parade and the distribution of campaign buttons on

June 8, John Kikulski, an organizer of butchers and meat cutters, outlined the goals of "this great campaign," in which "Polish, Irish, Lithuanian, and in fact every race, color, creed, and nationality is to be included. . . ." "While there will be varied differences in our physical makeup and thoughts," he continued, "there is one thing which we all hold in common, and that is our right to a living wage, and our rights in the pursuit of happiness as American citizens. . . ." In other attempts to organize black workers, and to convince them that labor's cause was also theirs, the C.F.L. devoted portions of its newspaper, *The New Majority*, to the Negro. The organ of the A.M.C.B.W., the *Butcher Workman*, likewise published pointed appeals to black workers. An article authored by a Negro woman appeared in the May issue. Entitled "The Negro's Greatest Opportunity as I See It," it was both a slashing attack on race prejudice and an announcement that the A.M.C.B.W. had "broken down the bars and . . . and invited us in." "Therefore, the black man should take advantage of this great opportunity [membership in the A.M.C.B.W.], so that he may be the instrument through which discriminiation may be driven out of this country—the home of the free and the home of the brave."

White and Negro workers paraded through the black belt on Sunday, July 6, and congregated in a playground near the yards. Brass bands led the way, and the marchers waved miniature American flags and carried placards, on one of which was printed: "The bosses think because we are of different colors and different nationalities that we should fight each other. We're going to fool them and fight for a common cause—a square deal for all." Union leaders delivered speeches at the playground. The seven speakers, of whom three were Negroes, did not betray the advertised purpose of the meeting—to organize Negro workers. "It does me good . . . to see such a checkerboard crowd," said J. W. Johnstone of the S.L.C. in welcoming the workers. "You are standing shoulder to shoulder as men, regardless of whether your face is black or white." John Kikulski then addressed the Polish in their native language to explain the need for "cooperation between blacks and whites."

Yet events just two days later belied the union leaders' rhetorical optimism. For on July 8, as a hot spell settled on the city, the most violent strike of the summer occurred. Two thousand employees of the Corn Products Refinery at Argo struck that morning, after the company's president had reneged on an agreement to hold a referendum on the closed shop. Anticipating trouble, the company had requisitioned a shipment of rifles and reinforced its special police force. The next day, during a fracas at the plant's entrance, armed guards shot and killed two strikers and seriously wounded eighteen others, one of whom soon died. A howling, stone-throwing mob of strikers' wives and daughters added to the turbulence by chasing the mayor of Argo, who was also superintendent of the company's machine shops, two miles to Chicago's city limits for threatening local grocers and druggists with discontinuance of the refinery's accounts if they extended credit to the strikers. The day after the shootings, the strikers and several thousand other Russian, Lithuanian, and Polish workers, mainly from the stockyards district, marched in a guard of honor at the funeral of the murdered men. During the funeral the rumor was rife that the company had asked numerous Negroes to "come back Monday and bring all of your friends." Argo's citizens feared that the introduction of Negroes would ignite another round of bloodshed; and on Monday refinery officials deputized a number of black men whom they strung out in a line in front of the plant. Their presence particularly incensed the strikers, and disorder erupted during which three strikers were wounded. A mother of four was shot in the leg and then beaten down from a trolley wire, but not before she had disengaged it in order to allow strikers to hurl bottles and bricks at a stalled streetcar filled with strikebreakers. Altogether 600 Negroes were brought in as strikebreakers in this bloody dispute; doubtless, the immigrant strikers in Argo and around the stockyards did not forget the Negroes' role.

A confrontation between labor and management in the yards was not long in coming. The first week of July witnessed the introduction of 300 mounted policemen to patrol the stockyards district, apparently to reverse the unions' organizing successes. As workers gathered around a union speaker, the police would ride into the crowd and disperse it. After protesting to the packers, 10,000 workers walked out on Friday, July 18. Although they returned to the stockyards Monday, it was evident that one of the most serious strikes in Chicago's history was imminent. That evening, union members voted to demand wage increases and other benefits, to submit these demands Saturday, July 16—just the day before the outbreak of the race riot—and to allow the packers forty-eight hours either to accept them or prepare for a strike. Ninety percent of the whites were unionized by that fateful weekend, while three-fourths of the Negroes, or 9,000 workers, were still outside the labor movement. What had retarded unionization among black workers?

Negroes in labor histories too often appear as faceless figures either to be praised, pitied, or damned. It is evident that black workers had very real reasons for resisting unionization. Many unions, of course, barred black craftsmen in order to control their portions of the labor market. These Negroes thus had to seek out unskilled positions, and it would be unreasonable for them then to unionize with common laborers, especially if they accrued employment benefits as non-union men. Unfortunately for the stockyards organization drive, neither all the A.F.L. national unions nor their members followed the lead of the C.F.L. Negroes were induced to join the federal locals recommended by Gompers, although some overzealous organizers enlisted black workers with the false promise that they would be transferred later to the locals of their respective crafts. A steamfitter expressed the dilemma of many of the Negro tradesmen in the yards: "I have worked as a steamfitter at the stockyards for fifteen years and tried to get into [all-white] Local 563 as have others of my race, but we have always been put off with some excuse until we gave up the attempt to get in." Other Negroes had become union members during labor disputes, only to be discharged after the strike was over. They felt betrayed, certain that unions were motivated not by a spirit of brotherhood but solely by self-interest. The exclusionist policies of southern unions had likewise alienated Negroes from the labor movement, and some of the migrants to Chicago during the war had traveled there to escape the job control exercised by the unions.

Other migrants had peculiarly individual motives for not unionizing; some Negroes' life insurance policies were even voided if they did. Still others hesitated to join with whites who, during earlier labor depressions, had replaced them in domestic services, in the operation of barber shops, bootblack parlors, and contractual janitorial services, and in cooking, waiting tables, and dishwashing.

Negroes who traveled from the South to work in Chicago's industries brought with them not only a rural psychology but, in many cases, a total ignorance of strikes and unions. Fully 90 percent of the northern-born black workers in the yards, for excample, wore the union button, but few of the migrants did. Other Negroes, however, were fully aware of how Negroes broke strikes, undermined wages, and reduced the white workers' bargaining power. Strikebreaking presented an opportunity to enter industries which formerly had been closed. Even if a Negro strikebreaker were employed at less than the union scale, he was generally paid more than he was accustomed to earning; and by refusing to go out on strike with whites, Negroes received promotions into more highly skilled fields which had not been previously open to them.

The readjustment from life on the farm to that of industrial wage-earner was so immense that Negro migrants often followed the advice of black leaders. Their advice was understandably more influential than that of white union members. A frequent source of counsel was the Urban League, the main employment agency in the black belt. The Urban League took a pragmatic view of unions, although the officers of the local branch were clearly cognizant of the danger of post-war labor conflict along racial lines. Robert E. Park, a white sociologist and president of the Chicago Urban League, feared that all the Negroes' perplexities after the Armistice would be "intimately bound up with the labor scene"; and, as early as November 1917, the League announced that it "would welcome any effort tending to an amicable settlement of this vital problem." It met with officers of the Chicago and Illinois Federations of Labor, and it advised the Women's Trade Union League during its campaign to organize Negro women in the yards, but these efforts accomplished little toward persuading unions to lower their color bars. The dilemma of the League, as of many Negro leaders, was that though it recognized the exigency of unionizing Negroes, it left little doubt that the first move had to be the unions' obliteration of all discriminatory membership policies. The League sought to plot a course between management and organized labor. For two reasons, however, it was more often on management's side: the unions did not lower their color bars, and Chicago's large industries could provide immediate opportunities for the migrants.

The attitude of Chicago's most widely circulated Negro newspaper, the *Defender*, paralleled that of the Urban League. "We have arrayed ourselves on the side of capital to a great extent," the *Defender* proclaimed in an editorial in late April 1919, "yet capital has not played square with us; it has used us as strikebreakers, then when the calm came turned us adrift." If it were to the race's "economic, social and political interest to join with organized labor now, it should not make the least bit of difference what was their attitude toward us in the past, even if that past was as recent as yesterday. If they extend the olive branch in good faith accept it today." In July, however, after the A.F.L. convention had done nothing to remove the exclusion clauses of some A.F.L. unions or the segregation clauses of others, the *Defender* complained: "Unwillingly we assume the role of strikebreakers. The unions drive us to it."

To most leaders in the black belt, exclusion and segregation were the roots of the problem. There was also a widespread attitude that employers were the Negroes' natural allies and that they, rather than unions, provided security and industrial opportunity. Negroes have found, Booker T. Washington wrote in 1913, that "the friendship and confidence of a good white man, who stands well in the community, are a valuable asset in time of trouble." For this reason, the Negro worker "does not always understand, and does not like, an organization [that is, a union] which seems to be founded on a sort of impersonal enmity to the man by whom he is employed. . . ." Mary McDowell recalled an example of the personal relationship which Negroes often believed existed between employer and employee. During the campaign to organize the stockyards, an organizer approached a newly-arrived Negro and explained to him the advantages of union membership. "It all sounds pretty good to me," the Negro replied, "but what does Mr. Armour think about it?"

Union leaders accused the packers of subsidizing black clergymen and other professional people, YMCAs, and welfare clubs to spread anti-union propaganda. Certain clergymen, among them unprincipled labor recruiters, did urge their parishioners to spurn union advances. Others, however, endorsed the endeavors of unions that were organizing without regard to race, arguing that union membership would help to minimize racial conflict; and among these were two of the city's most eminent ministers, L. K. Williams of the Olivet Baptist Church and John F. Thomas of Ebeneezer Baptist. In addition, black clerical associations, such as the Colored Baptist Ministers' Alliance and the AME Sunday School Convention, invited union organizers to use their groups as forums for outlining labor's views.

The YMCA, where at least two packers, Wilson and Armour, financed "efficiency clubs," was anti-union. Armour also gave an annual membership to the YMCA to each black worker after his first year of employment. Negroes at the club meetings, J. W. Johnstone charged, were "lectured and taught that the thing they have to do is to keep out of organized labor."

But were ministers and the YMCA witting instruments of the packers? Dr. George E. Haynes thought not. It was obvious, he reported after investigating the origins of the race riot, that certain black leaders were adamantly opposed to workers unionizing, "but there was no evidence that could be obtained that they were influenced to these opinions or used as tools of the employers."

It is not so difficult to determine the motives of Richard E. Parker, a notorious anti-union propagandist. Parker admitted that in 1916 he had distributed 20,000 handbills to "All Colored Working Men in the Stockyards," warning them not to "Join Any White Man's Union." He claimed that he had paid for these himself because of his "personal interest" in his race; but he also acknowledged that he had gone to the South in 1916 while working for several packing and steel companies, and had "imported more Negroes than any man in Chicago." Parker edited a newspaper in which he advised black workers not to join the established unions but to join the American Unity Labor Union, which he had founded and of which he was business agent. A card from his union, he boasted, would secure employment for Negroes in the building trades, steel mills, and stockyards. Parker was a demagogue and he was doubtless on the payroll of employers, but he might also have been working in the race's interest, as he perceived it. Because "the Negro happened to be born black," he wrote, "the Unions have labelled him inferior." As a result, they barred him not only from membership but also from apprenticeships and the chance to secure work in skilled jobs. "For this reason we formed the American Unity Labor Union," for we could expect "fairness from no local."

Above all, it was conflict between the white rank and file and their black counterparts that retarded unionization. Labor historians have wasted much energy debating the A.F.L.'s attitudes toward black workers, when the truly bitter, and functional, racial animosities were not at the national but at the shop level. Unions have too often directed their recriminations at anti-union Negroes, rather than conceding their own inability to control the racial hatreds of white members. Evidence of racial conflict at the shop level is scarce and difficult to find, but it is extant; and in few places was such conflict more pervasive than in the stockyards in 1919, where just a month before the race riot there was a series of spontaneous walkouts, all racially inspired.

"Well, are you going to join or not," the smokehouse floor steward impatiently asked the black worker. "No, I would rather quit than join the union." "If you don't join tomorrow, these men won't work with you." "Fuck you." "God Damn you." Then the black man drew a knife from the pocket of his overalls. "He was big enough to eat me . . . ," the floor steward recalled, so "I called for help." The union men, "practically all of them are in the union except . . . these three colored fellows," came to his assistance. It was after this encounter that the white men in the smokehouse walked out, declaring that they could no longer work with non-union blacks. Similar confrontations were occurring simultaneously in various shops at the yards. Leaving dead hogs hanging on the conveyor belt or after only partially dressing the beef, hundreds of workers informed their foremen that black men on the floor were non-union, and that they would not return until these men were discharged or made to join the union.

"We are paying the union and wearing the buttons," one member complained, "and they are getting just as much." Other members echoes this resentment. "Fuck the Union," a black worker had reportedly told one of them. "I am making as much money as you are. What is the use of joing the Union?" Another grievance was that Negroes allegedly received preferential treatment, such as not being docked for reporting late or punished for stealing meat.

Negro as well as white members accused certain black men who used abusive language and incited violence of being anti-union agitators. The only task of "Heavy" Williams, they said, was to bring new workers from the company employment office to the cattle-killing floor, and "he brings up all non-union men and keeps the non-union men from joining the union." " 'Let me tell you,' " he would instruct the new men, " 'when they get after you about this union, don't you join it. . . . You stay out. If you don't you won't be here long.' " Williams also fought with whites, among them "Tubs," whom he threatened to "split open" with a meat cleaver. Williams had been a union member; so had Joseph Hodge, until a black friend of his had been hit over the head with a blunt instrument. Hodge continually cast such vicious and obscene slurs at the union that whites warned that he would "agitate a race riot or perhaps . . . get killed." Another anti-union Negro stabbed a white man on the killing floor after damning the union and branding black union men "a lot of bastards," "a lot of white folks' niggers."

Negroes frequently replaced striking whites in the stockyards that summer. In the hair house, for example, the all-white union of spinners struck, and Negroes from various other departments were recruited to fill their jobs. Few whites in the yards could have been unaware of the strike; for, as one man reported, "at the noon hour these colored men are looking out of windows and doors, and these [white] men come out for lunch, and . . . it creates a dis-harmony and hard feelings among the races. . . ." It was also a fact, however, that sometimes Negroes who joined unions were also discharged.

Organizers and black workers had difficulty communicating with each other, and this was a major cause not only of friction but also of the unwillingness of Negroes to unionize. Numerous floor stewards and union committeemen spoke English poorly, if at all. How, a non-English-speaking Polish steward was asked by an interpreter, did he expect to explain the benefits of unions to black workers. He did not even try, he said, but there was a Negro committeeman who "talks the best way he can." Well, then, did he instruct the Negro committeeman? "I don't tell him nothing," he replied. "They have got to get it for themselves."

A Negro who did not "get it," however, would have "it made hot for him," with his "face pushed in" or bricks hurled at him. Frustration as well as racial bitterness provoked these acts of violence. "When I was coming in [to work]," recounted a Negro, "6 or 7 or 8 Polocks grabbed a colored fellow out there, and carried him on the [union] wagon, and said 'you son-of-a-bitch, you will join the union,' and made him go up, and one had him by this arm, and the other by this arm, and one fellow had him by the neck. . . ."

Black resistance—and, with it, interracial abuse and violence—only mounted in the weeks before the riot. "Fuck the union, fuck you in the [union] button," raged a black worker. Knives and revolvers proliferated on both sides. 'If I catch you outside I will shoot you," a Negro warned an insulting committeeman. Yet the unions became even more aggressive. "Where is your button?" demanded an organizer. "I ain't got non on," was the angry reply, "but [if I did] I would put it on the end of my prick."

Union leaders claimed that there was no racism involved in this bitterness—that it was simply a labor matter. But it was obviously much more than that by late July 1919; the two were inseparably fused. The Irish, Polish, Lithuanian, and other workers who clashed with Negroes in other spheres of human relations had their racial antagonisms reinforced if not initiated at the stockyards and in other industries. Labor in Chicago, moreover, was possessed of an intense class consciousness; anyone who was not with it was against it—and the black workers were notoriously not with it. The hostility was so intense that, as in 1905, hatred of Negro "scabs" could be generalized into hatred of an entire race. The factors retarding unionization—Negro distrust of unions and white workers, the economic advantages to be accrued as non-union workers, the manipulation of black workers by management, and, above all, the hatred of black workers by whites arising from racial antipathy and conditioned by strikebreaking and by other anti-union acts—left a legacy of twenty-five years of violence and helped produce a bloody race riot in 1919.

13   Carey McWilliams

BLOOD ON THE PAVEMENTS

On Thursday evening, June 3, 1943, the Alpine Club—made up of youngsters of Mexican descent—held a meeting in a police substation in Los Angeles. Usually these meetings were held in a nearby public school but, since the school was closed, the boys had accepted the invitation of a police captain to meet in the substation. The principal business of the meeting, conducted in the presence of the police captain, consisted in a discussion of how gang-strife could best be avoided in the neighborhood. After the meeting had adjourned, the boys were taken in squad cars to the street corner nearest the neighborhood in which most of them lived. The squad cars were scarcely out of sight, when the boys were assaulted, not by a rival "gang" or "club," but by hoodlum elements in the neighborhood. Of one thing the boys were sure: their assailants were not of Mexican descent.

Earlier the same evening a group of eleven sailors, on leave from their station in Los Angeles, were walking along the 1700 block on North Main Street in the center of one of the city's worst slum areas. The surrounding neighborhood is predominantly Mexican. On one side of the street the dirty brick front of a large brewery hides from view a collection of ramshackle Mexican homes. The other side of the street consists of a series of small bars, boarded-up store fronts, and small shops. The area is well off the beaten paths and few servicemen found their way this far

From *North from Mexico: The Spanish-speaking People of the United States* (New York: Greenwood Press, Inc., 1968), pp. 244-58. Reprinted by permission.

north on Main Street. As they were walking along the street, so they later stated, the sailors were set upon by a gang of Mexican boys. One of the sailors was badly hurt; the others suffered minor cuts and bruises. According to their story, the sailors were outnumbered about three to one.

When the attack was reported to the nearest substation, the police adopted a curious attitude. Instead of attempting to find and arrest the assailants, fourteen policemen remained at the station after their regular duty was over for the night. Then, under the command of a detective lieutenant, the "Vengeance Squad," as they called themselves, set out "to clean up" the gang that had attacked the sailors. But—miracle of miracles!—when they arrived at the scene of the attack they could find no one to arrest—not a single Mexican—on their favorite charge of "suspicion of assault." In itself this curious inability to find anyone to arrest—so strikingly at variance with what usually happened on raids of this sort—raises an inference that a larger strategy was involved. For the raid accomplished nothing except to get the names of the raiding officers in the newspapers and to whip up the anger of the community against the Mexican population, which may, perhaps, have been the reason for the raid. . . .

Thus began the so-called "Zoot-Suit Race Riots" which were to last, in one form or another, for a week in Los Angeles.

1. THE TAXICAB BRIGADE

Taking the police raid as an official cue,—a signal for action,—about two hundred sailors decided to take the law into their own hands on the following night. Coming down into the center of Los Angeles from the Naval Armory in Chavez Ravine (near the "Chinatown" area), they hired a fleet of twenty taxicabs. Once assembled, the "task force" proceeded to cruise straight through the center of town en route to the east side of Los Angeles where the bulk of the Mexicans reside. Soon the sailors in the lead-car sighted a Mexican boy in a zoot-suit walking along the street. The "task force" immediately stopped and, in a few moments, the boy was lying on the pavement, badly beaten and bleeding. The sailors then piled back into the cabs and the caravan resumed its way until the next zoot-suiter was sighted, whereupon the same procedure was repeated. In these attacks, of course, the odds were pretty uneven: two hundred sailors to one Mexican boy. Four times this same treatment was meted out and four "gangsters,"—two seventeen-year-old youngsters, one nineteen, and one twenty-three,—were left lying on the pavements for the ambulances to pick up.

It is indeed curious that in a city like Los Angeles, which boasts that it has more police cars equipped with two-way radio than any other city in the world (Los Angeles *Times*, September 2, 1947), the police were apparently unable to intercept a caravan of twenty taxicabs, loaded with two hundred uniformed, yelling, bawdy sailors, as it cruised through the downtown and east-side sections of the city. At one point the police did happen to cross the trail of the caravan and the officers were apparently somewhat embarrassed over the meeting. For only nine of the sailors were taken into custody and the rest were permitted to continue on their merry way. No charges, however, were ever preferred against the nine.

Their evening's entertainment over, the sailors returned to the foot of Chavez Ravine. There they were met by the police and the Shore Patrol. The Shore Patrol took seventeen of the sailors into custody and sent the rest up to the ravine to the Naval Armory. The petty officer who had led the expedition, and who was not among those arrested, gave the police a frank statement of things to come. "We're out to do what the police have failed to do," he said; "we're going to clean up this situation. . . . Tonight [by then it was the morning of June fifth] the sailors may have the marines along."

The next day the Los Angeles press pushed the war news from the front page as it proceeded to play up the pavement war in Los Angeles in screaming headlines. "Wild Night in L.A.–Sailor Zooter Clash" was the headline in the *Daily News*. "Sailor Task Force Hits L.A. Zooters" bellowed the *Herald-Express*. A suburban newspaper gleefully reported that "zoot-suited roughnecks fled to cover before a task force of twenty taxicabs." None of these stories, however, reported the slightest resistance, up to this point, on the part of the Mexicans.

True to their promise, the sailors were joined that night, June fifth, by scores of soldiers and marines. Squads of servicemen, arms linked, paraded through downtown Los Angeles four abreast, stopping anyone wearing zoot-suits and ordering these individuals to put away their "drapes" by the following night or suffer the consequences. Aside from a few half-hearted admonitions, the police made no effort whatever to interfere with these heralds of disorder. However, twenty-seven Mexican boys, gathered on a street corner, were arrested and jailed that evening. While these boys were being booked "on suspicion" of various offenses, a mob of several hundred servicemen roamed the downtown section of a great city threatening members of the Mexican minority without hindrance or interference from the police, the Shore Patrol, or the Military Police.

On this same evening, a squad of sailors invaded a bar on the east side and carefully examined the clothes of the patrons. Two zoot-suit customers, drinking a beer at a table, were peremptorily ordered to remove their clothes. One of them was beaten and his clothes were torn from his back when he refused to comply with the order. The other—they were both Mexicans—doffed his "drapes" which were promptly ripped to shreds. Similar occurrences in several parts of the city that evening were sufficiently alarming to have warranted some precautionary measures or to have justified an "out-of-bounds" order. All that the police officials did, however, was to call up some additional reserves and announce that any Mexicans involved in the rioting would be promptly arrested. That there had been no counterattacks by the Mexicans up to this point apparently did not enter into the police officers' appraisal of the situation. One thing must be said for the Los Angeles police: it is above all consistent. When it is wrong, it is consistently wrong; when it makes a mistake, it will be repeated.

By the night of June sixth the police had worked out a simple formula for action. Knowing that wherever the sailors went there would be trouble, the police simply followed the sailors at a conveniently spaced interval. Six carloads of sailors cruised down Brooklyn Avenue that evening. At Ramona Boulevard, they stopped and beat up eight teen-age Mexicans. Failing to find any Mexican zoot-suiters in a bar on Indiana Street, they were so annoyed that they proceeded to wreck the establishment. In due course, the police made a leisurely appearance at the scene of the wreckage but could find no one to arrest. Carefully following the sailors, the police arrested eleven boys who had been beaten up on Carmelita Street; six more victims were arrested a few blocks further on, seven at Ford Boulevard, six at Gifford Street—and so on straight through the Mexican east-side settlements. Behind them came the police, stopping at the same street corners "to mop up" by arresting the injured victims of the mob. By morning, some forty-four Mexican boys, all severely beaten, were under arrest.

2. OPERATION "DIXIE"

The stage was now set for the really serious rioting of June seventh and eighth. Having featured the preliminary rioting as an offensive launched by sailors, soldiers, and marines, the press now whipped public opinion into a frenzy by dire warnings that Mexican zoot-suiters planned mass retaliations. To insure a riot, the precise street corners were named at which retaliatory action was expected and the time of the anticipated action was carefully specified. In effect these stories announced a riot and invited public participation. "Zooters Planning to Attack More Servicemen," headlined the *Daily News*; "Would jab broken bottlenecks in the faces of their victims. . . . Beating sailors' brains out with hammers also on the program " Concerned for the safety of the Army, the Navy, and the Marine Corps, the *Herald-Express* warned that "Zooters . . . would mass 500 strong."

By way of explaining the action of the police throughout the subsequent rioting, it should be pointed out that, in June 1943, the police were on a bad spot. A man by the name of Beebe, arrested on a drunk charge, had been kicked to death in the Central Jail by police officers. Through the excellent work of an alert police commissioner, the case had finally been broken and, at the time of the riots, a police officer by the name of Compton Dixon was on trial in the courts. While charges of police brutality had been bandied about for years, this was the first time that a seemingly airtight case had been prepared. Shortly after the riots, a Hollywood police captain told a motion picture director that the police had touched off the riots "in order to give Dixie (Dixon) a break." By staging a fake demonstration of the alleged necessity for harsh police methods, it was hoped that the jury would acquit Dixon. As a matter of fact, the jury did disagree and on July 2, 1943, the charges against Dixon were dismissed.

On Monday evening, June seventh, thousands of *Angelenos*, in response to twelve hours' advance notice in the press, turned out for a mass lynching. Marching through the streets of downtown Los Angeles, a mob of several thousand soldiers, sailors, and civilians, proceeded to beat up every zoot-suiter they could find. Pushing its way into the important motion picture theaters, the mob ordered the management to turn on the house lights and then ranged up and down the aisles dragging Mexicans out of their seats. Street cars were halted while Mexicans, and some Filipinos and Negroes, were jerked out of their seats, pushed into the streets, and beaten with sadistic frenzy. If the victims wore zoot-suits, they were stripped of their clothing and left naked or half-naked on the streets, bleeding and bruised. Proceeding down Main Street from First to Twelfth, the mob stopped on the edge of the Negro district. Learning that the Negroes planned a warm reception for them, the mobsters turned back and marched through the Mexican east side spreading panic and terror.

Here is one of numerous eye-witness accounts written by Al Waxman, editor of *The Eastside Journal*:

> At Twelfth and Central I came upon a scene that will long live in my memory. Police were swinging clubs and servicemen were fighting with civilians. Wholesale arrests were being made by the officers.
>
> Four boys came out of a pool hall. They were wearing the zoot-suits that have become the symbol of a fighting flag. Police ordered them into arrest cars. One refused. He asked: "Why am I being arrested?" The police officer answered with three swift blows of the night-stick across the boy's head and he went down. As he sprawled, he was kicked in the face. Police had difficulty loading his body into the vehicle because he was one-legged and wore a wooden limb. Maybe the officer didn't know he was attacking a cripple.
>
> At the next corner a Mexican mother cried out, "Don't take my boy, he did nothing. He's only fifteen years old. Don't take him." She was struck across the jaw with a night-stick and almost dropped the two and a half year old baby that was clinging in her arms. . . .
>
> Rushing back to the east side to make sure that things were quiet here, I came upon a band of servicemen making a systematic tour of East First Street. They had just come out of a cocktail bar where four men were nursing bruises. Three autos loaded with Los Angeles policemen were on the scene but the soldiers were not molested. Farther down the street the men stopped a streetcar, forcing the motorman to open the door and proceeded to inspect the clothing of the male passengers. "We're looking for zoot-suits to burn," they shouted. Again the police did not interfere. . . . Half a block away . . . I pleaded with the men of the local police substation to put a stop to these activities. "It is a matter for the military police," they said.

Throughout the night the Mexican communities were in the wildest possible turmoil. Scores of Mexican mothers were trying to locate their youngsters and several hundred Mexicans milled around each of the police substations and the Central Jail trying to get word of missing members of their families. Boys came into the police stations saying: "Charge me with vagrancy or anything, but don't send me out there!" pointing to the streets where other boys, as young as twelve and thirteen years of age, were being beaten and stripped of their clothes. From affidavits which I helped prepare at the time, I should say that not more than half of the victims were actually wearing zoot-suits. A Negro defense worker, wearing a defense-plant identification badge on his workclothes, was taken from a street car and one of his eyes was gouged out with a knife. Huge half-page photographs, showing Mexican boys stripped of their clothes, cowering on the pavements, often bleeding profusely, surrounded by jeering mobs of men and women, appeared in all the Los Angeles newspapers. As Al Waxman most truthfully reported, blood had been "spilled on the streets of the city."

At midnight on June seventh, the military authorities decided that the local police were completely unable or unwilling to handle the situation, despite the fact that a thousand reserve officers had been called up. The entire downtown area of Los Angeles was then declared "out of bounds" for military personnel. This order immediately slowed down the pace of the rioting. The moment the Military Police and Shore Patrol went into action, the rioting quieted down. On June eighth the city officials brought their heads up out of the sand, took a look around, and began issuing statements. The district attorney, Fred N. Howser, announced that the "situation is getting entirely out of hand," while Mayor Fletcher Bowron thought that "sooner or later it will blow over." The chief of police, taking a count of the Mexicans in jail, cheerfully proclaimed that "the situation has now cleared up." All agreed, however, that it was quite "a situation."

Unfortunely "the situation" had not cleared up; nor did it blow over. It began to spread to the suburbs where the rioting continued for two more days. When it finally stopped, the Eagle Rock *Advertiser* mournfully editorialized: "It is too bad the servicemen were called off before they were able to complete the job. . . . Most of the citizens of the city have been delighted with what has been going on." County Supervisor Roger Jessup told the newsmen: "All that is needed to end lawlessness is more of the same action as is being exercised by the servicemen!" While the district attorney of Ventura, an outlying county, jumped on the bandwagon with a statement to the effect that "zoot suits are an open indication of subversive character." This was also the opinion of the Los Angeles City Council which adopted a resolution making the wearing of zoot-suits a misdemeanor! On June eleventh, hundreds of handbills were distributed to students and posted on bulletin boards in a high school attended by many Negroes and Mexicans which read: "Big Sale. Second-Hand Zoot Suits. Slightly Damaged. Apply at Nearest U.S. Naval Station. While they last we have your Size."

3. WHEN THE DEVIL IS SICK . . .

Egging on the mob to attack Mexicans in the most indiscriminate manner, the press developed a fine technique in reporting the riots. "44 Zooters Jailed in Attacks on Sailors" was the chief headline in the *Daily News* of June seventh; "Zoot Suit Chiefs Girding for War on Navy" was the headline in the same paper on the following day. The moralistic tone of this reporting is illustrated by a smug headline in the Los Angeles *Times* of June seventh: "Zoot Suiters Learn Lesson in Fight with Servicemen." The riots, according to the same paper, were having "a cleansing effect." An editorial in the *Herald-Express* said that the riots "promise to rid the community of . . . those zoot-suited miscreants." While Mr. Manchester Boddy, in a signed editorial in the *Daily News* of June ninth excitedly announced that "the time for temporizing is past. . . . The time has come to serve notice that the City of Los Angeles will no longer be terrorized by a relatively small handful of morons parading as zoot suit hoodlums. To delay action *now* means to court disaster later on." As though there had been any "temporizing," in this sense, for the prior two years!

But once the Navy had declared the downtown section of Los Angeles "out of bounds," once the Mexican ambassador in Washington had addressed a formal inquiry to Secretary of State Hull, and once official Washington began to advise the local minions of the press of the utterly disastrous international effects of the riots, in short when the local press realized the consequences of its own lawless action, a great thunderous cry for "unity," and "peace," and "order" went forth. One after the other, the editors began to disclaim all responsibility for the riots which, two days before, had been hailed for their "salutary" and "cleansing" effect.

Thus on June eleventh the Los Angeles *Times*, in a pious mood, wrote that,

> at the outset, zoot-suiters were limited to no specific race; they were Anglo-Saxon, Latin and Negro. The fact that later on their numbers seemed to be predominantly Latin was in itself no indictment of that race at all. No responsible person at any time condemned Latin-Americans as such.

Feeling a twinge of conscience, Mr. Boddy wrote that "only a ridiculously small percentage of the local Mexican population is involved in the so-called gang demonstrations. Every true Californian has an affection for his fellow citizens of Mexican ancestry that is as deep rooted as the Mexican culture that influences our way of living, our architecture, our music, our language, and even our food." This belated discovery of the Spanish-Mexican cultural heritage of California was, needless to say, rather ironic in view of the fact that the ink was not yet dry on Mr. Boddy's earlier editorial in which he had castigated the Mexican minority as "morons." To appreciate the iron aspects of "the situation," the same newspapers that had been baiting Mexicans for nearly two years now began to extol them.

As might have been expected, this post-mortem mood of penitence and contrition survived just long enough for some of the international repercussions of the riots to quiet down. Within a year, the press and the police were back in the same old groove. On July 16, 1944, the Los Angeles *Times* gave front-page prominence to a curious story under the heading: "Youthful Gang Secrets Exposed." Indicating no source, identifying no spokesman, the story went on to say that "authorities of the Superior Court" had unearthed a dreadful "situation" among juvenile delinquents. Juveniles were using narcotics, marihuana, and smoking "reefers." Compelled to accept drug addiction, "unwilling neophytes" were dragooned into committing robberies and other crimes. Young girls were tatooed with various "secret cabalistic symbols" of gang membership. The high pompadours affected by the *cholitas*, it was said, were used to conceal knives and other "weapons." Two theories were advanced in the story by way of "explaining" the existence of these dangerous gangs: first, that "subversive groups" in Los Angeles had organized them; and, second, that "the gangs are the result of mollycoddling of racial groups." In view of the record, one is moved to inquire, what mollycoddling? by the police? by the juvenile authorities? by the courts? Backing up the news story, an editorial appeared in the *Times* on July eighteenth entitled: "It's Not a Nice Job But It Has To Be Done." Lashing out at "any maudlin and misguided sympathy for the 'poor juveniles,' " the editorial went on to say that "stern punishment is what is needed; stern and sure punishment. The police and the Sheriff's men *should be given every encouragement* to go after these young gangsters" (emphasis mine).

Coincident with the appearance of the foregoing news story and editorial, the Juvenile Court of Los Angeles entered a most remarkable order in its minutes on July 31, 1944. The order outlined a plan by which Mexican wards of the Juvenile Court, over sixteen years of age, might be turned over to the Atchison, Topeka, and Santa Fe Railroad for a type of contract-employment. A form of contract, between the parents of the youngsters and the railroad, was attached to the order. The contract provided that the ward was to work "as a track laborer" at 58 1/2 cents per hour; that $1.03 per day was to be deducted for board, $2.50 per month for dues in a hospital association, and 10 cents a day for laundry. It was also provided that one-half of the pay was to be turned over to the probation officers to be held in trust for the ward. That this order was specifically aimed at *Mexican* juveniles is clearly shown by the circumstance that the court, prior to approving the arrangement, had first secured its approval by a committee of "representative" leaders of the Mexican-American community.

4. THE STRANGE CASE OF THE SILK PANTIES

All of this, one will say,—the Sleepy Lagoon case, the riots, etc.,—belongs to the past. But does it? On the morning of July 21, 1946, a thirteen-year-old Mexican boy, Eugene Chavez Montenegro, Jr., was shot and killed by a deputy sheriff in Montebello Park on the east side of Los Angeles. The deputy sheriff later testified that he had been called to the area by reports of a prowler. On arriving at the scene, he had stationed himself near a window of the house in question and had played his flashlight on the window. A little later, he testified, "a man" lifted the screen on the window, crawled out, and ran past him. When the "man" failed to halt on order, he had shot him in the back. At the coroner's inquest, the same deputy also testified that he had seen another officer remove a pair of "silk panties" from the dead boy's pocket and that the boy was armed with "a Boy Scout's knife."

While incidents of this kind have been common occurrences in Los Angeles for twenty years, in this case the officers had shot the wrong boy. For it turned out that young Montenegro was an honor student at St. Alphonsus parochial school; that his parents were a highly respectable middle-class couple; and that the neighbors, Anglo-Americans as well as Mexicans, all testified that the boy had an excellent reputation. Accepting the officers' version of the facts, it was still difficult to explain why they had made no effort to halt the boy, who was five feet three inches tall, when he ran directly past them within arms' reach. Before the hearings were over, the "silk panties" story was exposed as a complete fake. Despite a gallant fight waged by Mr. and Mrs. Montenegro to vindicate the reputation of their son, nothing came of the investigation. "Raging Mother Attacks Deputy Who Slew Son" was the *Daily News* headline on the story of the investigation.

... On January 23, 1947, the attorney general of California ordered the removal of two police officers for the brutal beating of four Mexican nationals who, with eight hundred of their countrymen, had been brought to Oxnard to harvest the crops. ... On March 30, 1946, a private detective killed Tiofilo Pelagio, a Mexican national, in a cafe argument. ... On the same day affidavits were presented to the authorities that confessions from four Mexican boys, all minors, had been obtained by force and violence. ... Esther Armenta, sixteen years of age, complained to her mother that she was being mistreated by Anglo-American classmates in a Los Angeles junior high school. "They would spit on her," said Mrs. Catalina Armenta, the mother, "and call her a 'dirty Mex.' Esther would come home in tears and beg me to get her transferred." A few weeks later the girl was in juvenile court charged with the use of "bad language." She was then sent to the Ventura School for Girls, a so-called "correctional" institution. When Mrs. Armenta finally got permission to visit her daughter, in the presence of a matron, the girl had "black and blue marks on her arm" and complained that she had been whipped by one of the matrons. ... On April 10, 1946, Mrs. Michael Gonzales complained to the Federation of Spanish-American Voters that her daughter had been placed in the Ventura School without her knowledge or consent and that when she had protested this action she had been threatened with deportation by an official of the juvenile court. ... On the basis of a stack of affidavits, the San Fernando Valley Council on Race Relations charged on May 16, 1947, that the police had broken into Mexican homes without search warrants; that they had beaten, threatened, and intimidated Mexican juveniles; and that they were in the habit of making "wholesale roundups and arrests of Mexican-American boys without previous inquiry as to the arrested boys' connection—if any—with the crime in question." ... In 1946 a prominent official of the Los Angeles schools told me that she had been horrified to discover that, in the Belvedere district, Mexican-American girls, stripped of their clothing, were forced to parade back and forth, in the presence of other girls in the "gym," as a disciplinary measure. ...

5. THE POLITICS OF PREJUDICE

I reported the zoot-suit riots in Los Angeles for *PM* and *The New Republic* and had a hand in some of the hectic events of that memorable week. Following the June seventh rioting, I chaired a meeting of a hundred or more citizens at which an emergency committee was formed to bring about, if possible, a return to sanity in Los Angeles. That same evening we communicated with Attorney General Robert W. Kenny in San Francisco by telephone and urged him to induce Governor Earl Warren to appoint an official committee of inquiry. The next day the governor appointed a committee of five which included four names from a panel which I had submitted. The fifth member was the governor's own selection: Mr. Leo Carrillo. Mr. Carrillo, like the sheriff of Los Angeles, is a descendant of "an early California family." The committee immediately assembled in Los Angeles where Mr. Kenny presented to them a proposed report, with findings and recommendations, which I had prepared at his request. With some modifications, this report was adopted by the committee and submitted to the governor. Out of the work of our emergency committee there finally emerged, after a year of negotiation, the present-day Council of Civic Unity.

Praising the report of the governor's committee—which I had prepared—the Los Angeles *Times* devoted several harsh editorials to certain "reckless" individuals, myself included, who had suggested that "racial prejudice" might have had something to do with the riots! "When trouble arose," said the *Times* in an editorial of June 15, 1943, "through the depredations of the young gangs attired in zoot-suits, it was their weird dress and not their race which resulted in difficulties. That is a simple truth which no amount of propaganda will change." In the same editorial, the charges of unfairness which I had raised in connection with the Sleepy Lagoon case were branded as "distortions," "wild charges," and "inflammatory accusations" (charges later confirmed in minute detail by the District Court of Appeals).

When Mrs. Eleanor Roosevelt innocently remarked in her column that the zoot-suit riots were "in the nature of race riots," she was severely taken to task by the *Times* in an editorial of June eighteenth under the caption: "Mrs. Roosevelt Blindly Stirs Race Discord." Even the president of the Los Angeles Chamber of Commerce felt compelled to reply to Mrs. Roosevelt. "These so-called 'zoot-suit' riots," he said, "have never been and are not now in the nature of race riots. . . . At no time has the issue of race entered into consideration. . . . Instead of discriminating against Mexicans, California has always treated them with the utmost consideration."

The zoot-suit riots in Los Angeles were the spark that touched off a chain-reaction of riots across the country in midsummer 1943. Similar "zoot-suit" disturbances were reported in San Diego on June ninth; in Philadelphia on June tenth; in Chicago on June fifteenth; and in Evansville, Indiana, on June twenty-seventh. Between June sixteenth and August first, large-scale race riots occurred in Beaumont, Texas, in Detroit, and in Harlem. The Detroit riots of June 20-21 were the most disastrous riots in a quarter of a century. The swift, crazy violence of the Harlem riot resulted, in a few hours' time, in property damage totalling nearly a million dollars. The rapid succession of these violent and destructive riots seriously interfered with the war effort and had the most adverse international repercussions. The spark that ignited these explosions occurred in *El Pueblo de nuestra Senora La Reina de Los Angeles de Porciuncula*, founded by Felipe de Neve in 1781, settled by Mexican *pobladores*.

None of these disturbances had more serious international consequences than the zoot-suit riots. On April 20, 1943, President Roosevelt had held his historic meeting with President Camacho on the soil of Mexico. At the time the riots occurred, Mexico was our ally in the war against Germany, Italy, and Japan. Large-scale shipments of Mexican nationals had just begun to arrive in the United States to relieve the critical manpower shortage. "Our two countries," President Roosevelt had said, "owe their independence to the fact that your ancestors and mine held the same truths to be worth fighting for and dying for. Hidalgo and Juarez were men of the same stamp as Washington and Jefferson." President Camacho, replying to this toast, had said that "the negative memories" of the past were forgotten in the accord of today. And then in the largest city in the old Spanish borderland had come this explosion of hatred and prejudice against Spanish-speaking people.

In response to a request from the Mexican ambassador, Secretary of State Hull had asked Mayor Fletcher Bowron for an official explanation. With a perfectly straight face, the mayor had replied that the riots were devoid of any element of prejudice against persons of Mexican descent! The same edition of the newspapers that carried this statement also carried another statement by the mayor under a headline which read: "Mayor Pledges 2-Fisted Action, No Wrist Slap"—a reference to police action contemplated against the Mexican minority. On June ninth Mr. Churchill Murray, local representative of the coordinator of Inter-American Affairs, wired Mr. Rockefeller that the riots were "non-racial." "The frequency of Mexican names among the victims," he said, "was without actual significance." If all this were true, asked Dan G. Acosta in a letter to the Los Angeles press, "Why are we consistently called hoodlums? Why is mob action encouraged by the newspapers? Why did the city police stand around saying very nonchalantly that they could not intervene and even hurrahed the soldiers for their 'brave' action? Not until these questions are answered, will the Mexican population feel at ease." What the riots did, of course, was to expose the rotten foundations upon which the City of Los Angeles had built a papier-mache facade of "Inter-American Good Will" made up of fine-sounding Cinco de Mayo proclamations. During the riots, the press, the police, the officialdom, and the dominant control groups of Los Angeles were caught with the bombs of prejudice in their hands. One year before the riots occurred, they had been warned of the danger of an explosion. The riots were not an unexpected rupture in Anglo-Hispano relations but the logical end-product of a hundred years of neglect and discrimination.

The riots left a residue of resentment and hatred in the minds and hearts of thousands of young Mexican-Americans in Los Angeles. During the rioting, one Los Angeles newspaper had published a story to the effect that the *cholitas* and *pachucas* were merely cheap prostitutes, infected with venereal disease and addicted to the use of marihuana. Eighteen Mexican-American girls promptly replied in a letter which the metropolitan press refused to publish: "The girls in this meeting room consist of young girls who graduated from high school as honor students, of girls who are now working in defense plants because we want to help win the war, and of girls who have brothers, cousins, relatives and sweethearts in all branches of the American armed forces. We have not been able to have our side of the story told." The letter, with a picture of the girls, was published in Al Waxman's *Eastside Journal* on June 16, 1943. Still another group of Mexican-American girls,—real *pachucas* these—bitterly protested the story in another letter which the metropolitan press did not publish. These girls insisted that they should be examined, as a group, by an officially appointed board of physicians so that they could prove that they were virgins. Long after the riots, I have seen Mexican-American boys pull creased and wrinkled newspaper clippings from their wallets and exhibit this slanderous story with the greatest indignation. Four years have now passed since the riots, but the blood has not yet been washed from the pavements of Los Angeles.

VII

THE SIXTIES

The decade of the sixties began with a glow of optimism and ended with a gloom of despair and pessimism. The non-violence of the civil rights demonstrators met with violent, entrenched racism. The March on Washington signaled an end to one phase of the civil rights movement, and the beginning of a new and more militant orientation. In 1966 the cry of "Black Power" was heard, and many frightened whites turned away from any commitment that they had had to blacks. A domestic arms race began, as both blacks and whites armed for an apparently inevitable confrontation.

On college campuses, students rejected formalized liberal education in favor of a more politicized search for relevancy. Teach-ins, which began peacefully on March 24, 1965, at the University of Michigan, became passe by the end of the decade. Violent methods expressed the new radical position. The young rejected the "system" for its failures; the war in Vietnam continued; racism seemed as rampant as ever; and the destruction of national resources in the name of progress continued apace. For many, only revolution seemed capable of halting our social decay. The writings of Franz Fanon, Regis Debray, Eldridge Cleaver, Lenin, Mao, Marx and Marcuse became best sellers in a troubled land.

In a chain-like reaction, the ghettoes exploded following the assassination of Martin Luther King, and the campuses erupted following Kent State and the invasion of Cambodia. Report after report, from the McCone Commission findings on the Watts Riot (1965), the *Kerner Commission Report on Civil Disorders* (1968), the Walker Report on "The Violent Confrontation of Demonstrators and Police in the Parks and Streets of Chicago . . . " (1968), to finally, the *Skolnick Report to the National Commission on the Causes and Prevention of Violence* (1969) and Hugh Davis Graham's and Ted Robert Gurr's, *The History of Violence in America* (1969), was started, completed, published, and ignored. Attempts to fix causation and prescribe prevention did not prove far-reaching. Like their historical ancestors, these reports and the ritual of their making were a part of the anesthesia administered after a riot. However, the conclusions of these reports were not so quieting. The causes were found to be more profound than agitation by radicals and militant blacks. The Kerner Commission indicated that the underlying causes for the summer riots of 1967 were societal, and proposed a program of widespread reform. Nor did The Walker Report mince its words: The major source of violence in Chicago during the Democratic National Convention in 1968 was a "police riot."

Riots in the past swirled around someone else in strikes, political rallies and ghettoes; in the 1960's, they spread closer to the homes of Middle America. Great shock and outrage did not follow the violent deaths on the black campuses at Orangeburg and Jackson State, but general horror was the reaction to Kent State, the University of California at Berkeley, Kansas State, and the University of Wisconsin. Can or will the violence stop? Shrill voices demand: Meet violence with violence; more money for riot control; tanks; guns; mace; specially trained riot forces; kill or be killed; I'd rather be dead than Red; America, love it or leave it; Get the Panthers; Get Whitey. These acts and demands are those of Gustav Le Bon.

The history of the United States can be considered in terms of conflict. A careful reading of this book will reveal that a historical continuum or process is apparent in our history. There is a direct and important link between the colonial riots and those of the past five years. No area of the nation has been without civil strife. The past should not be studied solely for its own sake, but rather the past should be examined with an eye looking for evidence of those processes which still pervade our society.

Many of the earlier articles present narratives detailing a chain of events. Others put forward a sophisticated interpretation trying to find the causes of group violence. Both types of articles force a number of questions to be asked about right and wrong, and cause and effect. Again, the articles should have an impact on one's opinions of riots, rioters, and accounts written about them. Yet, the response of the governing bodies involved has been consistent from our colonial period: apply more force, equip and train better the police and militia for riot duty, appoint a commission to investigate and report on a riot's causes and consequences, and determine steps that will avoid a repetition. This reflex response has obviously not worked, but where are the new alternative actions one might expect to find? Should not the question of whether or not civil strife is bad for a society be asked? In the totality of our history, such questions have not been asked very often. Why is that? To hesitate asking the question could imply a fear of the answer.

Confronted by a riot, value systems, both societal and individual, are subjected to extreme duress. Frequently, they are turned topsy-turvy. The following two articles demonstrated the incredible complexity that is a riot, as well as how one value system opposes another even when reporting observed facts how they are defined. This is frequently vital for, under stress especially, once someone or something is defined (labelled) the action that follows is all but pre-ordained and becomes irreversible. The events of My Lai are a case in point.

Regarding the Newark riot, most characterized it a race riot. Alternatively, others saw it to be revolution with the establishment of a heroic, insurrectionary state. This is a complex assessment. But what of the now all but stereotyped instance of a man, who usually is black, being shot to death for looting, a crime against property? Perhaps, as in Newark, this is a six-pack of beer. What type of value system is this? The Commission Report poses, or causes to be posed, questions and dilemmas such as these.

Sheldon Wolin and John Schaar together form one of our outstanding reporting teams. They have written articles on campus disorders reflecting their unique backgrounds, both were professors at the University of California at Berkeley during the time of the "peoples' park" conflict. Their article on "The Battle of Berkeley" is, therefore, a first-hand account, written by two men who observed many of those events.

Suggested Further Readings

The Kerner *Report of the National Advisory Commission on Civil Disorders* (1968) is an excellent beginning source to use when studying urban, racial violence in the 1960's. Robert Conot, *Rivers of Blood, Years of Darkness* (1967) offers a new approach for riot analysis, in this case Watts, (1965); Paul Jacobs, *Prelude to Riot* (1966) gives another analysis, the end of which is the prevention of renewed disturbance. John Hersey turns his talent as a writer-reporter to reporting a single event in the Detroit Riots of 1967 in *The Algiers Motel Incident* (1968). A riot of less notoriety is considered in Frank P. Besag, *The Anatomy of A Riot: Buffalo, 1967* (1968). The role of the police in urban riots is the subject of an article by Robert M. Folgelson, "From Resentment to Confrontation: The Police, The Negroes, and the Outbreaks of the Nineteen-Sixties Riots," *Political Science Quarterly*, LXXXII (1968), 217-47. The Winter Issue of the *Journal of Social Issues* is devoted to "Ghetto Riots." To date, surprisingly little has been written on the disorders surrounding the early civil rights demonstration; Anthony Lewis, *Portrait of a Decade: The Second American Revolution* (1964), gives some idea of what it was like then. An excellent account of the Newark uprising is Tom Haydon's, "The Occupation of Newark," *The New York Review of Books*, August 24, 1967, pp. 14-24. Interestingly, the cover of this issue is a diagram for the building of a molotov cocktail. Think about it!

On riots and campus violence, novelist James A. Michener has written of *Kent State: What Happened and Why* (1971). I. F. Stone has written on this subject, also, but no one has performed a similar service for Jackson State. James Simon Kunen, in *The Strawberry Statement* (1968) deals with the disorders at Columbia University," in *The New American Review No. 5* (1969), 81-101. Sheldon S. Wolin and John Schaar's articles on Berkeley which appeared in the *New York Review of Books* are now available in *The Berkeley Rebellion and Beyond* (1970).

14   Report of the National Advisory Commission on Civil Disorders

PROFILE OF DISORDER: NEWARK

The last outburst in Atlanta occurred on Tuesday night, June 20. That same night, in Newark, N.J., a tumultuous meeting of the planning board took place. Until 4 a.m., speaker after speaker from the Negro ghetto arose to denounce the city's intent to turn over 150 acres in the heart of the central ward as a site for the State's new medical and dental college.

The growing opposition to the city administration by vocal black residents had paralyzed both the planning board and the board of education. Tension had been rising so steadily throughout the northern New Jersey area that, in the first week of June, Col. David Kelly, head of the state police, had met with municipal police chiefs to draw up plans for state police support of city police wherever a riot developed. Nowhere was the tension greater than in Newark.

Founded in 1666, the city, part of the Greater New York City port complex, rises from the salt marshes of the Passaic River. Although in 1967 Newark's population of 400,000 still ranked it 30th among American municipalities, for the past 20 years the white middle class had been deserting the city for the suburbs.

In the late 1950's, the desertions had become a rout. Between 1960 and 1967, the city lost a net total of more than 70,000 white residents. Replacing them in vast areas of dilapidated housing where living conditions, according to a prominent member of the County Bar Association, were so bad that "people would be kinder to their pets," were Negro migrants, Cubans, and Puerto Ricans. In 6 years, the city switched from 65 percent white to 52 percent Negro and 10 percent Puerto Rican and Cuban.

The white population, nevertheless, retained political control of the city. On both the city council and the board of education, seven of nine members were white. In other key boards, the disparity was equal or greater. In the central ward, where the medical college controversy raged, the Negro constituents and their white councilman found themselves on opposite sides of almost every crucial issue.

The municipal administration lacked the ability to respond quickly enough to navigate the swiftly changing currents. Even had it had great astuteness, it would have lacked the financial resources to affect significantly the course of events.

In 1962, seven-term Congressman Hugh Addonizio had forged an Italian-Negro coalition to overthrow longtime Irish control of the city hall. A liberal in Congress, Addonizio, when he became mayor, had opened his door to all people. Negroes, who had been excluded from the previous administration, were brought into the government. The police department was integrated.

From the *Report of the National Advisory Commission on Civil Disorders,* Otto Kerner, Chairman, (March 1, 1968), pp. 30-38.

Nevertheless, progress was slow. As the Negro population increased, more and more the politically oriented found the progress inadequate.

The Negro-Italian coalition began to develop strains over the issue of the police. The police were largely Italian, the persons they arrested were largely Negro. Community leaders agreed that, as in many police forces, there was a small minority of officers who abused their responsibility. This gave credibility to the cries of "brutality!" voiced periodically by ghetto Negroes.

In 1965, Mayor Addonizio, acknowledging that there was "a small group of misguided individuals" in the department, declared that "it is vital to establish once and for all, in the minds of the public, that charges of alleged police brutality will be thoroughly investigated and the appropriate legal or punitive action be taken if the charges are found to be substantiated."

Pulled one way by the Negro citizens who wanted a police review board, and the other by the police, who adamantly opposed it, the mayor decided to transfer "the control and investigation of complaints of police brutality out of the hands of both the police and the public and into the hands of an agency that all can support—the Federal Bureau of Investigation," and to send "a copy of any charge of police brutality . . . directly to the Prosecutor's office." However, the FBI could act only if there had been a violation of a person's federal civil rights. No complaint was ever heard of again.

Nor was there much redress for other complaints. The city had no money with which to redress them.

The city had already reached its legal bonding limit, yet expenditures continued to outstrip income. Health and welfare costs, per capita, were 20 times as great as for some of the surrounding communities. Cramped by its small land area of 23.6 square miles—one-third of which was taken up by Newark Airport and unusable marshland—and surrounded by independent jurisdictions, the city had nowhere to expand.

Taxable property was contracting as land, cleared for urban renewal, lay fallow year after year. Property taxes had been increased, perhaps, to the point of diminishing return. By the fall of 1967, they were to reach $661.70 on a $10,000 house—double that of suburban communities. As a result, people were refusing either to own or to renovate property in the city. Seventy-four percent of white and 87 percent of Negro families lived in rental housing. Whoever was able to move to the suburbs, moved. Many of these persons, as downtown areas were cleared and new office buildings were constructed, continued to work in the city. Among them were a large proportion of the people from whom a city normally draws its civic leaders, but who, after moving out, tended to cease involving themselves in the community's problems.

During the daytime Newark more than doubled its population—and was, therefore, forced to provide services for a large number of people who contributed nothing in property taxes. The city's per capita outlay for police, fire protection, and other municipal services continued to increase. By 1967 it was twice that of the surrounding area.

Consequently, there was less money to spend on education. Newark's per capita outlay on schools was considerably less than that of surrounding communities. Yet within the city's school system were 78,000 children, 14,000 more than 10 years earlier.

Twenty thousand pupils were on double sessions. The dropout rate was estimated to be as high as 33 percent. Of 13,600 Negroes between the ages of 16 and 19, more than 6,000 were not in school. In 1960 over half of the adult Negro population had less than an eighth grade education.

The typical ghetto cycle of high unemployment, family breakup, and crime was present in all its elements. Approximately 12 percent of Negroes were without jobs. An estimated 40 percent of Negro children lived in broken homes. Although Newark maintained proportionately the largest police force of any major city, its crime rate was among the highest in the Nation. In narcotics violations it ranked fifth nationally. Almost 80 percent of the crimes were committed within 2 miles of the core of the city, where the central ward is located. A majority of the criminals were Negro. Most of the victims, likewise, were Negro. The Mafia was reputed to control much of the organized crime.

Under such conditions a major segment of the Negro population became increasingly militant. Largely excluded from positions of traditional political power, Negroes, tutored by a handful of militant social activists who had moved into the city in the early 1960's made use of the antipoverty program, in which poor people were guaranteed representation, as a political springboard. This led to friction between the United Community Corporation, the agency that administered the antipoverty program, and the city administration.

When it became known that the secretary of the board of education intended to retire, the militants proposed for the position the city's budget director, a Negro with a master's degree in accounting. The mayor, however, had already nominated a white man. Since the white man had only a high school education, and at least 70 percent of the children in the school system were Negro, the issue of who was to obtain the secretaryship, an important and powerful position, quickly became a focal issue.

Joined with the issue of the 150-acre medical school site, the area of which had been expanded to triple the original request—an expansion regarded by the militants as an effort to dilute black political power by moving out Negro residents—the board of education battle resulted in a confrontation between the mayor and the militants. Both sides refused to alter their positions.

Into this impasse stepped a Washington Negro named Albert Roy Osborne. A flamboyant, 42-year-old former wig salesman who called himself Colonel Hassan Jeru-Ahmed and wore a black beret, he presided over a mythical "Blackman's Volunteer Army of Liberation." Articulate and magnetic, the self-commissioned "colonel" proved to be a one-man show. He brought Negro residents flocking to board of education and planning board meetings. The colonel spoke in violent terms, and backed his words with violent action. At one meeting he tore the tape from the official stenographic recorder.

It became more and more evident to the militants that, though they might not be able to prevail, they could prevent the normal transaction of business. Filibustering began. A Negro former State assemblyman held the floor for more than 4 hours. One meeting of the board of education began at 5 p.m., and did not adjourn until 3:23 a.m. Throughout the months of May and June, speaker after speaker warned that if the mayor persisted in naming a white man as secretary to the board of education and in moving ahead with plans for the medical school site, violence would ensue. The city administration played down the threats.

On June 27, when a new secretary to the board of education was to be named, the state police set up a command post in the Newark armory.

The militants, led by the local CORE (Congress of Racial Equality) chapter, disrupted and took over the board of education meeting. The outcome was a stalemate. The incumbent secretary decided to stay on another year. No one was satisfied.

At the beginning of July there were 24,000 unemployed Negroes within the city limits. Their ranks were swelled by an estimated 20,000 teenagers, many of whom, with school out and the summer recreation program curtailed due to a lack of funds, had no place to go.

On July 8, Newark and East Orange police attempted to disperse a group of Black Muslims. In the melee that followed, several police officers and Muslims suffered injuries necessitating medical treatment. The resulting charges and counter-charges heightened the tension between police and Negroes.

Early on the evening of July 12, a cabdriver named John Smith began, according to police reports, tailgating a Newark police car. Smith was an unlikely candidate to set a riot in motion. Forty years old, a Georgian by birth, he had attended college for a year before entering the Army in 1950. In 1953 he had been honorably discharged with the rank of corporal. A chess-playing trumpet player, he had worked as a musician and a factory hand before, in 1963, becoming a cabdriver.

As a cabdriver, he appeared to be a hazard. Within a relatively short period of time he had eight or nine accidents. His license was revoked. When, with a woman passenger in his cab, he was stopped by the police, he was in violation of that revocation.

From the high-rise towers of the Reverend William P. Hayes housing project, the residents can look down on the orange-red brick facade of the Fourth Precinct Police Station and observe every movement. Shortly after 9:30 p.m., people saw Smith, who either refused or was unable to walk, being dragged out of a police car and into the front door of the station.

Within a few minutes, at least two civil rights leaders received calls from a hysterical woman declaring a cabdriver was being beaten by the police. When one of the persons at the station notified the cab company of Smith's arrest, cabdrivers all over the city began learning of it over their cab radios.

A crowd formed on the grounds of the housing project across the narrow street from the station. As more and more people arrived, the description of the beating purportedly administered to Smith became more and more exaggerated. The descriptions were supported by other complaints of police malpractice that, over the years, had been submitted for investigation—but had never been heard of again.

Several Negro community leaders, telephoned by a civil rights worker and informed of the deteriorating situation, rushed to the scene. By 10:15 p.m., the atmosphere had become so potentially explosive that Kenneth Melchior, the senior police inspector on the night watch, was called. He arrived at approximately 10:30 p.m.

Met by a delegation of civil rights leaders and militants who requested the right to see and interview Smith, Inspector Melchior acceded to their request.

When the delegation was taken to Smith, Melchior agreed with their observations that, as a result of injuries Smith had suffered, he needed to be examined by a doctor. Arrangements were made to have a police car transport him to the hospital.

Both within and outside of the police station, the atmosphere was electric with hostility. Carloads of police officers arriving for the 10:45 p.m. change of shifts were subjected to a gauntlet of catcalls, taunts, and curses.

Joined by Oliver Lofton, administrative director of the Newark Legal Services Project, the Negro community leaders inside the station requested an interview with Inspector Melchior. As they were talking to the inspector about initiating an investigation to determine how Smith had been injured, the crowd outside became more and more unruly. Two of the Negro spokesmen went outside to attempt to pacify the people.

There was little reaction to the spokesmen's appeal that the people go home. The second of the two had just finished speaking from atop a car when several Molotov cocktails smashed against the wall of the police station.

With the call of "Fire!" most of those inside the station, police officers and civilians alike, rushed out of the front door. The Molotov cocktails had splattered to the ground; the fire was quickly extinguished.

Inspector Melchior had a squad of men form a line across the front of the station. The police officers and the Negroes on the other side of the street exchanged volleys of profanity.

Three of the Negro leaders, Timothy Still of the United Community Corporation, Robert Curvin of CORE, and Lofton, requested they be given another opportunity to disperse the crowd. Inspector Melchior agreed to let them try and provided a bullhorn. It was apparent that the several hundred persons who had gathered in the street and on the grounds of the housing project were not going to disperse. Therefore, it was decided to attempt to channel the energies of the people into a nonviolent protest. While Lofton promised the crowd that a full investigation would be made of the Smith incident, the other Negro leaders urged those on the scene to form a line of march toward the city hall.

Some persons joined the line of march. Others milled about in the narrow street. From the dark grounds of the housing project came a barrage of rocks. Some of them fell among the crowd. Others hit persons in the line of march. Many smashed the windows of the police station. The rock throwing, it was believed, was the work of youngsters; approximately 2,500 children lived in the housing project.

Almost at the same time, an old car was set afire in a parking lot. The line of march began to disintegrate. The police, their heads protected by World War I-type helmets, sallied forth to disperse the crowd. A fire engine, arriving on the scene, was pelted with rocks. As police drove people away from the station, they scattered in all directions.

A few minutes later, a nearby liquor store was broken into. Some persons, seeing a caravan of cabs appear at City Hall to protest Smith's arrest, interpreted this as evidence that the disturbance had been organized, and generated rumors to that effect.

However, only a few stores were looted. Within a short period of time the disorder ran its course.

The next afternoon, Thursday, July 13, the mayor described it as an isolated incident. At a meeting with Negro leaders to discuss measures to defuse the situation, he agreed to appoint the first Negro police captain, and announced that he would set up a panel of citizens to investigate the Smith arrest. To one civil rights leader, this sounded like "the playback of a record," and he walked out. Other observers reported that the mayor seemed unaware of the seriousness of the tensions.

The police were not. Unknown to the mayor, Dominick Spina, the Director of Police, had extended shifts from 8 hours to 12, and was in the process of mobilizing half the strength of the department for that evening. The night before, Spina had arrived at the Fourth Precinct Police Station at approximately midnight, and had witnessed the latter half of the disturbance. Earlier in the evening he had held the regularly weekly "open house" in his office. This was intended to give any person who wanted to talk to him an opportunity to do so. Not a single person had shown up.

As director of police, Spina had initiated many new programs: police-precinct councils, composed of the police precinct captain and business and civic leaders, who would meet once a month to discuss mutual problems; Junior Crimefighters; a Boy Scout Explorer program for each precinct; mandatory human relations training for every officer; a Citizens' Observer Program, which permitted citizens to ride in police cars and observe activities in the stations; a Police Cadet program; and others.

Many of the programs initially had been received enthusiastically, but—as was the case with the "open house"—interest had fallen off. In general, the programs failed to reach the hard-core unemployed, the disaffected, the school dropouts—of whom Spina estimates there are 10,000 in Essex County—that constitute a major portion of the police problem.

Reports and rumors, including one that Smith had died, circulated through the Negro community. Tension continued to rise. Nowhere was the tension greater than at the Spirit House, the gathering place for Black Nationalists, Black Power advocates, and militants of every hue. Black Muslims, Orthodox Moslems, and members of the United Afro-American Association, a new and growing organization that follows, in general, the teachings of the late Malcolm X, came regularly to mingle and exchange views. Antiwhite playwright LeRoi Jones held workshops. The two police-Negro clashes, coming one on top of the other, coupled with the unresolved political issues, had created a state of crisis.

On Thursday, inflammatory leaflets were circulated in the neighborhoods of the Fourth Precinct. A "Police Brutality Protest Rally" was announced for early evening in front of the Fourth Precinct Station. Several television stations and newspapers sent news teams to interview people. Cameras were set up. A crowd gathered.

A picket line was formed to march in front of the police station. Between 7 and 7:30 p.m., James Threatt, executive director of the Newark Human Rights Commission, arrived to announce to the people the decision of the mayor to form a citizens group to investigate the Smith incident, and to elevate a Negro to the rank of captain.

The response from the loosely milling mass of people was derisive. One youngster shouted "Black Power!" Rocks were thrown at Threatt, a Negro. The barrage of missiles that followed placed the police station under siege.

After the barrage had continued for some minutes, police came out to disperse the crowd. According to witnesses, there was little restraint of language or action by either side. A number of police officers and Negroes were injured.

As on the night before, once the people had been dispersed, reports of looting began to come in. Soon the glow of the first fire was seen.

Without enough men to establish control, the police set up a perimeter around a 2-mile stretch of Springfield Avenue, one of the principal business districts, where bands of youths roamed up and down smashing windows. Grocery and liquor stores, clothing and furniture stores, drugstores and cleaners, appliance stores and pawnshops were the principal targets. Periodically, police officers would appear and fire their weapons over the heads of looters and rioters. Laden with stolen goods, people began returning to the housing projects.

Near midnight, activity appeared to taper off. The mayor told reporters the city had turned the corner.

As news of the disturbances had spread, however, people had flocked into the streets. As they saw stores being broken into with impunity, many bowed to temptation and joined the looting.

Without the necessary personnel to make mass arrests, police were shooting into the air to clear stores. A Negro boy was wounded by a .22 caliber bullet said to have been fired by a white man riding in a car. Guns were reported stolen from a Sears, Roebuck store. Looting, fires, and gunshots were reported from a widening area. Between 2 and 2:30 a.m. on Friday, July 14, the mayor decided to request Gov. Richard J. Hughes to dispatch the state police and National Guard troops. The first elements of the state police arrived with a sizeable contingent before dawn.

During the morning the Governor and the mayor, together with the police and National Guard officers, made a reconnaissance of the area. The police escort guarding the officials arrested looters as they went. By early afternoon the National Guard had set up 137 roadblocks, and state police and riot teams were beginning to achieve control. Command of antiriot operations was taken over by the Governor, who decreed a "hard line" in putting down the riot.

As a result of technical difficulties, such as the fact that the city and state police did not operate on the same radio wave-lengths, the three-way command structure—city police, state police and National Guard—worked poorly.

At 3:30 p.m. that afternoon, the family of Mrs. D. J. was standing near the upstairs windows of their apartment, watching looters run in and out of a furniture store on Springfield Avenue. Three carloads of police rounded the corner. As the police yelled at the looters, they began running.

The police officers opened fire. A bullet smashed the kitchen window in Mrs. D. J.'s apartment. A moment later she heard a cry from the bedroom. Her 3-year-old daughter, Debbie, came running into the room. Blood was streaming down the left side of her face: the bullet had entered her eye. The child spent the next 2 months in the hospital. She lost the sight of her left eye and the hearing in her left ear.

Simultaneously, on the street below, Horace W. Morris, an associate director of the Washington Urban League who had been visiting relatives in Newark, was about to enter a car for the drive to Newark Airport. With him were his two brothers and his 73-year-old stepfather, Isaac Harrison. About 60 persons had been on the street watching the looting. As the police arrived, three of the looters cut directly in front of the group of spectators. The police fired at the looters. Bullets plowed into the spectators. Everyone began running. As Harrison, followed by the family, headed toward the apartment building in which he lived, a bullet kicked his legs out from under him. Horace Morris lifted him to his feet. Again he fell. Mr. Morris' brother, Virgil, attempted to pick the old man up. As he was going so, he was hit in the left leg and right forearm. Mr. Morris and his other brother managed to drag the two wounded men into the vestibule of the building, jammed with 60 to 70 frightened, angry Negroes.

Bullets continued to spatter against the walls of the buildings. Finally, as the firing died down, Morris—whose stepfather died that evening—yelled to a sergeant that innocent people were being shot.

"Tell the black bastards to stop shooting at us," the sergeant, according to Morris, replied.

"They don't have guns; no one is shooting at you," Morris said.

"You shut up, there's a sniper on the roof," the sergeant yelled.

A short time later, at approximately 5 p.m., in the same vicinity, a police detective was killed by a small caliber bullet. The origin of the shot could not be determined. Later during the riot, a fireman was killed by a .30 caliber bullet. Snipers were blamed for the deaths of both.

At 5:30 p.m., on Beacon Street, W. F. told J. S., whose 1959 Pontiac he had taken to the station for inspection, that his front brake needed fixing. J. S., who had just returned from work, went to the car which was parked in the street, jacked up the front end, took the wheel off, and got under the car.

The street was quiet. More than a dozen persons were sitting on porches, walking about, or shopping. None heard any shots. Suddenly several state troopers appeared at the corner of Springfield and Beacon. J. S. was startled by a shot clanging into the side of the garbage can next to his car. As he looked up he saw a state trooper with his rifle pointed at him. The next shot struck him in the right side.

At almost the same instant, K. G., standing on a porch, was struck in the right eye by a bullet. Both he and J. S. were critically injured.

At 8 p.m., Mrs. L. M. bundled her husband, her husband's brother, and her four sons into the family car to drive to a restaurant for dinner. On the return trip her husband, who was driving, panicked as he approached a National Guard roadblock. He slowed the car, then quickly swerved around. A shot rang out. When the family reached home, everyone began piling out of the car. Ten-year-old Eddie failed to move. Shot through the head, he was dead.

Although, by nightfall, most of the looting and burning had ended, reports of sniper fire increased. The fire was, according to New Jersey National Guard reports, "deliberately or otherwise inaccurate." Maj. Gen. James F. Cantwell, Chief of Staff of the New Jersey National Guard, testified before an Armed Services Subcommittee of the House of Representatives that "there was too much firing initially against snipers" because of "confusion when we were finally called on for help and our thinking of it as a military action."

"As a matter of fact," Director of Police Spina told the Commission, "down in the Springfield Avenue area it was so bad that, in my opinion, Guardsmen were firing upon police and police were firing back at them. . . . I really don't believe there was as much sniping as we thought . . . . We have since compiled statistics indicating that there were 79 specified instances of sniping."

Several problems contributed to the misconceptions regarding snipers: the lack of communications; the fact that one shot might be reported half a dozen times by half a dozen different persons as it caromed and reverberated a mile or more through the city; the fact that the National Guard troops lacked riot training. They were, said a police official, "young and very scared," and had had little contact with Negroes.

Within the Guard itself contact with Negroes had certainly been limited. Although, in 1949, out of a force of 12,529 men there had been 1,183 Negroes, following the integration of the Guard in the 1950's the number had declined until, by July of 1967, there were 303 Negroes in a force of 17,529 men.

On Saturday, July 15, Spina received a report of snipers in a housing project. When he arrived he saw approximately 100 National Guardsmen and police officers crouching behind vehicles, hiding in corners and lying on the ground around the edge of the courtyard.

Since everything appeared quiet and it was broad daylight, Spina walked directly down the middle of the street. Nothing happened. As he came to the last building of the complex, he heard a shot. All around him the troopers jumped, believing themselves to be under sniper fire. A moment later a young Guardsman ran from behind a building.

The director of police went over and asked him if he had fired the shot. The soldier said yes, he had fired to scare a man away from a window; that his orders were to keep everyone away from windows.

Spina said he told the soldier: "Do you know what you just did? You have now created a state of hysteria. Every Guardsman up and down this street and every state policeman and every city policeman that is present thinks that somebody just fired a shot and that it is probably a sniper."

A short time later more "gunshots" were heard. Investigating, Spina came upon a Puerto Rican sitting on a wall. In reply to a question as to whether he knew "where the firing is coming from?" the man said:

"That's no firing. That's fireworks. If you look up to the fourth floor, you will see the people who are throwing down these cherry bombs."

By this time, four truckloads of National Guardsmen had arrived and troopers and policemen were again crouched everywhere, looking for a sniper. The director of police remained at the scene for three hours, and the only shot fired was the one by the guardsman.

Nevertheless, at six o'clock that evening two columns of National Guardsmen and state troopers were directing mass fire at the Hayes Housing project in response to what they believed were snipers.

On the 10th floor, Eloise Spellman, the mother of several children, fell, a bullet through her neck.

Across the street, a number of persons, standing in an apartment window, were watching the firing directed at the housing project. Suddenly, several troopers whirled and began firing in the general direction of the spectators. Mrs. Hattie Gainer, a grandmother, sank to the floor.

A block away Rebecca Brown's 2-year-old daughter was standing at the window. Mrs. Brown rushed to drag her to safety. As Mrs. Brown was, momentarily, framed in the window, a bullet spun into her back.

All three women died.

A number of eye witnesses, at varying times and places, reported seeing bottles thrown from upper story windows. As these would land at the feet of an officer he would turn and fire. Thereupon, other officers and Guardsmen up and down the street would join in.

In order to protect his property, B. W. W., the owner of a Chinese laundry, had placed a sign saying "Soul Brother" in his window. Between 1 and 1:30 a.m., on Sunday, J⸱ 'v 16, he, his mother, wife, and brother, were watching television in the back room. The neighborhood had been quiet. Suddenly, B. W. W. heard the sound of jeeps, then shots.

Going to an upstairs window he was able to look out into the street. There he observed several jeeps, from which soldiers and state troopers were firing into stores that had "Soul Brother" signs in the windows. During the course of three nights, according to dozens of eye witness reports, law enforcement officers shot into and smashed windows of businesses that contained signs indicating they were Negro-owned.

At 11 p.m., on Sunday, July 16, Mrs. Lucille Pugh looked out of the window to see if the streets were clear. She then asked her 11-year-old son, Michael, to take the garbage out. As he reached the street and was illuminated by a street light a shot rang out. He died.

By Monday afternoon, July 17, state police and National Guard forces were withdrawn. That evening, a Catholic priest saw two Negro men walking down the street. They were carrying a case of soda and two bags of groceries. An unmarked car with five police officers pulled up beside them. Two white officers got out of the car. Accusing the Negro men of looting, the officers made them put the groceries on the sidewalk, then kicked the bags open, scattering their contents all over the street.

Telling the men, "Get out of here," the officers drove off. The Catholic priest went across the street to help gather up the groceries. One of the men turned to him: "I've just been back from Vietnam 2 days," he said, "and this is what I get. I feel like going home and getting a rifle and shooting the cops."

Of the 250 fire alarms, many had been false, and 13 were considered by the city to have been "serious." Of the $10,251,000 damage total, four-fifths was due to stock loss. Damage to buildings and fixtures was less than $2 million.

Twenty-three persons were killed—a white detective, a white fireman, and 21 Negroes. One was 73-year-old Isaac Harrison. Six were women. Two were children.

15   Sheldon Wolin and John Schaar

THE BATTLE OF BERKELEY

Shortly before 5:00 a.m., on Thursday, May 16, a motley group of about fifty hippies and "street-people" were huddled together on a lot 270 x 450 feet in Berkeley. The lot was owned by the Regents of the University of California and located a few blocks south of the Berkeley campus. Since mid-April this lot had been taken over and transformed into a "People's Park" by scores of people, most of whom had no connection with the university. Now the university was determined to reassert its legal rights of ownership. A police officer approached the group and announced that it must leave or face charges of trespassing. Except for three persons, the group left and the area was immediately occupied and surrounded by about 200 police from Berkeley, Alameda county, and the campus. The police were equipped with flak jackets, tear gas launchers, shotguns, and telescopic rifles. At 6:00 a.m. a construction crew arrived and by mid-afternoon an eight foot steel fence encircled the lot.

At noon a rally was convened on campus and about 3,000 people gathered. The president-elect of the student body spoke. He started to suggest various courses of action that might be considered. The crowd responded to the first of these by spontaneously marching toward the lot guarded by the police. (For this speech, the speaker was charged a few days later with violating numerous campus rules, and, on the initiative of University officials, indicted for incitement to riot.) The crowd was blocked by a drawn police line. Rocks and bottles were thrown at the police, and the police loosed a tear gas barrage, scattering the crowd. Elsewhere, a car belonging to the city was burned. Meanwhile, police reinforcements poured in, soon reaching around 600. A rock was thrown from a roof-top and, without warning, police fired into a group on the roof of an adjacent building. Two persons were struck in the face by the police fire, another was blinded, probably permanently, and a fourth, twenty-five-year-old James Rector, later died. Before the day was over, at least thirty others were wounded by police gunfire, and many more by clubs. One policeman received a minor stab wound and six more were reported as having been treated for minor cuts and bruises.

Meanwhile, action shifted to the campus itself, where police had herded a large crowd into Sproul Plaza by shooting tear gas along the bordering streets. The police then formed small detachments which continuously swept across the campus, breaking up groups of all sizes. Tear gas enfolded the main part of the campus and drifted into many of its buildings, as well as into the surrounding city. Nearby streets were littered with broken glass and rubble. At least six buckshot slugs entered the main library and three .38 calibre bullets lodged in the wall of a reference room in the same building. Before the day ended, more than ninety people had been injured by police guns and clubs.

Under a "State of Extreme Emergency" proclamation issued by Governor Reagan on February 5th in connection with the "Third World Strike" at Berkeley late last winter and never rescinded, a curfew was imposed on the city. Strict security measures were enforced on campus and in the nearby business districts, and all assemblies and rallies were prohibited. The proclamation also centralized control of the police under the command of Sheriff Frank Madigan of Alameda County.

Roger Heyns, the Chancellor of the University, saw none of this, for he had left the previous day for a meeting in Washington. His principal Vice-Chancellor had gone to the Regents' meeting in Los Angeles. The Regents took notice of the events by declaring, "It is of paramount importance that law and order be upheld." The governor said that the lot had been seized by the street-people "as an excuse for a riot." A Berkeley councilman called the previous use of the lot a "Hippie Disney-land freak show."

The next day, May 17, 2,000 National Guardsmen appeared in full battle dress, armed with rifles, bayonets, and tear gas. They were called into action by the Governor, but apparently the initiative came from local authorities acting in consultation with University administrators. Helicopters weaved back and forth over the campus and city. Berkeley was occupied. (The next day one helicopter landed on campus and an officer came out to ask that students stop flying their kites because the strings might foul his rotors. A collection was promptly taken and the sky was soon full of brightly colored kites.)

During the next few days a pattern emerged. Each day began quietly, almost like any other day, except that people awoke to the roar of helicopters and the rumble of transports. As University classes began (they have never been officially cancelled), the Guardsmen formed a line along the south boundary of the campus. The Guard and the police would cordon off the main plaza and station smaller detachments at various points around the campus. Gradually the students crowded together, staring curiously at the Guardsmen and occasionally taunting them. The Guard stood ready with bayonets pointed directly at the crowd. This standoff would continue for an hour or two, and then the police would charge the crowd with clubs and tear gas. The crowd would scatter, the police would give chase, the students and street-people would curse and sometimes hurl rocks or return the tear gas canisters, and the police would beat or arrest some of them.

On Tuesday, May 20, the pattern and tempo changed. Previously the police had sought to break up gatherings on the campus, so now the protesters left the campus and began a peaceful march through the city. This was promptly stopped by the police. The marchers then filtered back to campus and a crowd of about 3,000 assembled. The group was pressed toward the Plaza by the police and Guardsmen and, when solidly hemmed in, was attacked by tear gas. A little later a helicopter flew low over the center of the campus and spewed gas over a wide area, even though the crowd had been thoroughly scattered. Panic broke out and people fled, weeping, choking, vomiting. Gas penetrated the University hospital, imperiling patients and interrupting hospital routines. It caused another panic at the University recreation area, nearly a mile from the center of campus, where many people, including mothers and children, were swimming. The police also threw gas into a student snack bar and into an office and classroom building.

The next day, May 21, was a turning point. More than 200 faculty members announced their refusal to teach; a local labor council condemned the police action; some church groups protested; and the newspapers and television stations began to express some criticism. Controversy arose over the ammunition which the police had used the previous Thursday. Sheriff Madigan was evasive about the size of birdshot issued, but the evidence was clear that buckshot had killed James Rector. The tear gas was first identified as the normal variety (CN) for crowd disturbances, but later it was officially acknowledged that a more dangerous gas (CS) was also used. The American army uses CS gas to flush out guerrillas in Vietnam. It can cause projectile vomiting, instant diarrhea, and skin blisters, and even death, as it has to the VC, when the victim is tubercular. The Geneva Conventions outlaw the use of CS in warfare.

On the same day the Chancellor issued his first statement. He deplored the death which had occurred, as well as "the senseless violence." He warned that attempts were being made "to polarize the community and prevent rational solutions," and he stated that a university had a responsibility to follow "civilized procedures." Heyns made no criticism of the police or National Guard tactics: that same day a Guardsman had thrown down his helmet, dropped his rifle, and reportedly shouted, "I can't stand this any more." He was handcuffed, taken away for a physical examination, and then rushed off to a psychiatric examination. He was diagnosed as suffering from "suppressed aggressions."

In Sacramento, where a deputation of Berkeley faculty members was meeting with the Governor, aggression was more open. The Governor conceded that the helicopter attack might have been a "tactical mistake," but he also insisted that "once the dogs of war are unleashed, you must expect things will happen . . . ." Meantime, the statewide commander of the Guards defended the gas attack on the grounds that his troops were threatened. He noted that the general who ordered the attack had said, "It was a Godsend that it was done at that time." The commander regretted the "discomfort and inconvenience to innocent bystanders," but added: "It is an inescapable by-product of combatting terrorists, anarchists, and hard-core militants on the streets and on the campus."

The next day, May 22, a peaceful march and flower planting procession began in downtown Berkeley. With little warning, police and Guardsmen converged on the unsuspecting participants and swept them, along with a number of shoppers, newsmen, people at lunch, and a mailman, into a parking lot, where 482 were arrested, bringing the week's total near 800. As those arrested were release; on bail, disturbing stories began to circulate concerning the special treatment accorded "Berkeley types" in Santa Rita prison.

These stories, supported by numerous affidavits and news accounts submitted by journalists who had been bagged in the mass arrest, told of beatings, verbal abuse, and humiliation, physical deprivations, and refusal of permission to contact counsel. Male prisoners told of being marched into the prison yard and forced to lie face down, absolutely motionless, on gravel and concrete for several hours. The slightest shift in posture, except for a head movement permitted once every half hour, was met with a blow to the kidneys or testicles. On May 24th a District Court judge issued an order restraining Sheriff Madigan's subordinates from beating and otherwise mistreating the arrestees taken to Santa Rita prison.

Despite all the arrests, the shotguns, gas, and clubs, the protesters have thus far shown remarkable restraint. Although both police and Guards have been targets of much foul language and some hard objects, nothing remotely resembling sustained violence has been employed against the police; and the Guard has been spared from all except verbal abuse. At this writing, the only damage to campus property, other than that caused by the police, has been two broken windows and one flooded floor.

After the mass arrests, the Governor lifted the curfew and the ban on assemblies, saying "a more controlled situation" existed. But he warned that no solution was likely until the trouble-making faculty and students were separated from the University. "A professional revolutionary group," he said, was behind it all. Charles Hitch, the President of the University of California, issued his first statement. (Much earlier, his own staff issued a statement protesting campus conditions of "intolerable stress" and physical danger.) The President ventured to criticize "certain tactics" of the police, but noted that these "were not the responsibility of university authorities."

In a television interview, the Chancellor agreed with the President, but added that negotiations were still possible because "we haven't stopped the rational process." A published interview (May 22) with the principal Vice-Chancellor found him saying, "Our strategy was to act with humor and sensitivity. For instance, we offered to roll up the sod in the park and return it to the people . . . . We had no reason to believe there would be trouble." Meanwhile the Governor was saying, "The police didn't kill the young man. He was killed by the first college administrator who said some time ago it was all right to break laws in the name of dissent."

The Governor also accused the President of the University, a former Assistant Secretary of Defense and RANDsman, of "trying to weasel" to the side of the street-people. Two days later the Governor refused the request of the Berkeley City Council to end the state of emergency and recall the Guard—requests, it might be added, that the University itself has not yet made. At this time the Mayor of Berkeley suggested that police tactics had been "clumsy and not efficient," to which Sheriff Madigan retorted: "If the Mayor was capable of running the city so well without problems we wouldn't be here. I advise the Mayor to take his umbrella and go to Berkeley's Munich . . . ."

On Friday, May 23, the Faculty Senate met. It listened first to a speech by the Chancellor in which he defined the occupation of the lot as an act of "unjustified aggression" against the University, and declared that the "avoidance of confrontations cannot be the absolute value." He said that the fence would remain as long as the issue was one of possession and control, and, pleading for more "elbow room," he asserted that the faculty should support or at least not oppose an administrative decision once it had been made. The faculty then defeated a motion calling fot the Chancellor's removal (94 voted for, 737 against, and 99 abstained). It approved by a vote of 737 to 94, a series of resolutions which condemned what was called "as irresponsible a police and military reaction to a civic disturbance as this country has seen in recent time."

The resolutions demanded withdrawal of "the massive police and military presence on campus"; the "cessation of all acts of belligerency and provocation by demonstrators"; an investigation by the Attorney General of California and the Department of Justice; and the prompt implementation of a plan whereby part of the lot would become "an experimental community-generated park" and the fence would be simultaneously removed. The faculty also resolved to reconvene in a few days to reassess the situation.

There is where events now stand (May 26). But pressures from all sides are increasing. A student referendum, which saw the heaviest turnout in the history of student voting, found 85 percent of the nearly 15,000 who voted favoring the use of the lot as it had been before the occupation. The students also voted to assess themselved $1.50 each quarter to help finance an ethnic studies department previously accepted by the University but now foundering. As of this writing, college students from all over the state are planning direct protests to Governor Reagan. Leaders of the protesters are preparing for a huge march against the fence on Memorial Day. The Governor remains committed to a hard line. All the issues remain unsettled.

2

What brought on this crisis? Like many of its sister institutions, the Berkeley campus has been steadily advancing its boundaries into the city. Back in 1956 it had announced its intention to purchase property in the area which includes the present disputed lot. Owing to lack of funds, very little land was actually purchased. Finally, in June, 1967, the monies were allocated and the University announced that ultimately dormitories would be built on the land, but that in the interim it would be used for recreation.

The lot itself was purchased in 1968, but no funds were then available for development. Undoubtedly the University was aware of the disastrous experience of other academic institutions which had attempted to "redevelop" surrounding areas. In fact, a short time ago the University announced, with much fanfare, its intention to mount a major attack on the problems of the cities. Despite these professions, the University's treatment of its own urban neighbors has consisted of a mixture of middle-class prejudice, aesthetic blindness, and bureaucratic callousness.

The victims in this case, however, have not been so much the Blacks as another pariah group, one whose identity is profoundly influenced by the University itself. For many years, Telegraph Avenue and "the south campus area" have constituted a major irritant to the University, the City fathers, and the business interest. It is the Berkeley demi-monde, the place where students, hippies, drop-outs, radicals, and run-aways congregate. To the respectables, it is a haven for drug addicts, sex fiends, criminals, and revolutionaries. Until the University began its expansion, it was also an architectural preserve for fine old brown shingle houses and interesting shops. It is no secret that the University has long considered the acquisition of land as a means of ridding the area not of sub-standard housing, but of its human "blight." The disputed lot was the perfect symbol of the University's way of carrying out urban regeneration: first, raze the buildings; next let the land lay idle and uncared for; then permit it to be used as an unimproved parking lot, muddy and pitted; and finally, when the local people threaten to use and enjoy the land, throw a fence around it.

Around mid-April, a movement was begun by street-people, hippies, students, radicals, and a fair sprinkling of elderly free spirits to take over the parking lot and transform it. Many possibilities were discussed: a child care clinic; a crafts fair; a baseball diamond. Soon grass and shrubs were planted, playground equipment installed, benches built, and places made for eating, lounging, and occasional speech-making. About 200 people were involved in the beginning, but soon the Park was intensively and lovingly used by children, the young, students and street-people, and the elderly. A week after the Park began, the University announced its intention to develop a playing field by July 1, and the Park people responded by saying that the University would have to fight for it. Discussions followed, but not much else. The University said, however, that no construction would be started without proper warning and that it was willing to discuss the future design of the field.

On May 8 the Chancellor agreed to form a committee representing those who were using the lot as well as the University. But he insisted as "an essential condition" of discussions about the future of the land that all work on the People's Park cease. In addition he announced certain guidelines for his committee: University control and eventual use must be assured; the field must not produce "police and other control problems"; and no political or public meetings were to be held on the land. Suddenly, on May 13, he announced his decision to fence in the area as the first step toward developing the land for intramural recreation. "That's a hard way to make a point," he said, "but that's the way it has to be . . . . The fence will also give us time to plan and consult. Regretfully, this is the only way the entire site can be surveyed, soil tested, and planned for development . . . hence the fence."

Why did it have to be this way? Because, as the Chancellor explained, it was necessary to assert the University's title to ownership. Concerning the apparent lack of consultation with his own committee, he said that a plan could not be worked out because the Park people had not only refused to stop cultivating and improving the land, but they had "refused to organize a responsible committee" for consultative purposes. In addition, he cited problems of health, safety, and legal liability, as well as complaints from local residents.

The first response came from the faculty chairman of the Chancellor's committee. He declared that the Chancellor had allowed only two days (the weekend) for the committee to produce a plan and that the "University didn't seem interested in negotiations." On May 14 a protest rally was held and the anarchs of the Park, surprisingly, pulled themselves together and formed a negotiating committee. Although rumors of an impending fence were circulating, spokesmen for the Park people insisted that they wanted discussion, not confrontation.

On May 15, the day immediately preceding the early morning police action, the Chancellor placed an advertisement in the campus newspaper inviting students to draw up "ideas of designs" for the lot and to submit them by May 21. The ad was continued even after the military occupation. On May 18, three days after the occupation had begun, the Chancellor announced that there would be "no negotiations in regard to the land known as People's Park," although discussions might go on, "while the fence is up anyway." His principal Vice-Chancellor, in an interview reported on May 22, stated that the University had not turned down a negotiating committee.

He also noted—and this was after the helicopter attack—that "the fence was necessary to permit the kind of rational discussion and planning that wasn't possible before." Once more the faculty chairman had to protest that he had not been informed of meetings between the Administration and representatives of the People's Park and that the Chancellor had consistently ignored the committee's recommendations. However, the principal Vice-Chancellor had an explanation for this lack of consultation: "I guess that's because the Chancellor didn't want him to get chewed up by this thing."

3

Why did the making of a park provoke such a desolating response? The bureaucratic nature of the multiversity and its disastrous consequences for education are by now familiar and beyond dispute. So, too, is the web of interdependence between it and the dominant military, industrial, and political institutions of our society. These explain much about the response of the University to the absurd, yet hopeful, experiment of People's Park.

What needs further comment is the increasingly ineffectual quality of the University's responses, particularly when its organizational apparatus attempts to cope with what is spontaneous, ambiguous, and disturbingly human. It is significant that the Berkeley administration repeatedly expressed irritation with the failure of the Park people to "organize" a "responsible committee" or to select "representatives" who might "negotiate." The life-styles and values of the Park people were forever escaping the categories and procedures of those who administer the academic plant.

Likewise the issue itself: the occupants of the Park wanted to use the land for a variety of projects, strange but deeply natural, which defied customary forms and expectations, whereas, at worst, the University saw the land as something to be fenced, soil-tested, processed through a score of experts and a maze of committees, and finally encased in the tight and tidy form of a rational design. At best, the most imaginative use of the land which the University could contemplate was as a "field-experiment station" where faculty and graduate students could observe their fellow beings coping with their "environment." In brief, the educational bureaucracy, like bureaucracies elsewhere, is experiencing increasing difficulty, because human life is manifesting itself in forms which are unrecognizable to the mentality of the technological age.

This suggests that part of the problem lies in the very way bureaucracies perceive the world and process information from it. It was this "bureaucratic epistemology" which largely determined how the University responded to the People's Park. Bureaucracy is both an expression of the drive for rationality and predictability, and one of the chief agencies in making the world ever more rational and predictable, for the bureaucratic mode of knowing and behaving comes to constitute the things known and done themselves.

Now this rational form of organizing human efforts employs a conception of knowledge which is also rational in specific ways (cf. Kenneth Keniston's analysis in *The Uncommitted: Alienated Youth in American Society*, 1967, pp. 253-272). The only legitimate instrument of knowledge is systematic cognition, and the only acceptable mode of discourse is the cognitive mode. Other paths to knowledge are suspect. Everything tainted with the personal, the subjective, and the passionate is suppressed, or dismissed as prejudice or pathology. A bureaucrat who based his decisions upon, say, intuition, dialectical reason, empathic awareness, or even common sense, would be guilty of misconduct.

The bureaucratic search for "understanding" does not begin in wonder, but in the reduction of the world to the ordinary and the manageable. In order to deal with the world in the cognitive mode, the world must first be approached as an exercise in "problem-solving." To say there is a problem is to imply there is a solution; and finding the solution largely means devising the right technique. Since most problems are "complex," they must be broken down by bureaucrats into their component parts before the right solution can be found. Reality is parsed into an ensemble of discrete though related parts, and each part is assigned to the expert specially qualified to deal with that part. Wholes can appear as nothing more than assemblages of parts, just as a whole automobile is an assemblage of parts. But in order for wholes to be broken into parts, things that are dissimilar in appearance and quality must be made similar.

This is done by abstracting from the objects dealt with those aspects as though they were the whole. Abstraction and grouping by common attributes require measuring tools that yield comparable units for analysis: favorite ones are units of money, time, space, and power; income, occupation, and party affiliation. All such measurements and comparisons subordinate qualitative dimensions, natural context, and unique and variable properties to the common, stable, external, and reproducible. This way of thinking becomes real when campus administrators define "recreation" in fixed and restrictive terms so that it may accord with the abstract demands of "lead-time." In a way Hegel might barely recognize, the Rational becomes the Real and the Real the Rational.

When men treat themselves this way, they increasingly become this way, or they desperately try to escape the "mind-forged manacles," as Blake called them, of the bureaucratic mentality and mode of conduct. In the broadest view, these two trends increasingly dominate the advanced states of our day. On the one side, we see the march toward uniformity, predictability, and the attempt to define all variety as dissent and then to force dissent into the "regular channels"—toward that state whose model citizen is Tocqueville's "industrious sheep," that state whose only greatness is its collective power.

On the other side we see an assertion of spontaneity, self-realization, and do-your-own-thing as the sum and substance of life and liberty. And this assertion, in its extreme form, does approach either madness or infantilism, for the only social institutions in which each member is really free to do his own thing are Bedlam and the nursery, where the condition may be tolerated because there is a keeper with ultimate control over the inmates. The opposing forces were not quite that pure in the confrontation over the People's Park, but the University and public officials nearly managed to make them so. That they could not do so is a comforting measure of the basic vitality of those who built the Park and who have sacrificed to preserve it.

4

But this still does not account for the frenzy of violence which fell on Berkeley. To understand that, we must shift focus.

Clark Kerr was perceptive when he defined the multiversity as "a mechanism held together by administrative rules and powered by money." But it is important to understand that the last few years in the University have seen more and more rules and less and less money. The money is drying up because the rules are being broken. The rules are being broken because University authorities, administrators and faculty alike, have lost the respect of very many of the students. When authority leaves, power enters—first in the form of more and tougher rules, then as sheer physical force, and finally as violence, which is force unrestrained by any thought of healing and saving, force whose aim is to cleanse by devastation.

Pressed from above by politicians and from below by students, the University Administration simultaneously imposes more rules and makes continual appeals to the faculty for more support in its efforts to cope with permanent emergency. It pleads with the faculty for more "elbow room," more discretionary space in which to make the hard decisions needed when money runs short and students run amuck. That same Administration is right now conducting time-and-motion studies of faculty work and "productivity." Simultaneously, both faculty and Administration make spasmodic efforts to give the students some voice in the governance of the institution. But those efforts are always too little, too late, too grudging.

Besides, as soon as the students get some power, unseemly things happen. Admit the Blacks on campus and they demand their own autonomous departments. Give the students limited power to initiate courses and they bring in Eldridge Cleaver and Tom Hayden. The faculty sees student initiative as a revolting mixture of Agitprop and denial of professional prerogatives. The Administration sees it as a deadly threat to its own precarious standing within the University and before the public. The politicians see it as concession to anarchy and revolution. The result is more rules and less trust all around—more centralization, bureaucratization, and force on one side, more despair and anger on the other.

Under these conditions, the organized system must strive to extend its control and reduce the space in which spontaneous and unpredictable actions are possible. The subjects, on the other hand, come to identify spontaneity and unpredictability with all that is human and alive, and rule and control with all that is inhuman and dead. Order and liberty stand in fatal opposition. No positive synthesis can emerge from this dialectic unless those who now feel themselves pushed out and put down are admitted as full participants. But that is not happening. More and more, we are seeing in this country a reappearance of that stage in the breakdown of political societies where one segment of the whole—in this case still the larger segment—determines to dominate by force and terror other segments which reject and challenge its legitimacy.

This dynamic largely accounts for the crushing violence and terror that hit Berkeley. When spontaneity appeared in People's Park, it was first met by a re-statement of the rules governing possession and control of land. When that re-statement did not have the desired effect, the University failed to take the next step dictated by rule-governed behavior—seeking an injunction. Nor did it take the step which would have acknowledged itself as being in a political situation—talking on a plane of equality, and acting in a spirit of generosity, with the other parties. Instead, it regressed immediately to the use of physical measures. In the eyes of the Administration, the building of People's Park was an "unjustified aggression," and the right of self-defense was promptly invoked.

Once force was called into play, it quickly intensified, and the University cannot evade its share of responsibility for what followed. He who wills the end wills the means; and no University official could have been unaware of the means necessary to keep that fence standing. But the administrators did not quite understand that their chosen agents of force, the police, would not limit their attention only to the students and street-people, who were expendable, but would turn against the University and the city as well.

Ronald Reagan reached Sacramento through Berkeley because, in the eyes of his frightened and furious supporters, Berkeley is daily the scene of events that would have shocked Sodom and revolutionary Moscow. All this came into intense focus in the behavior of the cops who were on the scene.

The police were numerous and armed with all the weapons a fertile technology can provide and an increasingly frightened citizenry will permit. Their superiority of force is overwhelming, and they are convinced they could "solve the problem" overnight if they were permitted to do it their own way: one instant crushing blow, and then license for dealing with the remaining recalcitrants. All the troublemakers are known to the police, either by dossier and record or by appearance and attitude. But the police are kept under some restraints, and those restraints produce greater and greater rage.

The rage comes from another source as well. Demands for a different future have been welling up in this society for some years now, and while those demands have not been unheard they have gone unheeded. Vietnam, racism, poverty, the degradation of the natural and manmade environment, the bureaucratization of the academy and its active collaboration with the military and industrial state, unrepresentative and unreachable structures of domination—all these grow apace. It seems increasingly clear to those who reject this American future that the forces of "law and order" intend to defend it by any means necessary. It becomes increasingly clear to the forces of law and order that extreme means will be necessary, and that the longer they are delayed the more extreme they will have to be.

Those two futures met at People's Park. It should be clear that what is happening this time is qualitatively different from 1964 and the Free Speech Movement. The difference in the amount of violence is the most striking, but this is largely a symptom of underlying differences. In 1964, the issues centered around questions of civil liberties and due process within the University. The issues now are political in the largest sense.

5

The appearance of People's Park raised questions of property and the nature of meaningful work. It raised questions about how people can begin to make a livable environment for themselves; about why both the defenders and critics of established authority today agree that authority can be considered only in terms of repression, never in terms of genuine respect and affection. These questions cannot be evaded. Those who honestly and courageously ask them are not imperiling the general happiness but are working for the common redemption.

It is increasingly clear that legitimate authority is declining in the modern state. In a real sense, "law and order" *is* the basic question of our day. This crisis of legitimacy has been visible for some time in just about all of the non-political sectors of life—family, economy, religion, education—and is now spreading rapidly into the political realm. The gigantic and seemingly impregnable organizations that surround and dominate men in the modern states are seen by more and more people to have at their center not a vital principle of authority, but a hollow space, a moral vacuum. Increasingly, among the young and the rejected, obedience is mainly a matter of lingering habit, or expediency, or necessity, but not a matter of conviction and deepest sentiment.

The groups who are most persistently raising these questions are, of course, white middle-class youth and the racial and ethnic minorities. The origins of protest are different in the two cases: the former have largely seen through the American Dream of meaning in power and wealth and have found it a nightmare; the latter have been pushed aside and denied even the minimal goods of the Dream. But the ends of the protest are remarkably similar: both are fighting against distortions and denials of their humanity. Both reject the programmed future of an America whose only imperative now seems to be: more.

The people who built the Park (there will be more People's Parks, more and more occasions for seemingly bizarre, perverse, and wild behavior) have pretty much seen through the collective ideals and disciplines that have bound this nation together in its conquest of nature and power. Having been victimized by the restraints and authorities of the past, these people are suspicious of all authorities and most collective ideals. Some of them seem ready to attempt a life built upon no other ideal than self-gratification. They sometimes talk as though they had found the secret which has lain hidden through all the past ages of man: that the individual can live fully and freely with no authority other than his desires, absorbed completely in the development of all his capacities except two—the capacity for memory and the capacity for faith.

No one can say where this will lead. Perhaps new prophets will appear. Perhaps the old faith will be reborn. Perhaps we really shall see the new technological Garden tended by children—kind, sincere innocents, barbarians with good hearts. The great danger at present is that the established and the respectable are more and more disposed to see all this as chaos and outrage. They seem prepared to follow the most profoundly nihilistic denial possible, which is the denial of the future through denial of their own children, the bearers of the future.

In such times as these, hope is not a luxury but a necessity. The hope which we see is in the revival of a sense of shared destiny, of some common fate which can bind us into a people we have never been. Even to sketch out that fate one must first decide that it does not lie with the power of technology or the stability of organizational society. It lies, instead, in something more elemental, in our common fears that scientific weapons may destroy all life; that technology will increasingly disfigure men who live in the city, just as it has already debased the earth and obscured the sky; that the "progress" of industry will destroy the possiblity of interesting work; and that "communications" will obliterate the last traces of the varied cultures which have been the inheritance of all but the most benighted societies.

If hope is to be born of these despairs it must be given political direction, a new politics devoted to nurturing life and work. There can be no political direction without political education, yet America from its beginnings has never confronted the question of how to care for men's souls while helping them to see the world politically. Seeing the world politically is preparatory to acting in it politically; and to act politically is not to be tempted by the puerile attraction of power or to be content with the formalism of a politics of compromise. It is, instead, a politics which seeks always to discover what men can share—and how what they share can be enlarged and yet rise beyond the banal.

People's Park is not banal. If only the same could be said of those who build and guard the fences around all of us.

VIII

CONCLUSION

What does the future portend? Is there hope for civil understanding, compromise and humanity? Or is there only knowledge of continuing civil strife? Must this assessment of the nation's past end with but the alternatives of justified, "moral" violence or with a foreboding fear of omnipresent violence and the spector of an oppressive police state?

The one response is a hopeless surrender to the simplistic attitude that man is inherently aggressive, so violence will always be with him for it has always been so. The alternative view does not deny violence, but rather places hope in the adaptability of the human personality so as to achieve an awareness of the fundamental nihilism of violence. Depriving a man of fundamental human rights either legally or socially is as violent an act as is a bullet in the back, only the speed of death is variable. Faced with no future, no hope, no humanity, men will always be violent; they have no reason to be otherwise. Imbuing ourselves and our society with a humanism that offers each man a future, we can each be free, not a prisoner of "the system."

A democracy presents a fundamental conflict between majority rule and minority rights. A majority can exert its power to the extent of oppression so that riots may appear to be the only available means for expression and change. This conflict stemming from "a tyranny of the majority" was pointed out first by deTocqueville in the 1830's.

This question of minority rights bothered Thomas Jefferson, almost wrecked John C. Calhoun, and challenges the mind of Herbert Marcuse today. It is a problem central to the first essay in this section by Professor Nieburg. And if he is right and riots are necessary for the expression of certain ideas, then is there any possibility of ending continual mass violence? Perhaps "participatory democracy" and "all power to the people" are more than jargon, and are viable expressions of an alternative to our present two party system. Would some form of multi-party government with proportionate representation be more likely to give expression to minority views, thereby bringing demonstrators off the streets? Would greater local control of schools and police departments make these institutions more in tune with the wishes of the people they serve? Would it be possible to reform our country without planning for a more equitable distribution of the national wealth? What of the other necessities of life—good housing, medical care, employment, education, and leisure—should these also be the common right of all? In short, it would seem to be necessary to alter the entire structure of our nation to bring about these changes, and this would be a revolution. Can such a revolution occur without violence; can there ever be a revolution without violence? This is the dilemma.

The conclusion to the Skolnick Report, the last essay in this volume, expresses the belief that it is possible to bring about far-reaching change in our society short of revolution. Only by such change will we avoid the terrible disorders that threaten this society. This article is a warning offering some hope of peaceful reform, but at the same time, it states that the alternative to "massive and widespread political and social reform" is "a society of garrison cities where order is enforced without due process of law and without the consent of the governed."

Suggested Further Readings

In addition to Edward C. Banfield, "Rioting Mainly for Fun and Profit" in *The Metropolitan Enigma* (1968), 283-308, (which gives an alternate view to those presented in this section), T. R. Gurr, *Why Men Rebel* (1969) and Hans H. Toch, *Violent Men* (1969) may offer some understanding of violence and social change. Nieburg's own ideas have been expanded into a book length study, *Political Violence: The Behavioral Process* (1969).

The following books are all of general interest to the readers of this volume: Hugh Davis Graham and Ted Robert Gurr, *Violence in America* (1969) (a task force report to the National Commission on the Causes and Prevention of Violence); The Arno Press and the New York Times have combined to bring out many interesting reprints in their series *Mass Violence in America* (1969); John W. Caughey, *Their Majesties the Mob* (1960) is a collection on vigilante justice; John Hope Franklin, *The Militant South* (1956); Richard Hofstadter and Michael Wallace, (eds.), *American Violence: A Documentary History* (1971); Robert H. Connery, (ed.), *Urban Riots Violence and Social Change* (1968); and finally a popular account is Ovid Demaris, *America the Violent* (1970).

Footnotes

1   Edward C. Banfield, "Rioting Mainly for Fun and Profit," in *The Metropolitan Enigma,* James Q. Wilson, (ed.) (Cambridge, Mass.: Harvard University Press, 1968), p. 285.

16   H. L. Nieburg

USES OF VIOLENCE

The threat of violence, and the occasional outbreak of real violence (which gives the threat credibility), are essential elements in conflict resolution not only in international, but also in national communities. Individuals and groups, no less than nations, exploit the threat as an everyday matter. This fact induces flexibility and stability in democratic institutions and facilitates peaceful social change.

I refer not only to the police power of the state and the recognized right of self-defense, but also to private individual or group violence, whether purposive or futile, deliberate or desperate. Violence and the threat of violence, far from being meaningful only in international politics, is an underlying, tacit, recognized, and omnipresent fact of domestic life, of which democratic politics is sometimes only the shadow-play. It is the fact that instills dynamism to the structure and growth of the law, the settlement of disputes, the processes of accommodating interests, and that induces general respect for the verdict of the polls.

An effort by the state to obtain an absolute monopoly over violence, threatened or used on the behalf of private interests, leads inexorably to complete totalitarian repression of all activities and associations which may, however remotely, create a basis of anti-state action. A democratic system preserves the right of organized action by private groups, risking their implicit capability of violence. By intervening at the earliest possible point in private activities, the totalitarian state increases the chance that potential violence will have to be demonstrated before it is socially effective. On the other hand, by permitting a pluralistic basis for action, the democratic state permits potential violence to have a social effect with only token demonstration, thus assuring greater opportunities for peaceful political and social change. A democratic system has greater viability and stability; it is not forced, like the totalitarian, to create an infinite deterrent to all nonstate (and thus

From *The Journal of Conflict Resolution,* VII (1963), pp. 43-54. Reprinted by permission of the author and publisher.

potentially anti-state) activities. The early Jeffersonians recognized this essential element of social change when they guaranteed the private right to keep and bear arms (Second Amendment). The possibility of a violent revolution once each generation acts as a powerful solvent of political rigidities, rendering such revolutions unnecessary.

The argument of this essay is that the risk of violence is necessary and useful in preserving national societies. This specifically includes sporadic, uncontrolled, "irrational" violence in all of its forms. It is true that domestic violence, no less than international violence, may become a self-generating vortex which destroys all values, inducing anarchy and chaos. However, efforts to prevent this by extreme measures only succeed in making totalitarian societies more liable to such collapses. Democracies assume the risk of such catastrophes, thereby making them less likely.

Violence has two inextricable aspects: its actual use (political demonstrations, self-immolation, suicide, crimes of passion, property, politics, etc.), or its potential use. The actual demonstration of violence must occur from time to time in order to give credibility to its threatened outbreak; thereby gaining efficacy for the threat as an instrument of social and political change. The two aspects, demonstration and threat, cannot be separated. The two merge imperceptibly into each other. If the capability of actual demonstration is not present, the threat will have little effect in inducing a willingness to bargain politically. In fact, such a threat may provoke "pre-emptive" counter-violence.

The "rational" goal of the threat of violence is an accommodation of interests, not the provocation of actual violence. Similarly, the "rational" goal of actual violence is demonstration of the will and capability of action, establishing a measure of the credibility of future threats, not the exhaustion of that capability in unlimited conflict.

POLITICAL SYSTEMS AND CONSENSUS

An investigation of the function of violence begins with an outline of concepts. We assume that all human relationships, both individual and institutional, are involved in a dynamic process of consensus and competition. These are opposites only as conceptual poles of a continuum. In real relationships, it is often difficult to distinguish objectively between the two. The distinction is sharp only subjectively, for the participant, and his perception of consensus or competition may change from moment to moment, depending on his political role and objective circumstances. A political role is defined in terms of the many political systems in which the individual objectively or subjectively (by identification of interests) plays a part. A political system operates through a hierarchy of authority and values. Each system constitutes a complex structure of leadership and influence but, because of the nature of its task (maximizing and allocating certain values), decision-making power is usually vested in one or a few roles (the elite) at the top of a pyramid of authority relationships. Formal and informal political systems exist at all levels of group life (children's play groups, families, lodges, gangs, work groups, nation-states, international alignments, etc.), interpenetrating each other among and between levels. Each isolated system has an interdependent structure of roles, in volving loyalty to certain values, symbols, leaders, and patterns of behavior according to system norms. The discreet individual, part of many different systems, must structure his own hierarchy of commitment to meet the simultaneous demands made upon him by many different roles.

Within the individual, the conflicting demands of these roles create tension. Similarly, within each system there are conflicting values among members which are constantly adjusted as roles change, maintaining a state of tension. Political systems have an objective, dynamic interrelationship, structured into the hierarchy of macrosystems. Within the latter, each subsystem has a role much like that of the individual in small constellations. Each subsystem may be part of several macrosystems, imposing conflicting demands upon it. Consequently, within macrosystems there is maintained a state of constant tension between subsystems. This objective tension, existing on all levels, is seen subjectively in terms both of competition and consensus, depending on the comparative degrees of collaboration and conflict which exist in the situation at any given moment.

Any two or more systems may appear as hostile at any given time. From the viewpoint of the participants, the conceptual framework of competition overrides underlying consensus. Decisions and policies of the rival elites are rationalized in terms of hostility to the values and leaders of the other system. However, if events conspire to place a higher value on a hostile tactical situation involving the macrosystem of which both smaller systems are a part, their relationship will be transformed quickly to a conceptual framework of consensus which will override and mute the unresolved competitive elements. Such an event may also bring about internal leadership changes in both subsystems, if the elites were too firmly wedded to the requirements of the now-irrelevant competitive situation.

Objectively, tension is always present among all roles and systems; that is, there is always present both elements of competition and consensus. The subjective emphasis which each pole of the continuum receives depends on the value which the tactical situation places on acts and attitudes of hostility or collaboration among the various systems at various times. Degrees of hostility and collaboration are structured by a hierarchy of values within and among all roles and systems all the time. All are involved in a dynamic process.

Conflict, in functional terms, is the means of discovering consensus, of creating agreed terms of collaboration. Because of the individual's personal role in the macrosystem of nation-states, he tends to view the Cold War in terms of competition. Similarly, because of his role in the subsystem of the family, he tends to view family problems in terms of consensus (until the system breaks down completely).

One can reverse these conceptual fields. The Cold War can be viewed in terms of the large areas of consensus that exist between the two power blocs, for example, the wish to prevent the spread of nuclear weapons to each other's allies; the wish to avoid giving each other's allies the power of general war and peace between the main antagonists; the common interest in reducing accidental provocations; the common interest in establishing certain norms of predictability in each others behavior; etc. Conflict can be considered merely as the means of perfecting these areas of consensus. In the same way, one can view the family situation negatively in terms of competition and hostility. As in an O'Neill drama, one would dwell on all of the things that divide the family members and interpret all actions in terms of maneuvers to subdue each other's will. Consensus becomes a residual category *hors de combat*, and therefore of no importance. One might dwell upon the collaborative aspects of international affairs or the disruptive aspects of family affairs. A policymaker should do both in the former area, just as a psychiatrist does both in the latter. The collaborative view of the Cold War should not, however, induce euphoria about the nature of the relationship (as it unfortunately does for some), since a high percentage of crimes of violence occur in families, or between lovers or ex-lovers (Frankel, 1938-39, pp. 687-8).

In performing this exercise, the relativistic nature of the concepts of consensus and competition becomes evident. It is impossible to reach any consensus without competition and every consensus, no matter how stable, is only provisional, since it represents for all of its members a submerging of other values. There is a constant effort by all collaborating individuals, groups, or nations to exploit any favorable opportunity to improve their roles or to impose a larger part of their own value structures upon a larger political system. In an important sense, all individuals, groups, or nations desire to "rule the world," but are constrained to collaborate with others on less desirable terms because of the objective limits of their own power.

The commitment required by a credible threat of violence, able to induce peaceable accommodation, is one of a very high order. Not all individuals nor all political systems are capable of credibly using the threat of violence in order to induce greater deference by others to their values. There is general recognition by all of the kinds of values which can and cannot elicit the high degree of commitment required to make the threat credible.

By and large, all violence has a rational aspect, for somebody, if not for the perpetrator. All acts of violence can be put to rational use, whether they are directed against others or against oneself. This is true because those who wish to apply the threat of violence in order to achieve a social or political bargaining posture are reluctant to pay the costs or take the uncertain risks of an actual demonstration of that threat. Many incoherent acts of violence are exploited by insurgent elites as a means of improving their roles or imposing a larger part of their values upon a greater political system. The greater the logical connection between the act and the ends sought, the easier it is to assimilate the act and claim it as a demonstration of the threat available to the insurgents if their demands are ignored. The rapidity with which insurgent movements create martyrs, often from the demise of hapless bystanders, and the reluctance of governments to give martyrs to the opposition, are evidence of this.

NATIONS, LAWS, AND BALLOTS

The nation is a highly organized, formal political system, whose structure is well defined by law and custom, reinforced by sanctions legally imposed by the police power of the state. The central problem of lawful societies is to develop principles, procedures, institutions, and expectations that create conditions of continuity and predictability in the lives of its members. The legal system is an abstract model of the society, designed to crystallize relationships of the status quo, maintain their continuity in the midst of political and social change, provide lawful methods of resisting or accommodating change. Law itself, however, tends to maintain the status quo and, with the instruments of state power, to resist change. But relationships in organized societies change anyway. The process for codifying changed conditions and relationships is called "politics." Formal political systems legitimize certain kinds of potential violence within controlled limits. However, law almost never serves the interest of all equally. Rather, it protects some against others or gives advantages to some over others. By placing the violence of the state behind the interest of some, law serves to neutralize the potential violence behind the demands of others. In a sense, it thus raises the threshold of violence required to make social protests against the law efficacious. This fact guarantees that the law cannot be changed easily or quickly by any group, thus giving it greater permanence and stability.

Pressures for political and social change must be substantial before the threat of violence and the fear of the breakdown of law and order rises above the threshold set by the reserves of force held by the state. While the threat and fear remain below the threshold, the status quo often responds to challenges against the law by more severe enforcement, augmented police and enlarged prisons. Just as soon as the threat and fear near or cross the threshold, there is a general tendency toward nonenforcement of the law. The status quo interests begin to share with the disaffected groups a desire to evade and to change the law.

Private demonstrations of violence are illegal in all domestic societies. Toleration is accorded to threats of potential violence, however, to the extent that the laws and institutions are democratic. In all systems, the state must apply adequate force to control all outbreaks of actual violence by private sources. If the state power is not equal to a private threat, the government in power ceases to rule. The private threat of violence becomes in fact the last resort of authority in the system. Why do governments fall when there is a general strike, or a street demonstration? Governments fall when their capabilities for dealing with threatened violence fail. The emerging political system which proves itself capable of raising a high threshold of violence becomes *de facto* the highest authority, and *de jure* the new government.

Laws are not merely the rules of a game of economic and political competition. They can also be a means of winning the game, if some of the players can, as they do in fact, write the laws. The ideal system is one in which the rules are written with perfect dispassion, so that they accord no special advantages to anyone. This ideal is never realized. The process of politics which underlies the making and unmaking of laws is not dispassionate. Indeed, it is one of the most passionate of the affairs of men. No matter how scrupulously fair may be the original constitution and representation of governing institutions, the tensions of political systems soon intrude historical hierarchies of advantage. Whomever enjoys early advantages in the game soon enjoys more by law, with the heightened threshold of the state to vouchsafe them.

Thus, the law tends always to become to some extent the instrument of the status quo and an instrument for resisting change.

However, in democratic societies the law also guarantees the rights of voluntary association, political liberties, and restrains (by a constitutional distribution of authority) arbitrary use of the police power. These permit opponents of the status quo to establish and maintain a formidable base of political action. It is difficult for the regime to find legal pretexts for controlling this base while its potential for anti-state violence is still within the state's control capability. Once the insurgent capability of demonstrating violence is equal or greater than that of the state, there is no realistic prospect of repressing it. Changing the law gains precedence over enforcing it, even for status quo leaders, who wish to preserve what control remains over informal political systems whose elite they are. Once the process of peaceful political change has been successfully established, all political elites, both emerging and declining, have a high interest in maintaining general freedom to threaten violence without initiating or provoking it, either on the part of the state or by other groups. For the insurgent elites, there is usually more to be gained in preserving the continuity of the laws than in appealing to the uncertain results of violence.

In democratic systems, the ballot becomes the nonprovocative symbol by which the elites may measure their capabilities for threatening direct action. In a real sense, voting is an approximation of picking sides before a street fight. Once the sides are picked, the leaders are able to gauge their bargaining strengths and make the best possible deal for themselves and their cohorts. The appeal to actual battle is not only unnecessary, but also, for the weaker side (the only side with an interest in challenging the results of the count), does not promise to change the results, and may in fact undermine the authority of the polls as a method of reversing one's position in the future.

The threat of violence implicit in the counting of heads is an ambiguous measure of the power available to the political systems into which people group themselves at election time. The extent of voter commitment in these systems is uncertain and probably, in most cases, unequal to demands for supporting action. There are very few national elections in the United States, although many elsewhere, in which the results prefigure a plausible threat of civil war as the means by which the defeated candidates can gain concessions and appointments from the winning side. In general, democratic political leaders share a common interest in resolving disputes without invoking real violence. Neither side is confident that the loyalty of voters will stand the test of a demonstration of strength. Voting is a very imperfect register of loyalty, but rather conveys a miscellany of emotions, difficult to pene-trate or to order rationally. Strenuous efforts are made by defeated candidates to restrain a show of violence by one's own followers. Public concessions of defeat, homiletic congratulations, and avowals of support for the winner, are designed to communicate to one's voters the finality of the verdict at the polls, which is subject to revision, not by a demonstration of violence, but by renewed peaceful efforts in the next election.

In 1960, after the close and somewhat questionable result of the Kennedy-Nixon election, what dangers could have been unleashed if Nixon had publicly repudiated the poll and openly supported minority efforts to hold recounts in California and Illinois? In a situation of this kind, it is clear how close to the surface lies the threat of violence implicit in the voting process.

THE INTERNATIONAL PROCESS

Many people blithely argue for law as a substitute for violence, as though there were a choice between the two. They call for international law and world govern-ment to eliminate war. This point of view reveals a blissful ignorance of the func-tions of violence in domestic legal systems. A viable system based on law protects the conditions of group action. Law always rests on violence. The threat of violence and the fear of the breakdown of law and order act to moderate demands and positions, thereby setting into peaceful motion the informal political processes of negotiation, concession, compromise, and agreement. Although there is no cen-tralized police power in the international forum, the processes of mediation and negotiation operate in much the same way. The credible threat of violence in the hands of the nations has a similarly stabilizing effect, providing statesmen are attentive to maintaining their national capability for demonstrating violence, and providing their ambitions are commensurate to the bargaining position which their armaments achieve. More comprehensive legal codes and a world government may not improve the stability of the world community in any case, since the possibility of civil conflict exists in all political systems. Civil wars are frequently bloodier and more unforgiving than wars between sovereign nations.

In international politics, the threat of violence tends to create stability and maintain peace. Here the threat is more directly responsive to police controls. The nation-state has greater continuity than the informal political systems that coalesce and dissolve in the course of domestic social change. The threat of violence can be asserted much more deliberately and can be demonstrated under full control, as in "good will" navy visits, army maneuvers near a sensitive border, partial mobiliza-tion, etc. Because of the greater continuity of these macrosystems, the national leaders must strive to maintain the prestige of a nation's might and will. If the reputation of a nation's military power is allowed to tarnish, future bargaining power will be weakened. It may be forced to reestablish that prestige by invoking a test of arms, as a means of inducing greater respect for its position from other nations. All strong nations are anxious to demonstrate their military power peaceably in order that their prestige will afford them the bargaining power they deserve without a test of arms.

Because the threat of violence is a conscious instrument of national policy, it generally lacks the random character which violence has domestically. This means that if the armaments of nations fall out of balance, if the prestige of nations is no longer commensurate with their ambitions, if the will to take the risks of limited military conflicts is lacking, if domestic political considerations distort the national response to external threat, then the time becomes ripe for the outbreak of violence, escalating out of control.

In general, the dangers of escalating international conflict induce greater, not lesser, restraint on the part of national leaders in their relations with each other. Attempts to achieve infinite security for the nation are as self-defeating as such attempts are for domestic regimes.

The functioning of consensus and competition between nations is not fundamentally different from that of domestic politics. The most striking difference is that in domestic politics the level of centralized violence available to the state creates a high threshold of stability against the threats brought to bear within the system by private groups. In the international forum, the closest approximation to such a threshold is the decentralized forces available to the Great Powers. A power interested in modifying the status quo must raise the level of its threat of violence, in order to induce other powers to choose between concessions to its demands or the costs and risks of an arms race. To the extent that the status quo powers are capable and willing to pay the costs and take the risks, their own levels can be raised, depriving the challenger of any political advantages from his investment. When all of the great powers are attentive to the equations of potential violence, no nation can hope to gain conclusive political advantages from an arms race. This situation makes possible international agreements for stabilizing arms and bringing about political settlements.

Diplomatic ceremonials, like the ceremonials of personal relations which we call "manners," serve to minimize the dangers of provocation and threat in the day-to-day relations between nations. Conversely, manners tend to minimize the dangers of provocation and threat in relations between people.

THE DOMESTIC PROCESS

Underneath all of the norms of legal and institutional behavior in national societies lies the great beast, the people's capability for outraged, uncontrolled, bitter, and bloody violence. This is common to totalitarian as well as democratic societies. Any group whose interests are too flagrantly abused or ignored is a potential source of violent unrest. This fact is a major restraint against completely arbitrary government. Even totalitarian regimes can hope for stability only if they reflect the changing currents of political interest of the people and if they are willing to recruit new elites from the potentially disaffected groups which they rule. Even totalitarian states must purvey some concept of fairness and flexibility, an ability to change in response to the changing internal and external demands put upon it. In fact, to the extent that a totalitarian regime permits the threat of violence to be raised against it in the form of political pressure, it has ceased to be totalitarian and has become, for all substantive purposes, pluralistic. However, the dynamics of totalitarianism generally make this kind of evolution difficult, if not impossible. Dictatorships of one or a few raise the level of official terror to offset or deter the threat of violence from below. The terror and counter-terror may escalate until the whole system collapses in an orgy of violence. The prospects for raising anything but another such dictatorship out of the wreckage are remote. Dictators may seek an escape from this iron logic by external adventures which unite the country behind the leader, postponing issues of internal dissension.

The threat to carry political dissent outside peaceable channels can distract the government from the pursuit of other values, can impose upon the government as its first and major responsibility the establishment of domestic peace and order, and can force the government into shortsighted measures to suppress violence, which may widen the base of opposition and increase the occasions for anti-government protests.

The mere threat of private violence directed against the government has very great power over government actions. By causing reallocations of the resources of the society into the essentially negative goals of internal security, the opposition is in a position to defeat or cripple the positive goals whose accomplishment might legitimize and strengthen government authority. To avoid this predicament, even totalitarian governments may go out of their way to appease their critics. The alternative to reform is ruthless suppression not only of the sources of the threat, but also of every symptom of united social action. Bowling clubs, assemblies of three or more people on street corners—there is no rational way to identify the first links of the chain which leads to social action. All must be broken up, and every symptom, however innocuous, must be stamped out. The hopeless search for infinite security begins in this way and often ends with the downfall of the regime.

With this choice before it, it is easy to see why social and political reform are the preferred reactions to the threat of violence. This is why so many kings and tzars, rather than destroying their opposition, sent them on enforced-vacations and educational tours abroad. In more recent cases, the State Department arranged scholarships in United States colleges for a number of leading anti-Yankee student agitators in Panama.

In democratic societies this sharp dilemma is avoided far short of infinite deterrence. The institutional distribution of authority (checks and balances, federalism, civil rights, etc.) precludes unilateral attempts to centralize all the police powers in the hands of one agent. Also, the law proscribes the overt threat of private violence and the existence of para-military forces, although it tolerates and protects the implicit threat of pluralistic political activities. Violence is demonstrated, not in organized forms, but rather in sporadic outbursts. Those disgruntled elites who possess a clear capability for causing a planned demonstration, i.e., they have organized groups with a deep sense of moral outrage and injustice, avoid incriminating themselves and avoid provoking counteraction against themselves. Instead, they carry out "peaceable demonstration" designed to reveal their numbers and the intensity of their commitment. These are likely to have the bonus effect of provoking violent action against them, causing government intervention, and/or causing their more inflammable followers to ignite into unplanned outbursts of violence. This potential exists implicitly in the situation.

The reformist leader is placed in a position of minimum risk and maximum effectiveness, that of playing the role of "responsible leader." He can bargain with formal authorities and with all the other members of the society in this way: "You must accept our just complaints and you must deal with us; otherwise, we will not be able to control our people." While playing this role, the reformist leader is not unhappy to have his prophesies fulfilled by a few psychotic teenagers. Events which demonstrate violence (and thus induce other elites to make concessions) do not have to be planned. Once the motions of a real social movement are churned up, the problem is to keep them from happening.

The irresponsible elements are, of course, disowned, but the bargaining power of the responsible leaders is enhanced. In the bargaining process, the moderate leaders often accept concessions which fall short of those demanded by some of their more extremist followers. Opportunists or "realists" often inherit the benefits wrought by the blood of martyrs. This is a healthy mode of exploiting the demonstration of violence without condoning it, enabling compromises to be reached which isolate the extremists and render them less dangerous to the body politic. The bulk of followers in social movements will follow responsible leadership through the gives-and-takes of compromise, because they share the general fear of unlimited violence and counter-violence, with their unpredictable results and the defeat of all rational goals. Accommodations can be reached, even if only provisionally, which preserve the general consensus in maintaining the form and continuity of society and law.

SOME CONCRETE EXAMPLES

Let us turn to some concrete examples of how this process works in practice.

A classical case of the actual demonstration of violence against the legality of existing authority is that of the founding of the state of Israel in 1949. The Irgun, an underground terror organization, created conditions in Palestine which made further British government occupation impossible. There is some doubt that the British government would have honored their commitment to the Jewish Agency or honored it when they did, had it not been for the Irgun's role. Yet it was the Jewish Agency, the responsible and moderate leadership, which negotiated the partition of Palestine and which played the major role in the founding of the new state, all the while disavowing the terrorist acts and methods of the Irgun. Before the launching of Irgunist terror, the British government stalled the Jewish Agency and accorded it little respect.

More instructive are cases of domestic violence where the actual demonstration is minimal and where the implicit threat is all, as in the current fight for Negro rights. Until the last decade, there has been little sustained pressure to improve the Southern Negro's position by governmental action. Even with the growth of Negro voting power in the big cities of the North, the Federal Administration has always shown great respect for the implicit capabilities of violence of well-organized White Supremacists. Partly because of the great power of the White South in the Congress, in Democratic National Conventions, and in the Electoral College, presidents have acted with restraint in protecting the rights of Southern Negroes. So long as the possibility of violence was asymmetrical, the Whites well-organized and armed, the Negroes apathetic, intimidated, and disorganized, Negro attempts to register to vote, to protest lynchings and other injustices, could easily be tranquillized by the County Sheriffs, the local police, and the KKK. In the last decade, the Negroes have been in the throes of a new self-consciousness, confidence, organization, and leadership. The Black Muslims, the Committee on Racial Equality, the National Association for the Advancement of Colored People, etc., have now demonstrated that the Southern Negro is capable of social action and of organized demonstrations of strength. As the capability grows for effective counter-violence against White Citizen Council provocation, or, what is more significant, nonviolent demonstrations which invoke violence by the extremist Whites, the Negro will gain increasing consideration for his demands, increasing support from "moderate" White leaders, and increasing attention and support from the Federal authorities. Just as the existence of the White Citizens Councils strengthened the hand of southern moderates in trying to restrain civil rights action from Washington, so the existence of the Black Muslims and Core now strengthen the position of the NAACP in seeking concessions from Southern Whites and action by the Justice Department. The threat of uncontrolled violent outbursts, hovering just beneath the surface, acts as a moderating influence, maintaining the institutions of peaceful process, inducing status quo groups to a greater readiness to yield some privileges, and restraining the responsible leaders of the insurgent Negroes from extremist demands.

The strategy of nonviolent social action (passive resistance or pacifism) does not abandon the threat of force as an instrument of social change. Rather, it is designed to operate within a civilized society by its provocative effects. By provoking the use of force by others, it forces the government to intervene on the behalf of the nonviolent demonstrators, while evoking the sympathies of those less intensely involved. As an international ideology, pacifism or unilateral nonviolence, may fail to achieve its objectives. Unless those who pursue it succeed in invoking some force in their behalf, they will be destroyed with impunity by their enemies.

The Douhabor Sons of Freedom (of Vancouver, British Columbia) have adopted a novel tactic of demonstrating violence as they conduct their immemorial campaign against compulsory public education. They set fire to their own homes and barns, standing by and watching the blaze. They also parade naked down the center of city streets. The significance of these demonstrations is plain. Their religion forbids them to threaten or use violence against others. Instead, they symbolically demonstrate their discipline and passionate commitment to their own way of life by inflicting violence upon their own property. The naked marches provoked arrests and imprisonment and the house-burnings forced the welfare agencies to provide temporary shelter. Both actions impose on the government responsibilities it is ill-prepared to carry out, especially if such demonstrations were to continue indefinitely and involve the entire Douhabor settlement. In addition, the demonstrations invoke public attention and sympathy for the believers. All of this may well give the local authorities incentive to ignore Douhabor defiance of school attendance laws. In fact, this is what has happened. Efforts to enforce the laws are spasmodic and half-hearted, while the law is generally evaded.

The relations of suicide and crime to social change are too large a subject for treatment here (Henry and Short, 1954, pp. 69-81). Durkheim studied these phenomena as an indicator or measure of social disorganization. They might be studied in terms of demonstrating violence as an instrument of political and social change. When teenagers commit crimes, the legitimate grievances which they have get more attention. When someone commits suicide, all those who may sense the circumstances that drove him to it reexamine their own lives, are strengthened in convictions concerning the society in which they live. A suicide of an over-extended installment buyer in Chicago led to efforts to reform state and national laws governing interest rates and collection of unpaid installment debts. A suicide, apart from its real motives, will be quickly exploited by those with a social cause. In effect, a suicide resembles a resignation from a government: it challenges values and institutions, evoking from all survivors a sense of the unresolved tensions which surround them, threatening the prospects for their own survival. Suicides and crimes, however obscure and ambiguous, threaten the world and thus change it.

SOME CONCLUDING REMARKS

There are several points that might be made in conclusion. Demonstrations of domestic violence serve to establish the intensity of commitment of members of the political system. The more intense the commitment, the greater the risks which the system will take in challenging the status quo. Accordingly, the greater will be the bargaining efficacy of future threats. Social change often occurs legalistically. Rationalization in terms of the continuity of abstract legal models is a useful means of stressing consensus over competition, adding to the stability of the whole society. However, it is obvious that a legal or ideological syllogism is meaningless except in terms of the emotional force which members of the society attach to the first principle. The infinite regress of syllogistic reasoning ends somewhere with a commitment of self. Such commitments cannot be explained or understood by reasoning alone. Efforts to adduce rational principles for explaining social and political change are futile unless one grapples with the often irrational and illogical intensity of self-commitment which marks social movements.

No system can hope to survive unless it can live with and adjust itself to the multitudinous threats of violence which are the basis of social change. Democracies have shown a greater ability to do this. However, this is not to rule out the possibility that, even within totalitarian forms, substantial democracy can be achieved. On the other hand, democratic forms can be subverted to become totalitarian in substance, if the search for infinite security in the international forum is reflected internally by the search for infinite deterrence of threats against the social and political status quo. Major social changes have major social causes; they are not the result of isolated conspiracies and plots. They cannot be arrested by an effort to stamp out all conspiracies and plots.

"Reason," as understood by Eighteenth Century Rationalists, Nineteenth Century Positivists, and Twentieth Century Pragmatists, plays an important role in conflict resolution as a means of gauging the possibilities of potential violence in bargaining situations. But conflicts cannot be resolved as merely legalistic, academic, or ideological abstractions. The dimensions of commitment and potential violence constitute the real substratum which give the myths of consensus reality.

17   Jerome H. Skolnick

SOCIAL RESPONSE TO COLLECTIVE BEHAVIOR

Throughout this report we have concentrated on showing the difficulty of determining what causes and what prevents violence, such as it is, in several protest movements. A common theme has emerged from the analysis of these movements. We have argued that they represent forms of political protest oriented toward significant change in American social and political institutions. In this concluding chapter we consider some of the implications of this perspective for public policy. In doing so, we narrow our focus to the question of the meaning of riots and civil disorder. We believe that conventional approaches to the analysis and control of riots have inadequately understood their social and political significance, and need to be revised.

In this section of this chapter we examine the perspective on riots developed in social-scientific theories of collective behavior. This is not merely an academic exercise. At least since the 1919 Chicago Commission on Race Relations, these perspectives have influenced the assumptions underlying official responses to civil

Jerome H. Skolnick, *The Politics of Protest:* A Report Submitted by Jerome H. Skolnick, Director Task Force on Violent Aspects of Protest and Confrontation of the National Commission on the Causes and Prevention of Violence.

disorders. Even where direct influence is unclear, it remains true that there has been a remarkable similarity between academic and official views on the nature, causes, and control of civil disorder. In the second section, we consider some of the themes in the official conception of riots in the light of historical and contemporary evidence. In the final section, we consider the implications of our findings for conventional approaches to the social control of disorder.

THEORIES OF COLLECTIVE BEHAVIOR

"Common sense" sees riots as threatening, irrational, and senseless. They are form-less, malign, incoherent, and destructive; they seem to raise to the surface those darker elements of the human character that are ordinarily submerged. Most of all, they are something others do: the lower classes, disadvantaged groups, youth, crimi-nals. By and large, this conventional view of riots has been adopted in the develop-ment of the study of collective disorder, although some of the most recent work in social science has come to perceive the relative and definitional aspects of such terms as "order," "violence," and "crime." As William Kornhauser has recently written, "The readiness to assimilate all politics to either order or violence implies a very narrow notion of order and a very broad notion of violence . . . what is violent action in one period of history becomes acceptable conflict at a later time." It is this more recent perspective that we attempt to apply to the analysis of collective behavior, especially in our consideration of social response.

The "Crowd"

The modern study of collective behavior has its origins in the nineteenth-century European writers on the "crowd." In the work of Gabriel Tarde, Gustave Le Bon, and others, the emergence of the "crowd" was identified with the rise of democ-racy. It was seen as both the catalyst and symbol of the decline of everything worthy in European civilization during and after the French Revolution. In becom-ing part of a crowd, wrote Le Bon, "a man descends several rungs in the ladder of civilization." Unlike civilized behavior, crowd behavior was impulsive, spontaneous, and uninhibited, rather than the product of reason, established tradition, and the restraints of civilized life. Ideas spread in the crowd through processes of contagion and suggestion. In this view, the crowd developed like a highly infectious disease; the crowd represented a pathological state. Like others after him, Le Bon had little to say about the origins of crowds; while exhaustively discussing their nature, he left the conditions of their emergence obscure. In this way, the "pathological" and "destructive" behavior of crowds was dissociated from its environmental and insti-tutional framework. Finally, Le Bon and other early writers tended to lump together indiscriminately what we today regard as distinct phenomena; in their aristocratic assault on the crowd, they included parliamentary bodies and juries as manifestations of "crowd behavior." This approach, while perhaps useful in dis-crediting the aspirations of rising social classes in a democratizing age, seriously undermined the analysis of specific instances of collective behavior.

Transplanted to American sociology and social psychology, the preconceptions of European theorists underwent considerable modification. Lacking a feudal tradition, American society was not receptive to the more explicitly anti-democratic biases represented in European theories of the crowd. The irrational behavior of crowds was no longer, for the most part, linked to the rise of democratic participation in government and culture. The simplistic disease model of collective behavior was for the most part replaced by a new perspective which, while discarding some of the older themes, retained many of their underlying premises.

The major change invoked in more recent analyses of collective behavior is toward greater interest in the *causes* of disorder. At the same time, early conceptions of the *nature* of riots have largely been retained.

The Nature of Riots

Social scientists usually place riots under the heading of "collective behavior," a broad concept which, in most treatments, embraces lynchings, panics, bank runs, riots, disaster behavior, and organized social movements of various kinds. Underlying this union of apparently diverse phenomena is the idea that each in some sense departs from the more routine, predictable, and institutionalized aspects of social life. Collective behavior, in the words of a leading social psychology text, is not only "extraordinary" and "dramatic," but also "likely to be foolish, disgusting, or evil."

The crucial element of "collective behavior" is not that it is collective—all group interaction is—but that it is qualitatively different from the "normal" group processes of society. Smelser, for example, acknowledges that although patriotic celebrations may erupt into riot, they are not to be considered as illustrative of collective behavior:

> True, they are based often on generalized values such as the divine, the nation, the monarchy of the *alma mater*. True, they are collective. True, they may release tensions generated by conditions of structural strain. The basic difference between such ceremonials and collective behavior—and the reason for excluding them—is that the former are institutionalized in form and context.

"Collective behavior" is thus conceived as nonconforming and even "deviant" group behavior. Under this conception, the routine processes of any given society are seen as stable, orderly, and predictable, operating under the normative constraints and cumulative rationality of tradition. The instability, disorder, and irrationality of "collective behavior," therefore, are characteristic of those groups that are experiencing "social strain"—for example, "the unemployed, the recent migrant, the adolescent." As such, "collective behavior" is characteristically the behavior of outsiders, the disadvantaged and disaffected. Sometimes, however, "collective behavior" becomes the property of the propertied, as when businessmen and bankers "panic" during a stock-market crash or the failure of a monetary system. Yet since the propertied rarely experience such "social strain," they likewise rarely inherit the derogation "panicky" and "crazy." When they do they are also relegated to the status of social outcasts, even though a bank run may in fact be an illustration of rational self-interest, narrowly conceived. Usually, however, "panicky" and "crazy" are terms reserved for social movements and insurrections, collective behavior theorists suggesting that a fundamentally similar departure from reasonable and instrumental concerns underlies all of them.

According to a recent theorist, what such phenomena have in common is their organization around ideas which, like magical beliefs, distort reality and "short-circuit" the normal paths to the amelioration of grievances. This distorted outlook is held responsible for the "crudeness, excess, and eccentricity" of collective behavior.

Related to this conception of collective behavior as irrational is an implicit notion that collective behavior is—particularly in its more "explosive" forms— inappropriate behavior. Just as many bewildered observers tend to view a riot in the same terms as a temper tantrum, so a social scientist categorizes collective behavior as "the action of the impatient." Implicit in this perspective is the application of different premises to collective as opposed to "institutionalized" behavior. To define collective behavior as immoderate, and its underlying beliefs as exaggerated, strongly implies that "established" behavior may be conceived as both moderate and reasonable, barring direct evidence to the contrary. Needless to say, such an approach has important political implications, which ultimately renders much of collective behavior theory an ideological rather than analytical exercise. This inherently judgmental aspect of collective behavior theory is made all the more damaging by being unexpressed; indeed, many of the theoretical traditions represented in current work on collective behavior stress the need for a "value-free" social science.

It should be emphasized that theories of collective behavior are not all of a piece, nor are they necessarily as internally consistent as this overly brief analysis implies. Several theorists, for example, recognize the potentially constructive character of collective behavior: all, however, remain deeply rooted in the tradition of viewing collective behavior as distinct from "orderly" social life.

Whereas much of modern social science remains close to its early forerunners in its assessment of the nature and quality of collective behavior, it departs from the traditional view in recognizing that the origins of collective disorder are neither mysterious nor rooted in the dark side of human personality. Rather, modern social theory usually focuses on two social sources of collective behavior: a condition of social "strain" or "tension," leading to frustration and hostility on the part of marginal or disadvantaged groups; and a breakdown of normal systems of social control, in the sense of both widespread social disorganization and the inability of local authorities to maintain order in the face of emergent disorder. When contemporary theorists attempt to deal with the causes of riot, one or both of these factors is generally invoked. On balance the latter factor—i.e., the breakdown of social control on a global or local level—predominates in these discussions. A major text in the sociology of collective behavior stresses as determinants of collective behavior both "social disintegration" and the failure of those occupying positions of social control to effectively perform their functions. Another, while stressing the importance of "frustration" as one kind of strain leading to "hostile outburst," also argues that firmness in the "agencies of social control" may play a role in preventing outbursts. This perspective is affirmed in a recent work directed specifically at the causes and control of ghetto disorders, where it is argued that while "social tensions" clearly underlie riots, they amount to only a partial explanation; "a key element in the outbreak of riots is a weakness in the system of social control."

Specifically, the failure of social control is said to be involved in a number of ways, and at a number of stages, in the emergence of ghetto riots. On one level, the breakdown of social control means the existence of "a moral and social climate that encourages violence," especially through the mass media. On another level, it means the failure of law enforcement agencies to stop the process of "contagion" through which riots spread. Left inadequately controlled, the riot escalates into widespread destruction and extensive sniper fire. Similarly, modern riot control manuals stress that riots are triggered by "social contagion," and "the level of mob frenzy . . . is reinforced and augmented by seeing others who are equally excited and also rioting."

The retention of the concept of contagion illustrates the degree to which most theories of collective disorder remain bound by earlier perspectives. The conception of the "escalated riot" involving heavy sniper fire illustrates the reciprocal relation between an inadequate theoretical framework and an inadequate attention to questions of fact, for, as the Kerner Commission exhaustively demonstrated, the existence of "heavy sniper fire" in the ghetto riots of the 1960's was largely mythical. It is the kind of myth, however, that fits very well the theoretical presuppositions dominating much collective behavior theory. It is also the kind of myth that may turn out to be self-confirming in the long run.

We find conventional theories of riots open to challenge on the following counts:

1. They tend to focus on the destructive behavior of disaffected groups while accepting the behavior of authorities as normal, instrumental, and rational. Yet established, thoroughly institutionalized behavior may be equally destructive as, or considerably more so than, riots. No riot, for example, matches the destructiveness of military solutions to disputed political issues. Further, available evidence suggests both that (a) armed officials often demonstrate a greater propensity to violence against persons than unarmed civilians; and (b) these actions often escalate the intensity of the disorder and comprise a good part of the "destructiveness" of riots, especially in terms of human deaths and injuries. Furthermore, as the reports of our Chicago, Cleveland, Miami, and San Francisco study teams well illustrate, riots are not unilaterally provoked by disaffiliated groups. Collective protest involves interaction between the behavior of "rioters" and the behavior of officials and agents of social control. Each "side" may on close inspection turn out to be equally "riotous." The fact that the behavior of one group is labeled "riot" and that of the other labeled "social control" is a matter of social definition.

2. They tend to describe collective behavior as irrational, formless, and

immoderate. As we will demonstrate in the next section, less emotional scrutiny of riots indicates that they show a considerable degree of structure, purposiveness, and rationality. Nor is "established" behavior necessarily guided by rational principle. While the beliefs underlying a riot may frequently be inaccurate or exaggerated, they are not necessarily more so than, for example, commonly held beliefs about racial minorities by dominant groups, the perception of foreign threats to national security, of the causes of crime, of threats to internal security, and so forth. A measure of irrationality, then, is not a defining characteristic of collective behavior generally or of riots in particular; rather, it is an element of many routine social processes and institutions *and* forms of collective behavior. The more significant difference may be that established institutions are usually in a more advantageous position from which to define "rationality."

The "inappropriateness" of riots is clearly variable, depending on the availability of alternative modes of action. Only by neglect of the relevant institutional setting can "inappropriateness" be considered a definitive characteristic of riots. Historically, riots have been used as a form of political bargaining in the absence of other channels of effective action. Where such channels are atrophied, nonexistent, or unresponsive, the riot may become a quasi-established, relatively standard form of political protest.

Hans W. Mattick, a consultant to the Kerner Commission, has described the underlying political character of recent urban riots:

> The content of the riot is reciprocal, like a broken bargain. It consists of claims and denials made in the substance and conceptions of life, liberty, and the pursuit of happiness. The parties to the bargain are the Negro community and the white majority, living under the rule of law, at some level of social accommodation. In process of time the predominant social forces come to shape the law in accordance with the differential distribution of power between the white majority and the black minority. Such consolidations of power are reinforced with irrational myths about black inferiority and white supremacy, and supported by discriminatory behavior patterns and prejudicial attitudes. As a result the Negro community experiences unfair treatment at the hands of the white majority and grievances accumulate. When claims of grievance are made, they are denied, minimized, and rationalized away. When legal attacks are made on discriminatory patterns, the formal law is changed in a grudging, rearguard action and represented as progress. Meanwhile informal procedures are devised to subvert the formal changes in the law. Grievances continue to accumulate and soon the grievance bank of the Negro community is full: almost every aspect of social life that has a significant effect on the life chances of Negroes seems blocked. The progress of the law has been too little and too late. At this juncture of history, after a series of prior indidents of similar character, the final incident takes place and violence erupts.

Any attempt to understand the nature of a riot based on final incidents is, more frequently than not, to deal with symptoms rather than causes. Indeed, final incidents are routine and even trivial. They are distinguished in retrospect because they happen to have been the occasion for the eruption of violence; otherwise they resemble ordinary events.

Beyond this, it is questionable whether there exists any necessary correlation between appropriate or moderate behavior and the use of established means. A strong preference for "normal channels" is discernible in many of the critiques of disorderly protest, black or otherwise. However, in human history, witches have been burned, slaves bought and sold, and minorities exterminated through "normal" channels. The "rioters" in Prague, for example, may not be "senseless" in believing that the Soviet Union is attempting to crush Czechoslovakian aspirations for democracy; nor are they necessarily "irrational" in perceiving unresponsiveness in "normal channels." The propriety—and to a large degree the rationality—of disorderly behavior is ultimately determined by historical outcomes, in the light of existing alternatives. Further, an assessment of the existing alternatives to disorderly protest must concern itself with the actual as well as the ideal, with substance as well as form. To suggest, for example, that disorderly protest has no justification in a society organized on democratic principles may obscure the fact that the society historically has offered less equality of political participation than its stated form would suggest. Which, of course, is not to suggest disorderly protest is always justified. Our point is that such labels as "normal channels" or "protest" do not automatically attach themselves to "goodness" or "badness' and that particular demands and grievances should be considered on their merits.

3. Finally, it is insufficient to analyze riots in terms of "tension" and "frustration." It is not that this perspective is wrong, but that it tells at once too little and too much. Too little, because the idea of "tension" or "strain" does not encompass the subjective meaning or objective impact of subordinate caste position or political domination. Too much, because it may mean almost anything; it is a catchall phrase that can easily obscure the specificity of political grievances. It is too broad to explain the specific injustices against which civil disorders may be directed; nor does it help to illuminate the historical patterns of domination and subordination to which the riot is one of many possible responses.

The difficulty with most traditional collective behavior theory is that it treats protest and riots as the "abnormal" behavior of social groups and derives many of its conceptual assumptions from phychological rather than from political premises. It may well be asked what remains of the idea of collective behavior if a political perspective is adopted. Does such a perspective imply that there is no such phenomenon, or that there is not a "carnival" element or "contagion" element in riots that have political roots? Such an implication is not intended. We recognize that there may well be an element of "fun" in being caught up in a collective episode, whether race riot or panty raid. (Some years ago, it was customary for Yale students to overturn trolley cars after football victories.) We also recognize that individual participants in disorders may have their share of disturbance or ignorance. What we object to is the *substitution* of a psychological analysis for a political one and, especially, the one-sided application of psychological premises to collective protest. We see no analytical justification for an arbitrary classification of *some* forms of political action as based, wholly or in part, on the cognitive or emotional inadequacies of the participants. We do not object to collective behavior theories that attempt to generalize about interaction and development in a nonjudgmental fashion. By contrast, we are most critical of those theories that are inherently ideological and that inadvertently use ostensibly "neutral" concepts and "scientific" language to discredit political action. From the point of view of a political analysis, the question has to be asked, "Why did Yale students move from overturning trolley cars to engaging in peace marches?" Collective behavior theory, as presently developed, does not offer adequate answers to that question, or to similar ones.

We have discussed collective behavior theories of riot to indicate how widespread and dominant certain assumptions concerning riots are. These assumptions sometimes spill over into analyses of less violent forms of collective protest, although this tendency to generalize has not been widespread. But it has been true that the view of riots as pathological has been adopted by officials who have analyzed riots. The next section deals specifically with these official views, and contrasts them with historical and contemporary evidence supporting the view that riots represent a form of instrumental political action.

OFFICIAL CONCEPTIONS OF RIOT

In Chapter IV, we discussed evidence indicating that the ghetto riots of the 1960's were participated in by a cross section of the ghetto communities, and given wide sympathy or support by those communities. Given these facts, few serious official treatments of riots now attempt to explain the resulting violence purely in terms of a criminal or "riffraff" element. Nevertheless, some official commissions, while generally appreciating that riots attract some popular support and participation, argue that riots are invariably aggravated or instigated by the criminal activities of a small group of provocateurs who take advantage of human weakness and transform basically nonviolent individuals into an irrational mob.

Thus, riots are widely characterized as outlets for pent-up frustrations and grievances sparked by a few. In Chicago, according to the 1919 report, even "normal-minded Negroes" exhibited a "pathological attitude to society which sometimes expresses itself defensively in acts of violence and other lawlessness." The Harlem riot also drew upon the participation of "normal" citizens:

> [Neither] the threats nor the reassurances of the police could restrain these spontaneous outbursts until the crowds had spent themselves in giving release to their pent up emotions. . . . Negro crimes result from the fact that normal individual impulses and desires are often forced to express themselves in a lawless manner in a disorganized social environment.

The Watts riot was characterized as an "insensate rage of destruction," a "spasm," and a "formless, quite senseless, all but hopeless violent protest." Similarly, the riots of 1968 were viewed as the product of a "sense of rage" and "years of frustration born and bred in poverty."

Implicit in this concept of frustration-aggression is the idea that riots are without purpose or direction. Though it is granted that "rioters" have some objective justification for their unhappiness and anger, it is also argued that they tend to exaggerate the importance of underlying grievances. According to the recent Chicago Commission, for example, "There is a conviction on the part of a clear majority of our black citizens that [political] representation is entirely unsatisfactory and must be improved. This conviction, *whether or not or to what extent it is true* [our emphasis], is of critical importance to the continued health of our city."

The essential problem with this perspective is that it neglects the intrinsically political and rational aspects of collective protest and fails to take seriously the grievances that motivate riots. Looting, for example, which distinguishes the riots of the 1960's, is a form of group protest and not merely individualistic or expressive action. Looting is widespread collective, public, and undertaken by a cross section of local residents whose behavior is perceived by most of the community as a legitimate form of protest. The instrumental nature of looting is evident in its selective character: stores and supermarkets with a reputation for discrimination and exploitation are usually singled out by looters. It is not accurate, therefore, to conceive of looting as merely random or senseless violence.

Finally, the emphasis on the irrational and "hypnotic" aspects of rioting tends to obscure the interactional nature of riots. It is misleading to ignore the part played by social control agencies in aggravating and sometimes creating a riot. It is not unusual, as the Kerner Commission observed, for a riot to begin *and* end with police violence.

Abnormality

Almost every official riot commission has pointed out that riots are abnormal and useless:

> The problem will not be solved by methods of violence.
> The avenue of violence and lawlessness leads to a dead end.
> [There] can be no justification in our democratic society for a resort to violence as a means of seeking social justice.
> [Unless] order is fully preserved, . . . no meaningful, orderly, and rational physical, economic or social progress can occur.
> Violence cannot build a better society.

This "violence doesn't pay" argument is misleading on two counts. First, it refers only to the domestic violence of disaffected groups, while ignoring the fact that systematic official violence for social ends is widely upheld in other spheres. Thus, the commissions of 1919, 1943, and 1968 do not even mention the possibility of a connection between war and domestic violence. It is a matter of moral judgment to attribute "normality" to one kind of violence—such as overseas war—but not to another. And it may be a glaring example of motivated obtuseness to ignore the possible connection between the public celebration of heroic military violence "over there" and the sporadic appearance of rebellious violence "back home." The breakdown of peaceful restraint during periods of war is among the most firmly established findings of social science.

Second, whether or not violence is "useless" is a problem for historical analysis, not a certainty. In any event, rioting has not been a particularly novel or unusual technique for expressing grievances. Instances of such rioting by both the respectable and disreputable poor in eighteenth- and nineteenth-century Europe have been well documented by historians. As Hobsbawm has noted, the preindustrial city mob "did not merely riot as a protest, but because it expected to achieve something by its riot. It assumed that the authorities would be sensitive to its movements, and probably also that they would make some sort of immediate concession." Like the modern riot, the classical mob was composed of a cross section of "the ordinary urban poor, and not simply of the scum." Moreover, one need not be fond of revolutions to observe that riots are sometimes the preface to an even more organized overthrow of existing arrangements with the substitution of new regimes. And one need not admire the consequence of the Russian Revolution to appreciate those of America or France. All three began with rioting. There is no intention here of making dire predictions. Our only point is that the viewpoint that holds that rioting is "useless" lacks a certain foundation in reality. At the same time, rioting is a "primitive" form of political action, which may lead to consequences undesired by the rioters.

Collective violence by powerless groups acts as a "signaling device" to those in power that concessions must be made or violence will prevail. Hobsbawm gives the example of the Luddites, whose "collective bargaining by rioting was at least as effective as any other means of bringing trade union pressure, and probably *more* effective than any other means available before the era of national trade unions." Similarly, Rimilinger notes that those involved in the development of European trade unionism were "convinced of the righteousness not only of their demands but also of the novel means proposed to enforce them."

The available evidence, then, suggests that contemporary urban riots are participated in by a predominantly youthful cross section of the lower-class black community, that they are supported (usually passively) by other segments of that community, that they are often instrumental and purposive, and that they are not a historically unique form of social protest.

SOCIAL CONTROL OF RIOTS

Official and academic conceptions of riots have strongly influenced the assumptions underlying governmental response to civil disorders in the past. We have argued that these conceptions seriously misconstrue the meaning of riots on several counts. It follows that riot-control efforts based on these conceptions may be inadequate and often self-defeating.

No recent treatment advocates a purely repressive approach to riot control. On the contrary, official conceptions of riots have usually been translated into recommendations combining a program for the reduction of social tensions with a call for the development of strategy and technology to contain disruption. On its face, this dual approach seems both reasonable and feasible. It suggests sympathetic response to legitimate grievances, and at the same time it offers the prospect of sophisticated, measured, and controlled force to protect civic order. After considerable analysis, however, we have come to question whether this two-pronged approach is ultimately workable.

Prospects of Support

First, implicit in the two-pronged theory is the assumption that, in practice, reform measures have about the same prospect of gaining executive and legislative support as control and firepower measures. Historical experience, however, suggests no such parity. On the contrary, commissions from the Chicago Commission of 1919 to the Kerner Commission have adopted the dual approach and have lived to observe control recommendations being implemented without concomitant implementation of social reform measures. Although it has generally been recognized that riots are motivated in part by legitimate grievances, the ensuing political response clearly reveals that order has been given priority over justice. After the Harlem riot in 1935, it was reported that "extra police stand guard on the corners and mounted patrolmen ride through the streets. . . . To the citizens of Harlem they symbolize the answer of the city authorities to their protest. . . . It offers no assurance that the legitimate demands of the community for work and decent living conditions will be heeded." Yet the Harlem Commission warned that riots would recur so long as basic grievances were not answered. Over thirty years later, the Kerner Commission reported a similar finding that "in several cities, the principal official response has been to train and equip the police with more sophisticated weapons." Following the Kerner Commission, there has been considerable development of riot-control weapons and programs in urban areas, without similar efforts, recommended by the Commission, to meet underlying and legitimate grievances. From the evidence, it appears that it has been found more expedient to implement recommendations for control than recommendations for altering the social reform, on the one hand, and for the development of sophisticated riot-control techniques and weaponry, on the other, will not suffer the same fate today.

We may suggest as a general rule that a society which must contemplate massive expenditures for social control is one which, virtually by definition, has not grappled with the necessity of massive social reform. There are various possible levels of social reform, ranging from merely token and symbolic amelioration of fundamental problems to significant changes in the allocation of resources—including political power. We feel that contemporary efforts at reform in this country remain largely at the first level. Precisely because society leaves untouched the basic problems, the cycle of hostility spirals: there is protest, violence, and increased commitment to social control: as we spiral in this direction, the "need" for massive social control outstrips the capacity of democratic institutions to maintain both social order and democratic values. Little by little, we move toward an armed society which, while not clearly totalitarian, could no longer be called consensual.

We need to reverse the spiral. A genuine commitment to fundamental reform will have positive effects, both reducing the need for massive social control and altering the quality and character of social control. We do not, of course, suggest that every demand of every protester or protest group be met. We do suggest, however, that a distinction be drawn between *demands* and *underlying grievances* and that grievances be considered on their merits. Too often attention is paid to disruption, but not to the reasons for it.

Law enforcement should be taken seriously. By this we mean to suggest that policing should take place within the framework of due process of law, using the minimum force required to effect the establishment of order. When actual crimes are committed, suspects should be arrested, charged, and tried in a court of law, not beaten in the streets. As suggested in Chapter VII, we should support reform of control agencies, not simply the addition of weaponry. The reduction and reformation of control should also occasion positive benefits by reducing polarization and hostility; that, in turn, should decrease disaffection, thus decreasing the need for force, and so forth. Only if the roots of disorder are attacked can the spiral be reversed and the problem of social order rendered manageable within a democratic framework.

The ramifications of reducing force and reforming the social structure, including the established policing services, are evident if we examine the connection between anti-war, student, and black protest. For example, a reduction of military spending and involvement overseas would reduce the level of anti-war and student protest, freeing resources that could then be used to combat the problems of the black communities. A greater understanding of black problems by control agents—a sympathetic understanding—would, in turn, also reduce the need for massive force.

Strategies of Control

The escalation of violence is related to strategies of social control. Our evidence suggests that a diversion of resources into domestic force and away from redress of social grievances is not only costly but self-defeating, since the heightening of force is likely to be a factor in creating still more violence. The ultimate result of force will probably *not*, in the long run, be to "channel the energy of collective outbursts into more modest kinds of behavior"; the eventual effects may be directly contrary.

Because the police are received with hostility in the black communities of America (for reasons discussed in Chapters IV and VII), the introduction of more and better-armed police will, we believe, only aggravate the situation. The contemporary ideology and behavior of police across America make it difficult to think otherwise. Furthermore, the introduction of sophisticated weaponry will likely be seen by protesting groups as evidence of governmental duplicity. The development of "nonlethal" weapons, for example, will not be perceived by the young man in the ghetto as a humane response to his condition; to him they will still be weapons—aimed at him—and will be viewed with hostility. Finally, as we have developed at length, the police, the military, and other agents of social control may themselves be implicated in triggering riots and in building up long-term grievances.

The Political Significance of Riots

The conventional approach underestimates the political significance of riots. Even given the possibility of efficient short-term control of riots, and ignoring its immediate destructive effects, the political nature of riots suggests that forceful riot-control techniques may channel expressive protest into more organized forms of political violence, thus requiring greater military and paramilitary force with its inescapable monetary and social costs. Thus it is not surprising that one expert finds that riots may be "giving way to more specific, more premeditated and more regularized uses of force." What is surprising, however, is his conclusion that "only surveillance and covert penetration supplies an effective technique of management."

We have learned from the Vietnam War that power and covert surveillance may well have the unanticipated effect of increasing resistance. Indeed, the literature of guerrilla warfare stresses that revolutionaries are made through violence. So, too, the young man who encounters the hostile actions of a policeman is likely to increase his hostility toward the society and to be attracted to groups that express such hostility. Moreover, in measuring the consequences of escalating domestic force, we must add the political and social dangers of depending on espionage as an instrument of social control, including its potential for eroding constitutional guarantees of political freedom.

For these reasons, we question the conventional two-pronged approach to contemporary American protest. An approach that gives equal emphasis to force and reform fails to measure the anticipated consequences of employing force; and it fails to appreciate the political significance of protest. If American society concentrates on the development of more sophisticated control techniques, it will move itself into a destructive and self-defeating position. A democratic society cannot depend upon force as its recurrent answer to long-standing and legitimate grievances. This nation cannot have it both ways: either it will carry through a firm commitment to massive and widespread political and social reform, or it will develop into a society of garrison cities where order is enforced without due process of law and without the consent of the governed.